DANCING AGAINST THE DARKNESS: A JOURNEY
THROUGH AMERICA IN THE AGE OF AIDS

ENDING THE HIV EPIDEMIC: COMMUNITY
STRATEGIES IN DISEASE PREVENTION AND
HEALTH PROMOTION (*Editor*)

WHEN SOMEONE YOU KNOW HAS

AIDS

A PRACTICAL GUIDE

by Leonard J. Martelli,
Fran D. Peltz, C.S.W.,
William Messina, C.S.W.,
and Steven Petrow

Foreword by Michael Callen

REVISED AND UPDATED

Crown Trade Paperbacks, New York

Material from interviews that first appeared in *Dancing Against the Darkness: A Journey Through America in the Age of AIDS* by Steven Petrow is reprinted with the permission of Lexington Books, an imprint of Macmillan, Inc. Copyright © 1990 by Steven Petrow.

Published by Crown Publishers, Inc., 201 East 50th Street, New York, New York 10022. Member of the Crown Publishing Group.

Random House, Inc., New York, Toronto, London, Sydney, Auckland

CROWN TRADE PAPERBACKS and colophon are trademarks of Crown Publishers, Inc.

Manufactured in the United States of America

Library of Congress Cataloging-in-Publication Data
When someone you know has AIDS: a practical guide / by
    Leonard J. Martelli [et al.].—Rev. and updated ed.
    Includes bibliographical references and index.
    1. AIDS (Disease)—Patients—Care.   2. AIDS (Disease)—
Patients—Home care.   3. AIDS (Disease)—Patients—Family
relationships.   4. AIDS (Disease)—Psychological aspects.
5. Caregivers.   I. Martelli, Leonard J.
RC607.A26M36   1993
616.97'92—dc20   93-2740

ISBN 0-517-88039-3

10 9 8 7 6 5 4 3 2 1

Revised Edition

This new edition is dedicated to Leonard J. Martelli (1937–1988). Len's care and concern for his lover, Evan, and for all people with AIDS and their loved ones led him to create the first edition in 1987. Guiding our work on this revised edition was Len's memory and his message: When we confront AIDS we are not alone; we can actively and wisely support and care for each other.

To Evan, the Nipper, who has been brave, courageous, and an inspiration throughout his illness and whose love has made me strong.

—L.J.M.

In memory of my father, David Peltz, who was always an inspirational force in my life. To my grandmother, better known as Bubby, who has taught me the gift of giving. I am very grateful to all the carepartners for the courage, care, and hope they shared with their loved ones.

—F.D.P.

To my lover, Larry Victor, who loved living his life to its fullest, who deeply and lovingly touched all those he knew, and who was and always will be the light in my life.

And with deep love and gratitude to Doreen, Nicole, Stanley, Linda, John, Fran, Charlie, Denise, Glynn, Margaret, Barbara, Hal, Allan, Abby, Terry, Charlie, Connie, Alberto, Russell, Annemarie, Jim, Maureen, Michael, Kathleen, Helen, Marie, Barbara, Bonnie, Linda, Edie, and the staff and clients of the Village AIDS Programs, all who know, deep in their hearts, why they are mentioned here.

—W.M.

For my parents, Margot and Richard Petrow, with love—and in memory of my dear friend, Julia Harper Day.

—S.P.

CONTENTS

APPENDIXES

ACKNOWLEDGMENTS

INDEX

FOREWORD

Trial and error was an awfully painful way to learn how best to deal with AIDS, but that's all we had a decade ago. It is a measure of how much we've learned that a book as practical as *When Someone You Know Has AIDS* can now find its way into the hands of those who choose to struggle alongside those of us with AIDS.

Like a stone dropped in a pond, the effects of AIDS radiate in concentric ripples affecting whole networks of friends, families, lovers, and associates. This refreshingly unsentimental, usefully specific guide to the changes that AIDS can bring will make a difficult struggle that much easier to bear for all concerned.

Make no mistake: AIDS is a messy business; and whether you are *in*fected or "merely" *af*fected by AIDS, the lessons contained in this book should soften the shock, if not the sorrow, of finding yourself in the same situations as those whose experiences form the guts of this book.

I'm something of an AIDS dinosaur, having been diagnosed back in the summer of 1982—before the term "AIDS" was even coined. One small advantage of having been struck so early was that I didn't have to experience the anxiety and uncertainty so characteristic of loving someone with AIDS. The agony of waiting for the other shoe to drop, so eloquently described by the subjects of this book, must be a terrible thing. But surely knowing that others have been there before and have left valuable signposts about how best to negotiate the terrain ought to provide some much-needed comfort.

Everyone's experience of AIDS will be unique; and yet, there are sufficient commonalities to make a book like this one useful. The problems that can present themselves are depressingly predictable, and this guide presents both the recommendations of professionals who have been dealing with AIDS for years as well as the firsthand, plainspoken experiences of actual carepartners. Over the course of the book, you come to recognize distinct voices and the specific ways in which carepartners tailor their responses based on the particular personalities of their loved one with AIDS. The cumulative effect of these different voices makes the important point that there is no single "right" way to deal with AIDS.

AIDS asks that most difficult of tasks: that we love and respect people with AIDS enough to let them make their own mistakes. The temptation to insist that your friend with AIDS should manage his or her illness as *you* would do must, painfully, be resisted. It's one of the many paradoxes of AIDS: You should love your friend enough to do your homework and then express your opinions firmly and clearly, but then you must stand back and let your friend do things his or her way. If the cliché of PWA "self-empowerment" is to have any real meaning, it must mean that we people with AIDS reserve the right to live—and to die—according to our own way of approaching the management of our illness.

AIDS is a world unto itself, and this book is an excellent travel guide. It will help you learn to speak a new language, full of abbreviations and medical terms and jargon. With this as your guide, you'll probably be amazed to discover skills you never knew you had. This book can help foster the endurance and pacing so necessary to loving someone who is ill.

One final observation: It's the feisty, difficult people who seem to live the longest. Just ask any nurse. We people with AIDS are often not easy to be around. But, as the message of this book makes clear, love and a humble sense of human limitation are usually sufficient to see this difficult journey through.

So much has gone wrong in our management of AIDS. There are many villains and much to complain about. As one notoriously feisty and difficult PWA, I don't often get the chance to say *nice* things. But I'd like to take this opportunity to acknowledge in advance how moved I am by those of you with enough love and charity to walk the difficult path of AIDS with someone you love. Good luck.

—Michael Callen, March 1993

1

AIDS:
EVERYTHING YOU'VE
EVER NEEDED TO KNOW

Jeffrey and Paul, both in their early thirties, had been together only a few months when Paul's health began to deteriorate. As Paul remembers: "I noticed that I started to feel a little run-down, and I was having a little trouble swimming—I used to swim five times a week. Then suddenly I realized I had dropped ten pounds on the weights I lifted twice a week. Some days I was even falling asleep at my desk. One or two people asked me if I was losing weight. I said that it was a conscious decision on my part—that I had been dieting and working real hard lately. Finally, I decided I needed a vacation, so I planned a trip to the Caribbean. While I was away, I not only missed Jeffrey, but I wasn't feeling any better, even after doing nothing but sleeping for the first two and a half days. I had no energy. I thought, 'There's definitely something wrong.' So, with a lot of juggling, I got a flight out early. I called Jeffrey as soon as I got back. We went to a movie that night, and I felt awful. The next day I decided to go to a nearby clinic and take the HIV [human immunodeficiency virus, which is believed to be the agent causing AIDS] antibody test."

Tom and Mart have been together for eighteen years. In many ways, they came of age on parallel tracks. They had met when they were in their early twenties and became lovers right away. Each gave up a promising acting career because the demands of the theater interfered too much with the time they wanted to spend together. Mart started a small business—which quickly became successful— while Tom put himself through college. By the time Mart became ill, they had had nearly two decades of a shared life. Mart had undergone seemingly minor surgery, which his doctors assumed would also bring down the high fevers he had been suffering. "On the day of Mart's surgery," Tom says, "I went to visit him. Afterward, I ran into his doctor and asked, 'How do you think it went with Mart?' The doctor was very brusque with me and said, 'Well whatever the problem is with the fevers, it won't be cured by this surgery.'"

Stella and David live in southern Kentucky. They had been married fifteen years, had two daughters, and had just recently built their dream house. David, a hemophiliac, had been injecting two blood-clotting factors for over a decade. "The first time we heard anything about AIDS," Stella says in her deep southern accent, "there was a little article in the paper, and it said that hemophiliacs had less than a one-percent chance of getting it. We weren't too concerned about it. Less than a one-percent chance, I said to myself, that means it's going to happen to someone else, not us. This all happened in the spring of 1983. About then, I started reading up on AIDS. David had developed some ailments I thought could be symptoms—a sinus infection that wouldn't go away, and frequent colds. Other than the hemophilia, he never had a cold, flu, whatever. He was the type that was very, very healthy. Then he started to have night sweats, too. I discussed it with David, and I said, 'We need to get you to a doctor.' He wouldn't hear of it. 'I don't have it,' he said. 'We won't worry about it. I'm not going to get it.'"

Joan and Barry are a successful couple who own several dry-cleaning stores in a midwestern state. Their four children have all graduated from college and left home. Joan tells this story: "My youngest son, David, came home at Christmastime, and I could tell immediately something was terribly wrong with him. He had no energy, and he seemed to be running a fever. He looked thin and very pale. He just wanted to sit around the house and rest or sleep. I asked him what was wrong, but he said he didn't know. He told me he had been to a doctor in California, but the doctor told him he was working too hard and needed a vacation.

"I was worried, so I went with him to Stanley, our family doctor, who called me into his office after he examined David. He told David to wait outside, as this matter didn't concern him. Then, out of the blue, Stanley told me he thought David had some of the symptoms of AIDS. I just looked at him, stunned. I actually felt I was having a hard time breathing. After a moment, I said: 'I can't say that to him, Stanley. We've never discussed that part of his life.' So then Stanley suggested that *he* tell David, 'but I'm not going to mention that I told you,' he said. So the doctor told him, and recommended that David be tested for HIV, and gave him a referral to a doctor in California. David never mentioned it during the trip, and neither did my husband, Barry, or I." Joan begins to cry. "I can't tell you how much I regret that we didn't talk about that with our son back then."

Linda is a real estate broker with her own business. She is divorced, and has two children, ages seven and nine. She remembers how her brother *Gary*, then twenty-nine, came to her office one day and shut the door. "At first I couldn't believe my eyes. I hadn't seen him in two months, even though we lived only about a hundred miles apart, and he looked terrible. He was thin and haggard, and he sort of slumped in the chair. Since college I had known Gary was gay. He had been living with another man, Bob, for about five years. But there was no way I could have been prepared for what he told me. He said, 'Linda, I'm really scared. The doctors tell me I'm HIV-positive and have some symptoms of AIDS. I barely have the strength to get to work anymore, and you can imagine that Bob is as scared as I am. We're just not making it.' He started to cry at that point, and I got up and went and hugged him. For years, I had been reading about AIDS because I was afraid for him. I kept thinking, 'How are we going to cope with this? How are we going to tell Mom and Dad?' And I said to him, 'Tell me what you want me to do. Tell me what you need. Do you need to come here, where the family can take care of you?' He had come to me, I knew, because he felt that we could help him get well. But he couldn't go to our parents first."

Meredith and Pete had been lovers for many years—and had two young children—when Pete was diagnosed with AIDS. All Meredith remembers from that time was her shock. "When I heard 'AIDS,' I had a mixture of disbelief and fear, because all I had read so far had been 'gay and AIDS.' " Pete died quickly, leaving Meredith as a single mom. A few months later she, too, developed the full-blown disease. After her initial hospitalizations, Meredith began to seek out support programs for heterosexuals like herself. She was appalled by what she found. "The fact that I was a woman made me ostracized. I was pushing for heterosexual education to get the stigma off the gay community. I kept saying, 'What about the women? What about the drug users?' All the services were being geared toward gay men. I kept saying, 'It's so important that AIDS is not known as the gay plague.' "

Jeffrey and Paul, Tom and Mart, Stella and David, Joan and Barry,

Linda and Gary, and Meredith are all people beginning to discover that HIV disease or AIDS is becoming a central factor in their lives or in the life of someone they love. As you read this book, you will meet many people who have grappled with the issue of caring about and caring for someone with AIDS. Those who speak on these pages are real people who have agreed to be interviewed by the authors and who have agreed to share their experiences. In some cases, their circumstances and names have been changed to protect their privacy, but these people have chosen to do whatever they can to help educate others about this disease.

What Do You Do When Someone You Care About Has AIDS?

Your involvement in the life of a person with AIDS could happen suddenly. You might get a phone call from a friend in great distress. "I need your help," he says. "I'm very sick." It could happen to you as it did to Linda, Joan, or Tom.

Or your involvement could happen gradually. You might notice that your friend, lover, son, daughter, brother, sister, husband, or wife hasn't seemed quite up to par lately. He or she seems to lack energy, to be fatigued, to catch more colds and flus than usual, to have strange rashes that come and go, and to be losing weight. Maybe you have been told enough to know what is going on; maybe you are just guessing that he or she may have tested positive for the HIV antibody, which is a primary indicator of infection. If you care and love this person, you may be on your way to becoming what we call a *carepartner* or a *caring friend*.

A *carepartner* provides continuing emotional support and/or physical care to a person with AIDS. A carepartner can be a friend, a parent, a sibling, a lover—anyone who is willing to become the primary caregiver, one who is willing to be responsible for a person with AIDS on a day-to-day basis. A *caring friend* is our term for a person involved with someone who has AIDS in the same ways that a carepartner is, but to a lesser degree, perhaps less intensely, or not on a daily basis. This relationship, too, is very important to someone confronting the challenge of AIDS.

When someone you care about is diagnosed with AIDS, you should be willing to be a friend in ways you might never have imagined before. You may find yourself learning about experimental drugs and treatments and how to get access to them, rearranging your life around your friend's hospital stays, confronting hurtful prejudice from strangers and outright meanness from family members, expe-

4

riencing anxiety about your own health as well as your friend's—but always hoping that a cure will be found. It is not easy to be either a carepartner or a caring friend, but the purpose of this book is to make it easier—by relating the stories of other real people who have traveled this road, and by giving you the most accurate and up-to-date information available about the disease, its treatments, experimental programs, and all necessary legal and financial planning. We also chart the emotional ups and downs you will experience as you and your friend confront AIDS; we will tell you how you both can sustain yourselves in difficult times. You should feel at liberty to pick and choose what you need from this book to help you at any given moment.

For the sake of simplicity, we will refer to the person who is sick as your *friend*. And we will refer to him or her as *he*, although 13 percent of all people with AIDS are women. We will refer to you not as a lover, mother or father, brother or sister, husband or wife, but also as a *friend*. We use these terms to try to include everyone.

What Are HIV Disease and AIDS?

From all documented scientific accounts, HIV has an extremely long incubation period—that is, the period of time from infection to the onset of actual symptoms may be from three to twelve years, or even longer. HIV infection is thought to be a lifelong condition, though increasingly, doctors are referring to HIV disease as chronic but manageable—especially as new drugs and treatments are developed.

The term "Acquired Immune Deficiency Syndrome," or "AIDS," was coined by the Federal Centers for Disease Control (CDC) in 1982. Since then, much has been learned about this disorder, though much remains to be deciphered. We know that AIDS is an infectious disease characterized by a weakening of the body's immune system. Its effects may vary from individual to individual, depending on many factors, but generally it is progressive and debilitating.

AIDS itself is the most visible and advanced stage of what scientists and doctors now refer to as HIV disease. The CDC currently estimates that at least 1.5 million Americans are infected with HIV. As HIV weakens a person's immune system over time, full-blown AIDS can develop, which is diagnosed by a number of serious infections and cancers. For better or worse, it's simply not possible to predict the future and answer your most important question: "What's going to happen to my friend?"

How Does the Immune System Become Damaged by HIV?

It is believed that HIV, when introduced into the body, first attacks a specific subset of white blood cells called T-4, or T-helper, cells, a key component in the body's defense system against invading organisms. The function of these cells is to alert other white blood cells that a foreign organism is present in the body, and to give an order to search for and destroy them. But once HIV invades a T-4 cell, it takes the cell over, stamping its own genetic code on that cell, which is then reproduced as the cell replicates. In this way, the virus is passed on quickly and quietly from cell to cell. The presence of the virus may go undetected for years as it reproduces, taking over and then killing more and more T-4 cells. Increasing numbers of scientists now believe that even at seroconversion—the time of infection—HIV begins to destroy and upset the delicate balance of the body's immune system. Eventually, all agree, the body has too few T-4 cells to recognize and attack infections as they invade the body. This progressive loss of immune function culminates in a profound and permanent immune deficiency. After a certain point, organisms that our bodies ordinarily fight off immediately and successfully can become life-threatening.

Suzanne, a suburban mother of two, describes her fears regarding one of her daughters, Michelle, a drug user. "As her drug problem increased, so did my fear for her health. She wasn't strong. I used to say that to her: 'Michelle, your body just won't support your lifestyle. Maybe some of the people you know can do this and get away with it for a number of years.' Of course, I chose to think she would outgrow this—that she would eventually take care of her health. She might have. It's not that unusual to be doing drugs at age twenty-four. But it wrecks your immune system, leaving you wide open. As soon as I started hearing about AIDS, something clicked in my brain. I was beside myself that this would happen to her. She was like a profile of someone who would get AIDS."

What Does It Mean to Be HIV-Positive?

Over the course of the last decade, this question has produced many different answers as science continues to unravel the mysteries of HIV.

Primary, or acute, HIV infection refers to the mild flulike illness associated with initial exposure to HIV. In most people, the symptoms of primary HIV infection go entirely unnoticed or are mistaken for an actual case of the flu. These symptoms, which occur two to six weeks after infection, may include fever, sore throat, swollen glands, skin rashes, fatigue, dry cough, and a variety of other aches and pains. The duration of the illness is usually short, between five and fourteen days. Some researchers believe that there is an association between the severity of these initial symptoms and the subsequent course of the disease; the more severe the primary infection, the worse the prognosis.

What happens next is less well understood. Because AIDS has been studied for little more than a decade, it remains difficult for experts to project what percentage of infected individuals will develop AIDS or in what period of time this could occur. The most current data indicate that about half of infected adults will develop AIDS within ten years of primary infection. It is not known what proportion of the remaining individuals will develop AIDS; some, perhaps, never will. Still, the longer the time elapsed since becoming infected, the greater the likelihood of developing AIDS. A small percentage of people who are HIV-infected find themselves free of symptoms and disease after ten years. These individuals also appear to have healthy immune systems. Evidence increasingly suggests that the antiviral drug AZT, along with other drugs like ddI and ddC, may slow the progress of the disease in individuals both with and without symptoms. Other treatments, such as Bactrim or Septra, used to ward off AIDS-related pneumonia (also called *Pneumocystis carinii* pneumonia, or PCP), may delay or retard the onset of symptoms. In general, maintaining a healthy life-style, which supports a strong immune system, may also assist in delaying the onset of symptoms.

How Many People Does HIV Disease Affect?

In the United States alone there were over 250,000 diagnosed cases of AIDS by the end of 1992. Over 170,000 of our brothers and sisters, mothers and fathers, friends and lovers, have died. The CDC predicts that nearly 650,000 Americans will have AIDS by 1995 and that 330,000 of them will have died. Here are some other startling facts:

- More Americans have died from AIDS than died in the Persian Gulf, Vietnam, and Korean wars combined.

- The number of cases of AIDS among young women has nearly doubled in the past two years.
- Between 1985 and 1988, cancer deaths fell 2 percent in the U.S. and deaths from heart disease were down 8 percent; deaths from AIDS surged 175 percent.
- The number of cases of AIDS among teens has increased 70 percent in the past two years. And those are just the reported cases.

These numbers do not tell the whole story. Every statistic is a life. And for every person with AIDS, researchers believe, dozens of other people's lives are directly affected. These are carepartners, lovers, and family members. AIDS is much like a stone tossed into a pond; the effect is ever-widening.

Who Is at Risk for AIDS?

It has long been said about AIDS that it is not *who you are* but *what you do* that puts you at risk. In other words, your sexual orientation, your race, where you live, and your gender are not what puts you at risk. It is what you do, or have done, that counts.

Those individuals at greatest risk are men and women who have had unprotected sexual contact with multiple partners since the middle to late 1970s. In the United States, this risk is the highest in heavily populated areas, such as New York, Miami, Los Angeles, and San Francisco, because of the greater concentration of people with the virus in those locales. However, the virus knows no geographical boundaries and people with HIV are found in every state across the land. In fact, the South reported the largest number of cases in 1991, as well as the greatest rate of increase over the previous year.

The following individuals are also at risk:

- Men and women who have shared syringes (or other drug paraphernalia) for the injection of drugs anytime since the middle to late 1970s. This risk is also highest in densely populated areas.
- Individuals who received transfusions of blood or any blood product before 1984. This group includes hemophiliacs.
- Women who have been artificially inseminated with sperm from individuals who are at risk for AIDS or who have the disease.
- Children of women infected by HIV through any of the

above behaviors, who are at risk in the womb and as a result of breast-feeding.

For much of the last decade, many if not most heterosexuals believed that AIDS was a gay disease or one of intravenous drug users. A recent survey by New York's Gay Men's Health Crisis (GMHC) shows that such beliefs remain steadfast. This is in spite of some very startling and frightening statistics—statistics that tell the stories of real men and women. More than 6 percent, or over fifteen thousand, of all AIDS cases nationwide are among heterosexuals. Among women with AIDS, the picture is even grimmer: More than one third of women with AIDS contracted the disease through sex with a male partner. Often misdiagnosed, women with AIDS die two times faster than men with AIDS. In New York City, AIDS long ago surpassed cancer and murder as the leading cause of death among women between the ages of twenty-five and thirty-four. By the end of 1992, AIDS was expected to become the leading cause of early death in the United States.

Despite these statistics and the lives they represent, many heterosexuals still do not take the risk of AIDS seriously. The consequences can be devastating.

Mirabel, a young mother of six children who lives in Queens, New York, has learned about the consequences firsthand. She had been married to her second husband only a short time when she learned she was pregnant. The father of her other children had died several years before. "Even though I shot up drugs for many years, I never thought I was vulnerable to this disease. I just thought that as a woman, and as a mother, it couldn't happen to me. I first learned that I was infected when I was pregnant two years ago. After much counseling, we decided that I would have an abortion, because we were afraid of the baby being infected. I can't tell you what it meant to have to do that.

"Since then, I've told some of my other children. My eldest daughter, then twenty-one, collapsed and became hysterical when I told her about the disease. It was even worse when we had to do some planning, like about who was going to be responsible for the kids if I died, what kind of funeral I wanted. These are things I never thought I'd be talking to my girls about."

Her daughter Eliza is also incredulous about what has happened. "I'm afraid of seeing my mother with tubes in her body, and all helpless. I want to scream out 'Don't leave me!' I think about her getting sick all the time. I pray to God for strength when she does get ill."

What Contributes to the Onset of Symptoms or Disease?

While the workings of the immune system are not totally understood, secondary factors, or what are called cofactors, almost certainly play a role in the development of disease in specific instances.
Among the most frequently named cofactors for AIDS are poverty
and malnutrition, stress, other infections, sexually transmitted diseases, surgery, and recreational drugs. Some researchers believe that
certain individuals may have a genetic predisposition to the onset of
disease once infected, but this has not been proven. No one, furthermore, has conclusively linked a particular cofactor to the onset
of a particular case of AIDS.

How Is AIDS Transmitted?

In order for HIV infection to occur, the virus has to travel from an
infected individual into the bloodstream of an uninfected person.
This is known to occur in three primary ways: (1) through sexual
activity (where semen or vaginal fluids are passed from one person
to another), (2) through the direct transfer of infected blood (by
the use of contaminated needles or as a result of a blood transfusion), and (3) perinatally, that is, from an infected woman to her
child (it is believed that infection may occur either during pregnancy, during the birthing process, or through the ingestion of
infected breast milk). Recent studies have also reported that oral sex
can lead to infection (pre-ejaculate fluid, semen, and menstrual
blood are all known to contain HIV in infected individuals).

Although trace amounts of HIV have been found in other bodily
fluids, such as saliva and tears, no evidence exists that transmission
has occurred by these fluids. Light or mouth-to-skin kissing is considered to be without risk. Deep kissing, where saliva is passed from
mouth to mouth and where bleeding gums may be a factor, poses a
theoretical, although low, risk of transmission.

There is *no* evidence, after more than ten years, that HIV can be
transmitted through casual contact with an infected person. This
means that no individual has gotten infected as a result of sharing a
glass, a plate of food, or a toilet seat with—or hugging or touching—a person with HIV disease or AIDS. No one is going to get
AIDS by living with someone with the disease, or from living in New
York, San Francisco, or Los Angeles. No one. Zero. End of discussion.

Much has been written about health-care workers becoming infected as a result of being stuck by needles containing infected blood. Despite frequently inflammatory news reports only three dozen documented cases of transmission resulting from accidental inoculation are known to exist. The risk of HIV infection to hospital and laboratory workers appears to be remarkably small, especially when the proper precautions are followed, that is, treating the body fluids of every patient as potentially infected.

Still, questions and fears remain. Experts have been unable to explain how a young woman, the patient of a Florida dentist who had AIDS, became infected with the virus. And there are, moreover, some cases of individuals who, because of lax hospital testing, received contaminated blood transfusions *after* 1984. Whenever you are uncomfortable about information you are being given, ask questions. Call a hot line. Ask more questions.

What Is the HIV Antibody Test?

Since March 1985, a blood test has been available to determine the presence of HIV antibodies, which are formed (in almost all cases) in response to the introduction of HIV into the body. It is called the ELISA test; there is also a more specific confirmation test, called the Western Blot. A positive ELISA test followed by a positive Western Blot almost always indicates HIV infection. Experts agree that these widely used tests have an accuracy rate that compares favorably with other diagnostic tests.

Since its inception, the HIV antibody test has been the subject of much controversy, most notably concerning an individual's right to privacy. Who else will find out the results: your health insurer, your employer, your landlord, the government? AIDS advocates have also stressed the importance of pre- and post-test counseling for the purpose of determining whether an individual will have access to adequate health care and treatment, and explaining what the test actually means for one's health.

If you decide to take the HIV antibody test, you should find a testing site that offers counseling. Because of the threat of being discriminated against, and even of losing your health insurance, you should go to a site where the results will be kept confidential, if not entirely anonymous. (A public health clinic or even your own doctor's office can suffice. Be sure to ask first.)

In cities like New York and San Francisco, among the other epicenters of the epidemic, a high percentage of gay men and many heterosexuals have been tested for HIV. In other areas of the country, where it is difficult to find appropriate counseling, where individuals fear someone will recognize them at the health department or clinic, where there is an even greater threat of discrimination, and where even less information is available about the importance of early detection and treatment, very few people have taken the HIV test.

Despite these caveats, there is no question that individuals who believe they may be infected can benefit from early detection through HIV antibody testing. The paramount benefit is the monitoring of the infection and of T-cell counts so that early intervention treatments can be administered. These treatments have been shown to slow the progression of the disease and to delay the onset of specific symptoms, such as PCP pneumonia. Testing could buy people time.

Early detection and treatment can also save dollars. For instance, it is ten times cheaper to *prevent* PCP with certain medications on an outpatient basis than to *treat* an individual with PCP in the hospital.

What Are the Symptoms of AIDS?

The best doctors in the world can't predict when medical symptoms related to AIDS will appear in someone who is infected with HIV. All of the symptoms listed below may be caused by other diseases. However, when not otherwise explained, the presence of these symptoms should be discussed with a doctor knowledgeable about AIDS and HIV infection. Remember, only a doctor can make a precise diagnosis. Still, here are some early warning signs:

- Fatigue, or a very low energy level, or an inability to be as active as usual, without any apparent reason, over a period of several months.
- Weight loss—perhaps fifteen pounds or more, or 10 percent of body weight—over a three-month period, without any dieting or other change of life-style habits.
- Swollen lymph glands in the groin, the neck, and/or the underarms that last for several months and have no apparent cause (such as the flu or other infection).
- Fevers persisting over several months for which there is no apparent cause. Sometimes these fevers "spike" (shoot up) suddenly.
- Chronic diarrhea.
- Night sweats (waking up in the night with the bed soaked from perspiration).

- Flu or other coldlike symptoms that last for a month or more.
- Rashes and other strange skin irritations that appear over a period of time and then may persist or disappear.

When Should Your Friend See a Doctor?

If your friend tests positive, he should see a doctor immediately for a complete physical, including a workup of his immune system. This is absolutely essential. If an individual does not know his antibody status and is exhibiting some combination of the above-mentioned symptoms, he should talk with his doctor or health-care provider about taking the HIV antibody test.

In addition to the cofactors we've discussed, early treatment can influence your friend's condition. If the two of you do not have a doctor who is knowledgeable about AIDS or with whom you feel comfortable discussing issues of life-style or treatment, you should seek references from friends, an AIDS hot line, or a public health clinic. Your friend will need a doctor who is up-to-date on all aspects of HIV disease and AIDS: This includes symptoms, treatments, experimental programs, and support programs. Unfortunately, many health-care providers still do not know what to look for or how to treat AIDS properly—and many don't wish to learn; this is especially true in smaller cities and suburban and rural areas.

Many tests exist that a doctor might recommend to determine the status of your friend's health. In addition to the HIV antibody test, these would include red blood cell (RBC) and white blood cell (WBC) tests; lymphocyte and platelet counts (which are often low in persons with HIV infection); a T-4 count, which would measure the strength of the immune system; and skin tests for such diseases as mumps, tetanus, and diphtheria, to determine immune function (people with HIV generally react very little, if at all, to these immune-function tests). Your friend's doctor may suggest these as well as other tests. One of you should always ask the doctor what the test is intended to determine and how accurate it is.

"I took the antibody test three years ago, so I've known I was infected since then," says *Stephen*, a San Francisco radio producer. "And I'll tell you, *that* was something. It took me two years just to get the courage up to go to the lab. I kept hearing two voices in my head: one saying 'I should know what's going on in my body' and the other saying 'I'm terrified, I'd just rather not deal with it.' You know, when you're feeling fine, a lot of people would rather not mess with it. But finally, reason prevailed. I had read enough by that time to know that I could be doing a really good thing for myself. I talked with my friend Craig forever about this, and then one day we both decided to go.

"We both tested positive. For about two months I was absolutely convinced my life was over. Everything went wrong, and I thought I wasn't going to be able to handle it. But you know what? It did get better. Craig and I went to a support group for newly tested people. We started to read about HIV . . . and eventually life took on some familiar guises. For now, I see my doctor every six months, when he usually runs a full battery of tests, mostly to see how my immune system is doing. Even though things have gone pretty okay, I still get totally stressed out when it's time to go in." With the anxiety clearly visible on his face, Stephen adds: "It's really hard to be in this kind of no-man's-land: infected, but not sick. I'm just really appreciative of my doctor, of Craig, and of my other close friends who let me do a lot of venting of my emotions."

Howard and Alex have been together for seven years. Both are in their forties; Howard is a businessman, and Alex is an architect. They live in a huge loft that Alex designed. "We were both seeing an internist," Howard explains, "and Alex had been complaining to the doctor repeatedly. Finally, the internist told us that Alex was suffering from chronic depression. The idiot! He knew Alex was gay. He knew all about him. Two years before, Alex had been so sick that his mother and sister came to stay with us. But the doctors never figured out what was wrong with him then."

A doctor more familiar with AIDS might have seen some familiar symptoms here. With greater knowledge, the doctor might have come to an appropriate diagnosis, which could have led to earlier treatment.

David's mother, Joan, explained what happened after she and her husband, Barry, learned that their son had AIDS. "I went back to see our family doctor after my son returned to California. I had been reading everything I could find about AIDS, but it was very confusing. So one evening I went to see Stanley, our family doctor, after all his other patients had left. I didn't have an appointment; I just dropped by. I said, 'Tell me what your diagnosis of David means. I'm really worried. Does this mean that David is going to die?'

"Stanley and I had been friends for years. He had taken care of all my children, so I felt I could trust him. But his answer didn't really help. 'I don't know what it means,' he said. 'Some people with David's symptoms just stay that way. Others get AIDS and die. Many are taking AZT and other prophylactic, or preventative, treatments.

14

These are proving very beneficial to a lot of people.' Then he stopped a minute and looked at me. 'Does David live alone?' he asked. 'Yes,' I answered. 'That's too bad,' he said. 'If he becomes very ill, it's going to be harder for him to take care of himself and his health.'

"For just a moment the thought went through my mind that Stanley was telling me to get David home. But a lot of other thoughts crowded in. 'I have to think about what to tell Barry,' I said. As I got up to leave, Stanley came around the desk and hugged me. He'd never done that. 'This is an awful thing to have to face,' he said. I felt very confused and depressed. On the one hand, something told me that this was a terrible and serious situation. On the other, something inside me just wanted to believe it would all go away.''

Further Symptoms

Following are the symptoms of the opportunistic diseases and cancers that may develop in someone who is infected with HIV. These diseases include, besides Kaposi's sarcoma (KS) and other cancers, infections caused by viruses, fungi, and protozoa, as well as by parasites and bacteria.

- A dry, persistent cough that lasts for a month or more and/or shortness of breath. This could be related to PCP.
- Purple or reddish areas on the skin, or lumps, boils, or sores on top of or beneath the skin, usually appearing on the arms or legs but also occurring on the mucous membranes in the mouth, throat, anus, and nose. These could be signs of Kaposi's sarcoma.
- A persistent thick, whitish coating on the tongue or inside the mouth and throat that may also cause a sore throat. This could be a symptom of thrush (candidiasis). Thrush may appear with oral hairy leukoplakia of the tongue, which looks like little pieces of cottage cheese affixed to the sides of the tongue. Some researchers believe that thrush and hairy leukoplakia are predictive symptoms of AIDS.
- Shingles (herpes zoster), a usually painful infection consisting of clustered small blisters, surrounded by reddened, swollen, and, later, itchy skin, which are usually found near nerve endings. It is most common for shingles to appear along the back and around the sides of the torso, but shingles are also found on the neck and face.
- Easy bruising as well as unexplained bleeding; this could be

15

a sign of immune thrombocytopenic purpura (ITP), which is evidenced by a decreased level of blood platelets.

- Persistent loss of memory or changes in gait or balance; tremors or seizures; changes in vision, hearing, taste, or smell; difficulty in swallowing; changes in mood and other neurological problems. These could be signs of AIDS dementia.

Michael and Joe had been friends for ten years. Michael, a student and part-time taxi driver, had not seen his friend for over two years when Joe moved from Louisiana and took an apartment in a nearby city. Michael remembers their first visit: "First of all, he looked horrible. He was real skinny and appeared exhausted. I ascribed the exhaustion to his just having driven cross-country nonstop, and the fact that he was thin to begin with. Then, a week later, he called me, and he said he couldn't breathe. He came over to visit, and he was exhausted just from climbing the stairs. He said he had been visiting friends, and that he had smoked some pot, and it had hurt his lungs. 'Maybe that's why I can't breathe,' he said. So I asked him when that had been, and he said, 'Three days ago.' 'That's ridiculous,' I said. 'That stuff doesn't last for three days.' A week later I called him, and he said he was lying on his bed and felt horrible and couldn't do anything. So I told him he should go to the doctor."

Jack and Bruce lived in the heart of Houston's gay district—Jack worked as a carpenter, Bruce on a crew repairing city streets—but they loved to spend time outdoors. They almost always went on weekend trips: to Galveston's beaches, camping in east Texas, and even once to a hunting ranch. But it was a trip to southern Mexico that they remember with horror.

Jack explains what happened: "When we got back to Houston, we were both a mess. Both of us had those intestinal bugs, with diarrhea and all that. We went straight to the doctor, who gave us some medication. In about a week I was all right, but Bruce didn't seem to get better. The parasites went away, but then he felt weak, and he was having trouble breathing. Worst of all, he was coughing all the time. I had noticed, too, that he had a white coating on his tongue. Then one night we went out, and he said he couldn't stand the smoke, so we sat outside, although it wasn't warm, and then we walked over to his place. I was really worried about him, so I spent the evening. All night he couldn't breathe. He was actually gasping for air, and I really didn't know what to do about it.

"Early the next morning, I took Bruce to the emergency room at a hospital nearby. I called the doctor who had been treating us, and he said we were in the right hospital. He was a gay doctor who had treated a lot of venereal diseases and people with AIDS. Around noon he came by—we were still in the emergency room—took one look at Bruce, and told us that he was going to call in a pulmonary specialist. He looked in Bruce's mouth and shook his head. 'Damn it' was all he said.''

Linda, the real estate broker whose brother Gary has the virus, remembers the devastation she felt after he told her he was ill. ''I must have made a hundred phone calls that night after Gary left. I called everyone in the country who could tell me anything about AIDS. One person led me to another, and that one to another. I kept hearing over and over that no one knew for sure what would happen to him. But everyone agreed it would certainly be better for him to be at home, where someone could look after him all day. I mean, he was too sick to work. I have to say, I also worried about catching it myself. But everyone told me the same thing: 'No one will get the disease from him unless they have unprotected sex with him or exchange blood with him.' The family was safe. So late that next afternoon, I felt I knew how to approach the whole problem, and I called him and told him to come down that weekend, and we would speak to our parents. He seemed so relieved that he started to cry on the phone.

''You know, before those two days, I never remember Gary crying about anything. He got his tough, athletic manner from our father. Yet he was so unsure of us—his family—that he'd left his lover, Bob, in the car outside when he came in to see me that first evening. Almost like he was afraid I'd throw him out. I keep wondering where that fear came from. I had never hesitated to show him I loved him. Neither had our stepmother, Rose. Of course, our father had always done his masculine thing.''

What Can You Do When Your Friend Becomes Ill?

If your friend develops symptoms of HIV disease, you should urge him to seek treatment from a doctor informed about AIDS if he has not done so himself. If you think it would make your friend feel more comfortable, ask if you can accompany him. If you have been a sexual partner of your friend, then you, too, should consider taking the HIV antibody test if you haven't already. At this point, you should be extremely careful about how your friend's medical bills are submitted to his health insurer. Make sure there is no mention of HIV or T-cell counts. Unfortunately, there are many insurance companies that will attempt to cancel coverage at the first hint of AIDS.

If your friend is diagnosed with HIV disease or AIDS, and if he wants, you should assist him in obtaining as much medical information as he might need at that time. Sooner, rather than later, he may also need information about government entitlement programs (like Social Security Disability), private financial and emotional support organizations, wills, powers of attorney, and a host of other things. Often, your local AIDS organization can provide answers to many of these questions or referrals to other individuals and agencies. (See Appendix C.) You both may find all this overwhelming; many people do. Try to take things one day at a time.

After Meredith, who was infected by her lover, Pete, was diagnosed with AIDS, she realized that much of her energy was going toward supporting her friends, educating them and alleviating their fears, rather than the other way around. "I'm horrified that I had to turn to my gay friends for support, for love, for affection, for an ear, for someone I could tell, 'I'm scared, I'm tired.' But I have to constantly educate the people I grew up with who have remained my friends. They haven't taken the time to inform themselves. The responsibility for AIDS education has fallen on me. It's put a strain on my friendships. I say, 'Get printed material. Call a hot line. Don't put that strain on my friendship, because I don't feel good now. And I need your love. I don't need to be your teacher.' "

Once your friend is diagnosed with AIDS, there are many things he can do to live a healthier life that you can help him with. Your friend may immediately incorporate many of these elements into his life when he learns that he is HIV-positive. But if not, you two should begin to talk about behavior change.

Practice Safe Sex

Your friend should practice safe sex with any and all partners *all* the time. He will also need to be touched, hugged, massaged, and otherwise comforted during this highly stressful time. The safe-sex guidelines are printed in Appendix B. If the two of you are sexual partners—and are both HIV-positive—you should still have *protected* sex between yourselves. Scientists believe that repeated reintroduction of the HIV virus will further weaken the immune system. Evidence also indicates that there are other strains of HIV; the effect of being infected by more than one strain is not completely understood but could be dangerous and hasten the onset of further symptoms. You would also not want to pass on any other sexually transmitted diseases to your friend at this time—or vice versa.

Maintain a Healthy Regime

Your friend should start taking the best possible care of his health. It is not always practical to incorporate many life-style changes at once, so it is important to be both realistic as well as dedicated to change. Here is a list of things for your friend to do, composed by the leading medical, psychological, and nutritional experts:

- Eat a balanced diet, one full of vitamins, minerals, proteins, and carbohydrates. Try to eat three meals a day; avoid junk foods. If your friend is losing weight, your doctor may prescribe a nutritional supplement that, while expensive, can be highly beneficial.
- As much as is possible, reduce stress both at home and at work. Stress and depression may contribute to the further deterioration of the immune system. Getting enough sleep every night is also important to your friend's health.
- Stop using all recreational drugs—no poppers, pot, crack, cocaine, amphetamines, tobacco, or alcohol. All these substances, some of them highly toxic, can further damage the immune system, making it less resistant to disease.
- Use antibiotics only as prescribed. Indiscriminate use can bring on fungal infections and encourage the development of antibiotic-resistant strains of bacteria. Sedatives, aspirin, or Tylenol-like products prescribed by a physician can be used. If your friend's platelet count is low, then his intake of analgesics should be monitored closely by a physician.
- Minor injuries, like scrapes and cuts, should be cleaned immediately with hydrogen peroxide, Mercurochrome, or soap and water, and then further protected with an antiseptic ointment or cream and appropriate bandages. Wounds that do not heal should be seen by a doctor knowledgeable about AIDS. Infections are to be avoided at all costs because they can quickly get out of hand.
- Trips abroad should be planned carefully and not be taken to areas where sanitary conditions are poor. The reason for this is quite simple: Your friend's body has little natural resistance to infections (like intestinal parasites).
- Crowds should be avoided, when possible, to lessen your

friend's exposure to colds and flus—and especially to tuber-culosis—as well as to any other airborne germs that might be present.

- Your friend should try to stay out of intense sunlight. There is evidence that, over time, strong sunlight weakens the immune system.
- Pets should be approached with caution because they may carry disease-causing organisms. This is especially true of cats, which have parasites in their stools known to cause toxoplasmosis (a severe infection of the brain). Use rubber gloves and face masks when handling pet wastes.

What's Left?

After this list of don'ts, you and your friend might ask, "What's left?" Some people have found it easier to make changes when they let go of the question "Will AIDS change my life?" and replace it with "*How* will AIDS change my life?" But accepting the reality of having a life-threatening disease takes time. No doubt about it.

The main lesson is that your friend needs to begin paying more attention to his body. You should pay attention to *your* body as well, since you may now be under greater stress than you have ever known. Your body will try to let you know when you are using it too hard, when you are not feeding it right, when it is not getting enough sleep. "Am I getting too tired?" "Does eating this food make me feel good?" Help your friend to notice by noticing *yourself* and talking about what you see and feel.

What's Ahead?

With all the changes happening, try to keep some things—as many things as possible—the same as before. For instance, try to include your friend in activities you might have done together previously—from skiing trips to shopping trips. If you can manage it without upsetting him, pay attention to what he eats, how much he drinks, and when he sleeps. But don't irritate him or make him feel as if he's unable to do these things for himself.

Whatever you do, don't run away. Don't avoid him. Of course, there will be times when you think, "I can't handle this anymore. I'm out of here." Or, "This is just too painful to be a part of. I'm leaving." Nearly everyone has these thoughts at some point when they care about someone with AIDS. Listen to yourself. And then stop and think, "What's really going on? Am I afraid for him? Am I afraid for me? Do I feel powerless? Is he shutting me out? What would happen if I took a break?" Above all, remember that no one ever said this would be easy. You should also remember that one of the most important components of health is the desire to be healthy—in other words, motivation. Someone who feels the companionship and love of his friends will have more reason to maintain his health.

2

WHEN YOU BECOME A CAREPARTNER OR CARING FRIEND

Most likely you will be reading this chapter if your friend's health has taken a significant turn for the worse. Perhaps this is his first hospitalization, or he is being plagued by an infirmity or disability that requires a great deal of your time and energy. As HIV disease progresses, you will find your relationship with your friend changing. Over time, this is likely to mean he will require different—and more—attention from you as a friend. As small problems and decisions give way to larger ones, you will find yourself redefining the friendship. Although it may sound dramatic, much about your life and your friend's life will change radically as his health fluctuates. Be prepared for a roller-coaster ride as you begin to deal with your friend's illness on a regular basis.

Whether you notice it right away or not, your interests will probably change, as will your priorities. You may even find that your core values begin to look different. Like many others, you may find yourself wondering: "What is happening to me? Why is my job suddenly less satisfying? Why do my other friends seem irrelevant? Why do I always seem to want to be somewhere else, like with my friend who is ill?" By asking these sorts of questions and becoming aware of the changes, you will begin to see and feel how your life is dovetailing with your friend's; you will find you have become a carepartner or a caring friend of someone with AIDS.

What to Expect Now that Your Friend Is Sick

There are some events and experiences that almost all carepartners share, some characteristics and attitudes that you, too, will most likely develop. These are part of the definition of a carepartner or caring friend.

A Feeling of Urgency

As a carepartner, your sense of time and urgency will undoubtedly speed up. Often, when this is all very new, you may feel that you have put your life on hold for the duration of your friend's illness. This may be troubling to you for a variety of reasons. You may actually feel that you are waiting for the day when you can begin to live your own life again. Then one day it will probably occur to you, as it has to many others, "What am I waiting for? If I am waiting for something, then I must be waiting for my friend to die." This is a normal response, and the guilt you may feel is natural, too.

Once the initial crisis of an AIDS diagnosis or opportunistic infection has passed, you'll come to realize that your friend may live for quite some time, and may go months, if not years, between serious illnesses. Although not a cure, the use of AZT and other medications has been clearly shown to delay the onset of symptoms in many individuals. People with AIDS are living longer and better lives than was the case earlier in the epidemic. Most likely, you will find yourself working to turn the time you spend with your friend into a positive and fulfilling experience. Once you get past the attitude of "I am doing all I can to help you live, but I will never be free until you die," you'll find yourself and your friend very much alive.

Still, you should each acknowledge the enormous stress that faces you and begin to learn to "live for each day." Although it may sound simplistic, a slogan like that can be helpful.

Tom explains how he and his longtime lover, Mart, who is infected with HIV, learned to look beyond the immediate future. "Because Mart and I both had been so sure it was going to be a quick, dismal, dreary end, each day that we had—each good thing that happened to us—we became aware of. It was a gift. Each addi-

tional day and joyful experience was a bonus that we hadn't expected to have. Therefore, we valued it even more. And do you know
what? We were wrong. We had a lot of time.''

A Deepening Relationship

As a carepartner, you will probably develop a deeper, symbiotic
relationship with your friend. Because of the experiences, good and
bad, you are sharing—panic attacks, doctor visits, and hospitalizations as well as dinners, movies, and family holidays—you can only
become closer. When your friend goes through a period of being
relatively healthy and all is well, you and he may get the sense that
everything will end happily after all. Perhaps you'll feel that you will
both wake up to discover that this whole AIDS thing was just a bad
dream—a nightmare you somehow shared. This kind of hope can
bring you closer.

But when the next crisis occurs, you may both go through the
exact same fear and dread as before. Then one of you will grab on
to reality. "Look, we got through this before. We'll do it again. We'll
just have to deal with whatever comes along. We owe that to each
other.'' Indeed, even the down times can result in more intimacy
and trust between you.

Len and Evan have been through many highs and lows during
Evan's illness. Len, a book editor in his forties, was in Texas visiting
family when Evan called from his parents' home in Florida, explaining that he was sick again. "We both flew back home to New York
immediately,'' Len recalls. "On the plane, my mind was in turmoil.
'How did he get sick again so soon? He's only been out of the
hospital six weeks.' I felt so depressed and angry. When I got home,
Evan was there with two friends who had picked him up at the
airport. He, too, was discouraged. 'How can I get sick so often?' he
asked. 'My body's not going to be able to take that.' But we sat
together for a while, sort of leaning against each other, and slowly
we began to calm down. Then Evan's friends left, and we began to
get things ready for him to take to the hospital. Without saying
anything, we both knew that we would do what we needed to do.
The panic, depression, all of that was gone.''

Memory can also play its tricks with a disease like AIDS. Often,
we tend to forget the quieter, easier times in the wake of tougher
ones. In fact, even though Len said that Evan had "only been out of
the hospital six weeks,'' at other times they had gone many, many

months between illnesses. You, too, can maintain the hope that you and your friend will be as fortunate.

As the level of trust deepens between the two of you, you'll probably find that you are becoming a more active participant in your friend's life and treatment. You may arrange for doctors' visits, argue with insurance companies, bring back information about government entitlement programs or experimental therapies. The more you help out, give guidance when asked, and become an informed partner, the more gratified and fulfilled you will feel. You will probably wake up one day and realize, "Yes, I made a difference."

Giving Basic Care

As a carepartner, you will find yourself providing practical as well as emotional and spiritual support. You will run errands, wash clothes, cook meals, change sheets, take temperatures, dress sores, keep company, and wake up in the night to give medicine. The list is truly endless. Usually, you will do all this while you continue with your own life: going to work, paying the bills, taking care of the children.

Hugh and John, both in their late thirties, went through drastic changes as John became sicker, first with chronic diarrhea, then with other infections. Hugh, John's lover, a contractor, describes his life this way: "The first few months that John was sick, I just didn't believe it. I mean, what do you do? It was like every conceivable problem in the world was there. I got a big job renovating a kitchen, and I was trying to do all the work myself so I could make more money. Meanwhile, I got up at six and made breakfast every morning for the both of us, then went to work, ran home to make John lunch, and ran back to work. So naturally, everything got all screwed up and I lost the job. At one point, John owed two months' back rent. I owed a month's rent. I told John everything was taken care of."

Suzanne, meanwhile, went from "zero to sixty" in no time when it came to taking care of her daughter Michelle. But there was a price to pay. "I don't know how much of it was that I didn't want to think. I was constantly running. Anything she wanted, I ran for. Even when I was visiting her in the hospital, I was running to Sixth Avenue, Seventh Avenue. 'So you want a grape, no problem.' Somehow, I think running that fast is also running away from what's happening. It's too large a problem to really digest."

25

Why Taking Care of Someone with AIDS Is Different

Being a carepartner of someone with AIDS is a vastly different experience from being the primary caregiver of someone with any other devastating illness, such as cancer or Alzheimer's disease. Carepartners and friends of people with AIDS encounter a great many painful and difficult circumstances that make this illness unique. Here are some attitudes and problems specific to AIDS.

A Disease and a Stigma

For many people, AIDS is much more than an illness: It is the twentieth-century version of the Scarlet Letter. In her 1988 book, *AIDS and Its Metaphors*, Susan Sontag compared the stigma of AIDS with that of cancer.

> With AIDS, the shame is linked to an imputation of guilt; and the scandal is not at all obscure. Few wonder, Why me . . . ? It is not a mysterious affliction that seems to strike at random. Indeed to get AIDS is precisely to be revealed, in the majority of cases so far, as a member of a certain "risk group," a community of pariahs. The illness flushes out an identity that might have remained hidden from neighbors, jobmates, family, friends. It also confirms an identity and, among the risk group in the United States most severely affected in the beginning, homosexual men, has been . . . an experience that isolates the ill and exposes them to harassment and persecution.

Fear and ignorance drive the discrimination and persecution, which can lead to hurtful, deeply painful actions.

Ricky, Robert, and Randy Ray were three young boys in grammar school when, in 1986, they learned that they were HIV-positive as a result of the clotting factor they were taking for their hemophilia. After their parents wrangled in the courts for a year, desperately trying to keep the boys in school, near panic swept the Rays' small Florida town when they won their case. "I was scared at the beginning when Mom and Dad said [that people in town] were trying to kill us," then ten-year-old Ricky explained. "Sometimes when we were in our tree house, other boys would be down on the ground shouting, 'Where are those queers? Where are those fags?' " A week after school started, a stranger called the Ray house and said, "Your children will die." That night, someone torched the family house, destroying everything.

Meredith found that when her lover, Pete, was at his worst, discrimination based on fear weighed in heavily. "One day I went to see him at home, and his urine was the color of black coffee. I panicked, begged someone, anyone, 'Please let me use your car, just to take us to the medical center.' I said, 'I'll hold him,' because he wasn't bigger than a pea by then. I went to the newspapers and said, 'We need help.' They actually wrote a story, but the only replies we got were threatening phone calls: 'He's a nigger, let him die.' Or 'He's a junkie, let him die.' I mean, the man's a man. Who are any of us to judge him?"

The majority of people afflicted with AIDS continue to be gay men and intravenous drug users. Women, blacks, and Latinos are disproportionately represented in the tally of AIDS cases. These are the very groups in this country that are already subject to bigotry and prejudice. With an AIDS diagnosis, these prejudices are often exacerbated.

Suzanne lives in a beautiful town house with her husband, Bob, and Michelle's sister, Camille. "I always wish that I could paint a really good picture of Michelle," Suzanne says. "She was unusual, but the fact that she was a drug addict paints a certain picture. The stigma attached to anyone who is a drug addict is tremendous. It almost makes them modern-day lepers, and not just the addict, but the entire family: me, my daughter Camille, and my husband, Bob."

People often blame addicts for everything that happens to them. But the truth is more complicated than that. "Michelle was *always* such a difficult child," Suzanne recalls. "She was born with four defects in her heart. I think the medication that she received during all those years of operations and pneumonia just grew into street drugs. She grew up with the notion 'If there's a problem, there's a drug to fix it.' That was a big part of the problem."

For much of the epidemic, discrimination has been visible and widespread. Ryan White, an Indiana teenager, was forced to leave his school and home because of threats and name-calling, not to mention gunshots aimed at his home and slashed tires on the family car. John Chadbourne, an analyst at the Raytheon Company in southern California, was denied his job after a short hospital stay for PCP. A friend recalled that the company "said some of John's coworkers believed they could get AIDS just from working with him." Chadbourne, who died penniless, won his AIDS-discrimination case posthumously. And because of her health status, Janice Campion, a woman with AIDS, could not find a surgeon to operate on her. "They were afraid," she said. "But was that my problem?"

Prejudice is not limited to any place or any kind of person. As a carepartner, you should always be on the alert for possible discrimination against your friend. At times, you will have to be your friend's voice, taking timely and appropriate action. Ryan White's mother, Jeanne, stood alongside her son in his crusade against AIDS discrimination; John Chadbourne's friend Ann Wood got him an attorney. For a long time, Janice Campion had no one, and she almost died because she could not get her surgery. You may not like conflict or confrontation; you may never have fought for your rights or anyone else's. But now, you must be prepared—for your friend's sake.

The Fear of Infection

The infectious aspect of AIDS make it different from other catastrophic diseases, especially when lovers or spouses are involved. Usually, people caring for someone with a very serious disease do not fear that they themselves may contract the illness. For instance, no one worries that cancer could be contagious. But once again, AIDS raises unique issues. Carepartners who have had sexual relations or shared needles with their friend or who are themselves HIV-infected may have real and justified fears. "Am I infected?" you may ask, if you don't know. Or if you are infected, you may find yourself asking: "Will I become as ill as my friend?" That is scary.

Raoul is a gay psychotherapist in Los Angeles whose practice consists exclusively of gay men—among them, people with AIDS. Despite his work, he says he will not seriously date anyone with AIDS. "It's a lot of different things," he explains cautiously and with some embarrassment. "Even though I know a lot about AIDS, I am still afraid that I could become infected. I can't explain it. Beyond that, I just don't want the responsibility of caring for someone who will become so ill. I've watched many, many friends die. . . . I see it in my work. . . . I just can't do it anymore. After a pause, Raoul continues: "Earlier this year I was seeing a guy who was HIV-positive. And early on I told him, 'Look, this can't get serious.' As you can imagine, he found this very hurtful. At one point he said, 'You know, you're no better than some of those Jesse Helms types.' In the end, I broke off the relationship because of his health status."

Parents and nonsexual friends do not have to deal with these fears. Still, even the most well-meaning and loving friends or relatives, not to mention uncaring strangers, may be beset with fears of contagion that have nothing to do with reality. You may be afraid to drink from a glass in your friend's home or hospital room, to eat off his plates, to sit on a toilet he's used, to touch a doorknob he's touched. You might seat yourself as far across the room from your friend as is possible. "Will I get infected by spending time in close contact with my friend?" you may worry, even if you know better. While you realize that all these reactions are based on irrational fears, they can be very hurtful, nonetheless. As best you can, steady yourself and talk yourself through your reactions. If you have questions about the transmission of HIV, ask the right people for answers.

A Note About Other Infections

While AIDS is not infectious through casual contact, there are other infections and viruses that can be more easily transmitted. Recently, tuberculosis has become epidemic in American cities, especially among people with AIDS. If you are taking care of someone with TB, you should be checked regularly, at least annually, to see if you have become infected. At times during your friend's course of treatment for infectious TB, it may be advisable for you to wear a mask in his presence and to take other precautions. For more information, you should speak with your doctor, local health department, or an AIDS organization.

Similarly, if your friend develops acute hepatitis (yellow jaundice) or is a carrier of the hepatitis B virus, then anyone coming in close contact with him (i.e., anyone living with him, as well as his current or recent sexual partners) should speak to a health-care provider about receiving treatment and/or a vaccine to prevent infection.

Other diseases that your friend may have, including diarrhea, chicken pox or shingles, and fever blisters or cold sores, require special precautions. You should speak to your doctor or a local AIDS agency to find out more about how to protect yourself and yet remain an integral and intimate part of your friend's day-to-day life. But remember, *HIV itself is not transmissible through casual contact.* When you are caring for someone with AIDS-related illnesses, you should take the same sort of precautions you would take in caring for anybody with a serious illness.

How and When to Talk About "The News"

The decision about when to tell and whom to tell of an AIDS diagnosis (or infection with HIV) can be difficult and wrenching for your friend. "Will my parents disown me? Will my job be safe? How will my friends treat me?" These are only some of the many questions that will arise. At this time, you can be of the greatest service to your friend by acting as a nonjudgmental sounding board. "What are the pros and cons?" you might ask. "What will you gain? What might you lose?"

There may be occasions when your friend will ask you to tell others or, because of his condition, when you will find that you *have* to. If a situation like this occurs, you should state the facts as you know them and, if your friend agrees, refer those you've told to a doctor or other sources of reliable AIDS information.

When your friend tells others that he is HIV-positive or has AIDS, it often means the simultaneous disclosure of other aspects of his life, elements that he may have chosen not to reveal in the past, such as the fact that he is gay or was a needle-user. For some, these disclosures can be very anxiety-producing. There are no rules concerning whom to tell or how. Your friend should use his own best judgment—and that of his carepartner. You should be available for support, and you may even ask your friend if he would like you to be present during certain conversations.

The contractor, Hugh, became frightened because his lover, John, was very sick and had not yet told his family anything about his illness. As Hugh explains: "I called his family and told them I thought they should come up to see John. I had never spoken to these people before in my life. I told his brother that he should visit, but I didn't mention anything about AIDS. Later, when they were in New York with us, I was talking to John's mother and brothers in the hospital waiting room. She was this very proper southern lady, who chain-smoked constantly, tailored to a T, very charming. Finally she asked me, 'What's wrong with John?' So I told her that John had no immune system left. 'What does that all mean?' she asked. And I told her that John had AIDS. That must have been a huge shock to her, because she turned to one of her other sons and said, 'I didn't know that John had that style of life.' At that point, I'm sure she was in denial, because she turned to another one of her sons and said, 'I think we should go eat.' Then they left for lunch."

"I went numb for a long time," explains Mirabel, the young mother of six, talking about the period after her AIDS diagnosis. "I just couldn't believe it. I didn't want to hear about it, talk about it, or anything. I shelved it. But after working in therapy on what the diagnosis meant to me, and could mean for my family, I decided to talk to my two eldest girls. I mean, I had to. I had to be responsible about the future. The time wasn't perfect, but I asked myself: 'When will that perfect time be?' I knew the answer to that one. Never.

"What happened? My girls were very upset. I had to educate them at the same time I was dealing with my own feelings. But I needed them to know, because they are my family." Mirabel begins to cry as she speaks about her daughters. "I love my kids so much. My whole world revolves around them. I knew we'd get through it one day at a time."

Support or Abandonment

When people contract illnesses other than AIDS, their friends and carepartners will often get a great deal of support from their own family, friends, and co-workers. But where AIDS is concerned, in all too many cases, both the ill person and the caring friend find themselves alone—ignored by those closest to them precisely at the time they need the greatest support. Disclosure of an AIDS diagnosis can have ramifications from employment to insurance to where your friend lives. Moreover, it's not just a family but a support group or a network of friends that can disappear—to be replaced or altered over the course of the disease. Help your friend think things through, to make decisions carefully.

Michael explains what happened to his friend Joe. "The minute that I heard Joe was in the hospital, I went to see him. Once the diagnosis was confirmed, Joe called his family, and his family—well, his mother, anyway, initially sounded like she was going to let him come home. She said to him, 'I talked to the doctors in New Orleans, and I'm finding out that I can't get it from kissing you on the cheek, and we can share the same glasses and plates, so everything sounds okay.' It sounded like he was going home. I was relieved. Then, twenty-four hours later, his father had flipped out, called up, and said: 'You can't come home.'

"Joe didn't know what he was going to do. I said, 'You can come stay with me if you want.' I said it pro forma, strictly ritualistic. I really believed his family was going to get over their temporary aberration, and he was going to go home. That's really what I thought was going to happen. Of course, it didn't."

Mart had a very different experience. His mother came to stay with him four days after he came out of the hospital. "I had never told her I was gay," he says. "She had asked me once, a year ago, if I was gay, and I had denied it. When she got here, she was going on about how much healthier I looked and that I was going to be fine.

31

Tom took me aside and said, 'You've got to tell her. Right away. You can't let her think that.' You see, we hadn't told anyone what was wrong with me.

"Tom went out and left me and my mother here together. And I said to her, 'I've got to tell you something pretty bad.' And I started to cry. She said, 'Tell me, just tell me.' So I told her I had AIDS. I think I told her first that I was gay and that Tom and I had been more than roommates all these years. That was a difficult thing to do, but once it was over, I felt relieved. She was supportive and has been since then."

Rose, Linda and Gary's stepmother, tells of the Saturday afternoon Linda and Gary came to visit her and their father, Charlie. "When I saw them," Rose says, "I touched Charlie's arm, and we both knew something was terribly wrong with Gary. He had that look about him that said 'serious illness.' We hugged him and had him sit in the big stuffed chair. Linda explained it all to us. I guess that's what makes her such a good businesswoman. She knows all the facts, she lays out the alternatives, then she makes recommendations. 'He has symptoms related to AIDS,' Linda said, 'and some of them are very serious.'

"I decided he should come home, where I can take care of him. He's my son and my responsibility. No mother ever loved her son more. I looked at Charlie, and he looked at Gary. 'Yes, by all means, come home,' Charlie said. 'If there's any place in the world where you can get well, it's under the care of Rose.' He reached over and put his hand on mine. So it was settled that afternoon. Gary planned to move the following weekend. Not one of us brought up the fact that Gary had just told us he was gay."

Denial: A Way to Avoid the Real Issue

Sometimes when a gay man comes out to his family or to his co-workers at the same time he reveals his AIDS diagnosis, the response focuses on the question of "How did you get it?" rather than on the fact of the illness itself. Intravenous drug users have run into the same difficulty in telling their loved ones and acquaintances. In both cases, the double whammy can be very difficult for many to assimilate. Unfortunately, some people with AIDS have been abandoned by friends and family at the very time when they are most in need. As your friend's carepartner, you will find that any kind of abandonment increases the burden on your shoulders. It will mean that your friend will have less support from other sources. And the abandonment may raise new issues for your friend and, as a result, for you. Be aware of these new issues, and as best you can, continue to take things one step at a time.

Joan explains her husband's reaction to the news of their son's illness: "Basically, Barry was flabbergasted. 'You mean, David is a homosexual? I just can't believe it. He didn't get that from me!' I wanted to say to him that it was obvious all through high school and college that David was different. David didn't date many girls, and he never seemed very interested in them. So I repeated: 'Barry, David may come down with full-blown AIDS. He may get very sick.' But Barry couldn't focus on David's illness. It was almost like he wasn't interested in it. 'They'll figure that out,' he said, sort of dismissing the whole thing. But then he added, 'What if our friends find out?' "

A different tragedy exists when someone with AIDS has no one to call on. After *Eddie*, a clerk with a local telephone company, became too ill to live on his own in San Francisco, he contacted his family in Kansas to see if he could return home. Despite his parents' divorce and despite his having been abused as a child, Eddie harbored illusions of being taken back into the fold. But he had not seen his family in over thirteen years, and when he asked them to take care of him, they could not forget the real reason for the schism: Eddie's homosexuality. During the nearly two years Eddie was sick, no family member ever came to visit him in San Francisco. He spent much of his time lying alone in his bed in a city-funded residence for people with AIDS.

For some, though, to be abandoned by family has led to an unexpected positive outcome—namely, a closer relationship with a carepartner. The intensity, the closeness, the loving, and the sharing in the relationship tend to build to a level many people with AIDS have never experienced before, not even when they were well.

With the epidemic growing uncontrollably in Los Angeles, *Samantha* had volunteered to become a "buddy" for someone with AIDS; her first client was a seventeen-year-old named Rocky, whose family could not accept his gayness or his disease. Samantha, a lesbian, had also become estranged from her family over the issue of sexual orientation. "We talked a lot about his relationship with his family. His mother was all over him—'Don't do this, do that'—and his father was, like, as they say, 'not there.' " For five months, Rocky and Samantha spent every afternoon together. "We talked about everything," Samantha says, smiling knowingly. And then, suddenly, Rocky died. "I missed him intensely," she says. "I felt really close to him, and I loved him, and I felt like he loved me a lot. I don't know how we got so close, but it was a very special relationship."

Lack of Support from Medical Professionals

Doctors, nurses, and other hospital staffers sometimes don't provide people with AIDS the kind of support or care that they need. In a major opinion poll taken in 1991, nearly one third of responding physicians said they saw nothing wrong in refusing to treat HIV-infected individuals. Some doctors have refused to perform elective surgery on patients with HIV disease. But those are the more glaring problems. Less obvious, more subtly discriminatory, are the doctors and other medical professionals who isolate or withdraw from a person with HIV because they are not capable of dealing with the many ramifications of the disease. Some of them are fearful of becoming infected themselves; some harbor prejudice; others have difficulty facing the all too predictable outcome.

Regardless, doctors do not have a choice about whether or not they will treat someone with AIDS. According to the American Medical Association:

> A physician may not ethically refuse to treat a patient whose condition is within the physician's current realm of competence solely because the patient has been infected with [HIV]. . . . When an epidemic prevails, a physician must continue his labors without regard to the risk to his own health. . . . The doctor has a special social status, and in return society expects that the doctor will shoulder certain risks and take care of the sick, including people with AIDS. . . . A person with AIDS needs compassionate treatment. Neither those who have the disease nor those who have been infected with the virus should be subjected to discrimination based on fear or prejudice, least of all by members of the health care community.

If you feel that a health-care provider has discriminated against your friend, and your friend is not capable of dealing with the problem, then you will need to step forward as his advocate. If this occurs, you should know your rights and what it is you want for your friend. Be clear, be direct, and follow up all conversations in writing.

Another problem faced by some carepartners is that there are medical professionals who do not provide them the same recognition and access they would to a parent or a legal spouse. Again, ask your friend to verbalize his wishes and then have him follow up with a letter, to be placed in his chart, naming you as his primary carepartner.

Meredith found that Pete's doctors went the extra mile to accommodate her. "They had set up a cot for me in his room. The doctors were very open with me, given that I wasn't his wife. Because it was a medical center, every day there would be teams of students coming in with the doctors. I got to hear them ask questions, and I was allowed to ask them questions. As his neurological problems became more prominent, he would often use me to interpret. After they'd leave the room, he'd get quiet and ask me, 'What did they mean when they said . . . ?' He actually got the words right, but backward. I became his interpreter. I became his right hand because he couldn't function."

Many carepartners have expressed surprise at the sheer number of issues and problems that come to rest in their hands. At times you may feel overwhelmed. Or you may say, "I only signed on to help with my friend's medical problems. Now it seems like I'm carrying the whole world." These feelings are not uncommon. Talk about them with your friend and with other friends. You may decide to join a support group specifically designed for carepartners. Remember, you are not alone. Nor are you the first to travel this path.

What Are the Special Fears and Needs of Carepartners?

All our friends make demands on us from time to time as they come to us with their vices and virtues. Generally, we accept and overlook a friend's more difficult sides because we like and enjoy this person. The situation is the same with our friends who have AIDS. While the demands they make on us may be greater and more frequent than those of our other friends, the rewards they give us can be greater as well: the intimacy, their gratitude, our appreciation of the routine heroics of being ill with AIDS.

Still, when someone you know is diagnosed with AIDS, your inclination may be to stay away, to try to distance yourself from your friend. Why? The reasons include a complex web of psychological issues as well as the personal experiences each of us carries. If you yourself are also HIV-positive, the diagnosis of full-blown AIDS in a friend may be very personally threatening. "I don't want that to happen to me," you may say. If you have already lost dozens of friends, you may say to yourself: "I just can't do it again." Whatever the reasons, they are commonplace and to be expected, and you will find yourself experiencing them and coming to terms with them as you and your friend confront AIDS. Following are some of the specific fears you may realize. Later in the book, we'll talk more about how to handle them.

Fear of Contagion

You may be afraid that your friend will give you AIDS, even though you know better. You have undoubtedly heard television reports or seen tabloid stories proclaiming the presence of the live virus in saliva and other bodily fluids. AIDS VIRUS LIVES 100 YEARS OUTSIDE HUMAN BODY could be one such headline! Or you're afraid that, despite all the evidence to the contrary, you may contract the virus by sharing a glass, hugging or kissing, or just breathing the same air as your friend. All these fears can be heightened when you go to the hospital and see the precautions the medical staff takes—*to protect the patient from you and outside germs.* But still, you may say quietly: "If these people are supposed to know what they're doing—and the disease is spread only by sexual contact or needle sharing—what are they afraid of? Why are they wearing masks just to deliver a food tray?" These are reflexive, natural fears, particularly in light of all that is still not known about the disease and the fact that it remains, to date, incurable.

Suzanne's first experience with hospital procedures was terrifying. "That first Sunday when Michelle was in the hospital, I remember arriving at her room and seeing this orange ISOLATION sign. People were running in and out of the room, and they were all wearing masks and gloves. I became terrified. And I began to worry about the rest of my family, about my other daughter. My God, Michelle had been going into the refrigerator and drinking from the milk carton. She shared the bathroom with us, even though there's two bathrooms. We had all been taking care of her. So I spent a couple of days chasing the young men up and down the hospital corridors, asking about the rest of us. I needed to be reassured. And they did; they all assured me that AIDS was not easy to get. These procedures, they explained, are for the protection of the patient. They should say that right off. That was such a frightening experience. I mean, they would come into her room covered in plastic just to take out the garbage."

Bill, a forty-year-old newspaper editor, had been admitted to a Honolulu hospital on very short notice, presumed to have a case of PCP. As a journalist, he has a keen eye for the important details: "I was looking for any sign from anyone that they thought I was loathsome or scary or immoral or unpleasant or whatever. You can really become attuned to that, to the point of paranoia. I developed an acute sense of how people treated me. The doctor stood against the wall when he talked to me; was that because he was fearful? He put on gloves to examine me—just to palpate my abdomen—which certainly wasn't necessary. I came to dread the sound of gloves being put on.

"I was staying on the penthouse floor of the hospital, and as I was lying in bed, I noticed a workman was nailing the sliding glass doors shut. I asked him why, and he said to keep the air-conditioning in. I thought they were worried about me committing suicide. I realized this is the hospital's way of dealing with people with AIDS. It didn't say anything about me. It was like a machine taking over—a mechanical response."

Nearly every person who has been a carepartner has, at some point, had an irrational fear of contagion. This feeling almost always dissipates with time and experience. After the initial shock, you will begin again to see your friend as your friend—and not only as a person with AIDS.

Fear of Similar Life-styles

If you have ever had gay sex or been a needle user at any time, you may see a lot of similarities between your life and your friend's. "He and I used to party all the time," you may remember. "We also went to the same clubs, baths, and private parties. If he's gotten sick, will I, too?" The underlying question is clearly "Is my fate already sealed?" And there is no doubt that these fears can cause enormous additional anxiety, particularly if you know you are HIV-positive.

Mark and Sam have been friends since high school. Mark, now twenty-six, is a computer programmer living in Los Angeles. "It seems like Sam and I have always been friends," he says. "We had fooled around a little in the beginning, but sex never really worked for us. So with that out of the way, we became really good buddies. We did so many things together—you know, go out to the bars, the discos, the beach, the movies. We went up to San Francisco on weekends. We bought grass from the same guy. We always discussed all our little affairs. So when he got sick, I freaked out. How long was it going to be before it happened to me? I started looking in every mirror for KS lesions. I couldn't believe that I was having these really negative feelings toward Sam. In addition to being scared, I started to blame Sam in my mind. I needed someone to blame, someplace to focus my fear. I chose Sam."

Our first instinct is often to blame, particularly when we're scared. You will probably have a lot of questions and conflicting feelings if you and your friend traveled in the same circles. There are no answers to questions like "Why him, not me?" or "After him, will it be my turn?" The best you can do is take care of your friend, take care of yourself, and keep open the lines of communication.

Fear of Helplessness

There are times when you will feel powerless or helpless to do anything for your friend. You may find that he becomes depressed, angry, or withdrawn for no discernible reason. In fact, he may lash out at you—since you may well be the closest target. These will be difficult times. You won't always know what to say or do. Your friend, when asked, may not even be able to tell you what he would like from you at a particular time.

Linda tells what happened when her brother Gary came home to stay with their parents. "When everyone—I mean my mother and father and my other brother—got over the shock of finding out not only that Gary was gay but that he was sick, then we all settled in to help him get well. After a few weeks, though, everyone started getting so depressed because Gary wasn't getting any better. We all felt so helpless because nothing we did seemed to make any difference. He was still losing weight, and no one could get him to eat much, and the medicines were nothing but analgesics to keep his fever down. I remember one day my mother called me and said, 'God forgive me, Linda, for even thinking such a thing, but sometimes I want to send Gary away. I don't want to see him. I want to shut the door to his room and pretend that he's still living in Chicago. I feel so helpless. I go out and sit in the car and cry so he can't hear me.'"

Helplessness is not a state many of us are accustomed to or experienced with. Acceptance of helplessness is the recognition of our limited ability to change a situation. At times, it means that we must "let go." With someone you care about or love, this step can be very painful and difficult.

Fear of Death

Except in wartime, when circumstances are, perhaps, unique, we do not live with the specter of the prospective deaths of many or even all of our friends, especially at an early age. In many communities, gay men and intravenous drug users have watched their entire friendship network evaporate. These deaths are out of the normal chronological sequence as we have come to understand it. Parents lose children, friends lose friends, lovers lose lovers, all before they expect it. Confronted with the relentless progression of death, so many of us don't know what to do. The situation makes no sense. As a carepartner, you should expect it to raise your own fears as well.

In October 1992, the AIDS Memorial Quilt was laid out once again on the Washington Mall, blanketing the grass with the handiwork of those who had survived the death of a loved one to AIDS. Over twenty-one thousand panels were unfolded, each representing another AIDS death. One man, who had traveled over five hours to pay homage to his friends who died from AIDS, recalls, "As far as I could see, there were panels representing the dead. I've lost count of how many friends I've lost and how many the government says have died. Death just seems omnipresent. Sometimes I want to escape those feelings, but that would mean abandoning my friends who are sick now and jettisoning my memories of those who are gone. That, I'd never do."

Some philosophers have written that the fear of death is the greatest of all fears, and that the fear of death that visits too early is supreme. With your friend, acknowledge that it is okay to be afraid, because there *is* great pain in losing friends, lovers, and family members.

Overcoming Your Fears

At this point, you may feel exhausted or overwhelmed. You may ask, "Will I be able to be a good carepartner for my friend?" You should expect to feel this way and to ask yourself questions of this nature. Remember, you are not alone. Many others have already traveled this same road, while countless others will, sadly, follow in your footsteps. In a subsequent chapter, we will discuss these fears in greater detail and talk more specifically about what you can do to alleviate them: how you can break down your fears and problems to make them manageable. For now, keep talking with your friend and with other friends about how you are feeling. Try to gauge your limits and, when necessary, express them. There's nothing wrong with saying to your friend, "I need a break today. I'll call you later and see you tonight."

Day by day, you will get through. And day by day, you will come to feel strengthened by what you have accomplished. These small victories will continue to collect, and you will be able to continue to draw on them and on your experiences as you go about meeting the challenge of caring for someone with AIDS.

3

WHEN YOUR FRIEND GETS SICK

If you call a friend to ask how he is doing or are visiting him in the hospital and he tells you he has AIDS, how do you react? What do you say? There is no easy or right answer, but in general, it is best to allow your friend to focus on himself. In fact, it is best to follow your friend's lead in any conversation. He may want to talk about his diagnosis and what he's going to do or how he's feeling—or he may not want to talk at all. He may want or need information. He may need you to make some phone calls, take care of his home, or just be an attentive ear.

All you can do is tell your friend that you are very sorry to hear this news, and let him know how you feel. Then ask, "But how do *you* feel? Can you tell me? Who have you told? Tell me if there is anything I can say or do right now beyond telling you that I love you and will stick by you."

Concurrent with your friend's diagnosis, you will be entering the strange new world of AIDS: a world of daunting medical terms, experimental treatments, government assistance programs, and some very difficult choices. At first, you may find yourself confused, even by the list of drugs, which sounds like alphabet soup: AZT, ddC, ddI. . . . So it makes sense to deal with first things first, because you can't do everything at once. What information does your friend need now? Where can either you or he get it? How can you be of the most help to him?

At the same time you are helping your friend, you will also be riding your own rough seas regarding the diagnosis. Undoubtedly, this will be one of the most painful and sad times you have experienced. Reactions can be as different as personalities, but most carepartners respond with some combination of anger, intense fear, denial—even a certain numbness, or shock. In this chapter, we will focus first on the medical aspects of your friend's diagnosis or initial illness: what *you* need to know, how you can help your friend in a very practical and real way. The second part of the chapter will deal with the emotional ramifications of the diagnosis: for you and your friend individually, and for the two of you together.

The Medical Aspects

Seeking to find the cause and then a cure for John's chronic diarrhea, Hugh and John had been to many doctors who specialized in intestinal parasites. Finally, they found a knowledgeable doctor. After an office visit, he told them to come back the following day for the results of some cultures. "The next day, I didn't go with him," Hugh recalls. "But he got back about eleven o'clock, and he was crying. . . . He said that the doctor had told him he had AIDS. I said, 'Who told you that you had AIDS? You just can't tell someone they have AIDS.' I held him, just trying to get him to calm down. I mean, there I was comforting this person, and I was freaking out myself. I'm giving comfort, and any second I'm ready to lose just about everything."

Jack and Bruce waited for the pulmonary specialist in the small holding area of the hospital's emergency room. "The specialist came in about three in the afternoon," Jack said. "He was a young man, kind of rugged-looking, like he grew up on a ranch in west Texas. He seemed like one of us. After a couple of minutes, he looked at Bruce. 'Can I talk in front of him?' he asked, meaning me. 'That's Jack,' Bruce said. 'Anything you say to me you can say in front of him.' The doctor stuck out his hand, first to me, then to Bruce. 'I'm Dr. Bill. Glad to make your acquaintance. I may have seen you guys around.'

"Then without any more introductions, he said to Bruce, 'You've got AIDS. The problem with your lungs is *Pneumocystis carinii* pneumonia. That's the AIDS pneumonia. We're getting a hospital room ready for you now. You'll probably be here for about five days. We can treat your pneumonia.' Then he asked us: 'What do you know about AIDS?'

"Bruce and I were both too stunned to answer. 'AIDS. It can't be,'' I said. Bruce was shaking his head back and forth with his eyes sort of shut. 'Shit my yellow rose of Texas,' he kept repeating. The doctor seemed to get uncomfortable, and he said, 'Look, I'll leave you alone for a while. I'll be back later, when they've got you in a room.' As soon as the doctor left, I went and hugged Bruce. We held on, rocking back and forth for the longest time. Later, they came to take him to a room.''

Joan and Barry flew to the West Coast after their son David called to say he was in the hospital. Joan says, "When I walked into the room and took one look at him, I knew what the problem was, but something inside me was holding on to a thread of hope. But then David told us that he had AIDS. I felt my heart sink. Instinctively, I reached out and grabbed Barry's arm. My head spun around for a minute, and tears welled up in my eyes. Through my tears I could see that David was looking at me, and he was afraid. I said to myself, 'He's so scared. I can't cry.' So I said, 'I love you,' and I got up and went over to the bed and hugged him. Barry just sat there speechless.''

Marilyn and Tim, a married couple in their late twenties, were both part of a very high-fashion scene in New York. Tim was the sales manager and top account executive for a well-known clothes designer, and Marilyn was a model who worked steadily and had appeared in all the top magazines. Over the years, they had shot up drugs a few times but never worried that they could be placing themselves at risk for AIDS. Then, one fall, Tim began to feel sick, all the time, for what finally amounted to two to three months. Marilyn took Tim to their doctor, who then sent them to a specialist. Marilyn says of their visit: "It didn't register. The doctor may as well have been from Planet X. He had just told us that Tim had PCP. 'And that means AIDS,' he added. But I was either numb or freaked out or something, because I just said, 'How long will he have to be in the hospital? We're planning a trip to London next month, and if we have to put it off, we have to give them a month's notice.' After I said that I thought, 'What are you saying? Have you lost your mind?' You see, it didn't register for days. It just wasn't possible. And for days, Tim just shut down. He didn't say anything."

Dealing with Your Friend's Immediate Needs

At this point, you do not have to confront what the diagnosis means. You do not have to deal with where all this might lead over a period of months or years. You have to deal with *right now and the very near future.* Your friend is probably going through the same reactions you are. A little bit of denial is healthy and sanity-preserving. Yet you both need to concentrate on what needs to be done right now. Taking appropriate action will help you get over this period of shock. Stay busy. Make plans. Get yourselves set up.

Your immediate concern is to make sure that your friend has the best of everything that can be provided to him by medical professionals and hospital staffs. You need information. You need resources.

Finding the Right Doctor

What should your friend seek in a doctor? He will want someone who has treated AIDS before, who keeps up-to-date on the latest research findings, who is informed about government-approved treatments *and* underground therapies, who is affiliated with a respected and convenient hospital, and who has a personal style your friend finds comfortable, if not comforting. He'll also want to choose a doctor who is board certified in either internal medicine, infectious diseases, or a related specialty, and who has a wide range of contacts in case he needs additional referrals.

Gay Men's Health Crisis, a New York–based education, client-service, and public-policy organization, tells prospective patients to ask themselves these additional questions before settling on a physician:

- Are you interested in taking an aggressive approach with your illness? Do you want to become as informed as possible about new drugs and new medical treatments? Do you want to take an active role in the decision-making process with your doctor? If so, will your doctor be receptive to your wishes?
- Will you want to be involved in new drug trials or new research protocols? Will your doctor monitor you on such protocols? Will he work to help you get a slot in a research study?
- Are you interested in exploring alternatives to established Western medicine, such as homeopathy, vitamin therapies,

and macrobiotics? Is your doctor supportive of these approaches?

- Will your doctor follow your wishes with regard to ending life support or establishing a living will? Who will be responsible for making medical decisions if you become incompetent?

Are you and your friend satisfied with his doctor? If not, you or he should speak to friends who may have other referrals. Get references from organizations dealing with AIDS patients. Talk to other doctors and nurses to find out about who in your vicinity is well known for treating people with AIDS. You may even call local hospitals for recommendations. And remember: Just because a particular doctor diagnosed your friend's condition, do not think your friend has to remain with him. Whatever you do, you should make sure your friend has confidence in his doctor, because the selection of a primary doctor is one of the most crucial decisions he will make about his health care. Above all, your friend should have a doctor who is a good communicator, who respects the relationship between the two of you (especially if yours is not a legally defined relationship), and who is free of any prejudice or bigotry.

Howard and Alex had to solve this problem. Immediately after Alex was diagnosed with KS, Howard went to see their regular doctor, the same internist who had been seeing Alex, to get a checkup. But the doctor didn't seem to understand Alex's condition or, apparently, anything about AIDS. "After a while I realized that Alex was his first patient with HIV disease and that he was totally green in this field," Howard says. "It would have meant a lot if our doctor had referred Alex out much earlier. You know, he dillydallied around with us for over two months.

"The doctor who diagnosed the KS heard our story and agreed that Alex shouldn't go to this internist anymore because he didn't know anything about AIDS or AIDS-related diseases. That was a difficult decision to make, because we had been going to this internist for years. We knew him; he knew us."

Finding the Right Hospital

Is your friend satisfied with his hospital? What kind of reputation does it have? Find out. Ask friends. Ask doctors. Ask agencies dealing with AIDS. If you live in or near a city, you may find hospitals that have a great deal of expertise with AIDS patients, such as San Francisco General—which has a dedicated ward—and St. Vincent's in New York—which has a special program. If you live outside an urban area, your friend should be especially careful about what medical center he selects. It is important to know that medical professionals have the experience, the patience, the common sense, the compassion, and the expertise to do their job properly.

Stella tells about her odyssey to find the right hospital for her husband, David. "At first, David was having a lot of trouble with his ankle joints. He saw an orthopedic surgeon in Louisville, who suggested that David have ankle surgery, which he did. In my own mind, I'm positive David had AIDS before the surgery. But of course, there was just no way to convince David. So he went ahead with the surgery and developed what the doctors here thought was pneumonia. They treated him for approximately six weeks. We did go back to the doctor in Louisville, and he said pneumonia, too. Finally, when David wasn't getting better, I took him to the emergency room at a bigger hospital and convinced them that there was a bad problem. So they admitted him. The doctor was very nice, and he did the best he could. I tried to explain to him that David had HIV, but I couldn't make him understand or believe me, especially around here, where we've had so few cases. The doctor kept saying, 'But he's married,' like that was some kind of vaccine. When they didn't know what to do with him anymore, they transferred him to the University of Kentucky. They tested him there. Five days later, we got the results: He was HIV-infected and did indeed have *Pneumocystis*. He had a hard time recovering from that because it had gone on for six weeks. He spent seven and a half weeks in the hospital that time, but he finally did recover. I wish I had moved him to the university medical center much earlier. Even though he got better, I always felt that waiting had greatly weakened him."

Getting the Recognition You Need from Medical Professionals

Sometimes the doctors and nurses you and your friend have to deal with may not treat you as a key person in the life of your friend. Some may not take your relationship seriously. Others may have had no previous experience with certain kinds of relationships. You will probably be surprised at the number of health-care professionals who become involved in your friend's case, which means you will encounter the same problem over and over again. At the outset, you and your friend should jointly answer these questions: Does your friend want you present, when possible, for medical examinations? For medical consultations? Does he want you informed about medical procedures? At some point, you two may have to decide whether he wants you to have the power to sign consent forms for treatments or medical procedures; this is what is called a health proxy.

If the answer to any of the questions above is yes, then you should explain your decision to the doctor *together.* It should be put in writing, too. You can simply state: "I am the primary caregiver to my friend, and I want to be present, when possible, at all examinations and consultations. I want to be kept informed of medical procedures used on him, and I want the right to consult with him before any procedure is performed."

If you are not a legal relation or a blood relative and the doctor asks, "Who are you?" then tell him that you are the "significant other" or the "caring friend" in this person's life, and that you expect to have the same rights and privileges as a spouse, sibling, or parent. If the doctor seems hesitant, then have your friend repeat the message. (It's not a bad idea in any case to have your friend repeat the request.) Have your friend tell you not to leave the room if the doctor or nurse so orders, and have your friend inform all medical professionals that whatever they have to say to him, they should say in front of you as well. It would certainly be a good backup to write a letter to the same effect—and have your doctor place such information in your friend's medical chart.

"For a long time, when the doctors came in to see David," Stella says, "I was polite and left the room because they wanted me to. Then, one time, David was trying to tell me something but, you know, with the cytomegalovirus, he wasn't speaking too clearly, and then finally I realized what he was telling the doctor. 'She doesn't have to leave anymore,' he said, giving me a quick wink. 'She wipes my butt, and she can stay.' After that, I stayed in the room when the doctors were there. I was sure glad he said that. He had a great sense of humor—all the way through."

Tom and Mart also had to confront the problem of lack of recognition from medical professionals. "One afternoon, Dr. K. came in. He said, 'Hi, can I speak to you?' " Tom recalls. "Mart said, 'Sure.' Dr. K. looked at me and said, 'I mean alone.' Like that. After I left, he told Mart that he had a confirmed diagnosis of *Pneumocystis* and that it was AIDS. So Mart told him that anything he had to tell him, he should tell me at the same time. Dr. K. came out and called me into the room and apologized for excluding me, but, he said, he always handles these things privately with the patient first."

"Somehow, because of Dr. Bill," Jack says, "Bruce and I knew not to take any crap from the other doctors and nurses—even the cleaning people in the hospital. Right from the beginning, I think we scared everybody, anyway. I mean, we're both big men, and we don't always act friendly. They gave me some kind of pass so that I could come and go when I wanted to, and I used to stay there with him a lot and sleep on a cot in the room. You know, his family was way up in the Panhandle, and he didn't want to tell them anything. So we stuck together in that hospital. I didn't care what anybody who worked there thought about us."

You should remember that in many cases, medical professionals are not accustomed to dealing with gay men or gay couples, I.V. drug users, or, for that matter, people with AIDS. Often, they do not know how to react. It's up to you and your friend to educate them about how you expect to be treated. It's a continuing battle, but they will learn to respect you.

In the event that you find yourself dealing with a doctor who is disrespectful or discriminatory in any fashion, think seriously about switching to another physician. There are also some steps you might take in the interim. If that doctor is part of a hospital staff, one of you should tell him that you are going to report him to the administration, and if the offending behavior continues, do so. If that fails, contact the hospital's patient representative or ombudsman to make your case, or call your local medical association (which you can find by calling the American Medical Association in Washington, D.C.). Finally, if all else fails, you can make a complaint to the state agency that regulates physician accreditation and hospitals. They *will* investigate your complaint.

Along with protesting within the medical system, you can also call your local health department and your local AIDS agency to register a complaint. In cases of outright discrimination, you may also want to speak to city or state officials about taking legal recourse.

Learning About AIDS

Carepartners, parents, friends, spouses, and people with AIDS often become practical experts on the disease; they know all the opportunistic infections and other conditions associated with it, as well as the drugs and alternative methods used to combat both AIDS and these infections. They read extensively, go to lectures and conferences, and do research in medical libraries. Learning about AIDS helps both you and your friend make better and more informed decisions in dealing with doctors and the treatments they prescribe. Moreover, it will give you some sense of control over what too often seems like an uncontrollable situation. Remember: AIDS is still relatively new to medical professionals, too, and in some situations they might not be aware of the latest findings, experimental treatments,

47

or holistic remedies that you may have heard or read about in your research. You should always ask your doctor about anything you might have discovered in your research. Don't be shy. Medical professionals are working for *you.*

You and your friend should also endeavor to learn as much as possible about the administration of all medical treatments and procedures. "Is this necessary? What is the purpose? What are the potential side effects, short-term and long-term?" You and your friend might decide that some of the tests and medications may cause him more discomfort than they are worth; you can demand that they be discontinued.

Both of you should take an active part in your friend's therapy. The more the two of you know about what is going on, the more you will feel part of the fight. This is very important, not just physically but emotionally and psychologically as well. If your friend feels that he is a helpless victim both of the disease *and* of medical professionals and hospital staff, then it could be much more difficult for him to fight. How strongly he challenges AIDS is a crucial factor in his therapy.

Tom feels that his knowledge and intervention may have saved Mart's life, or at least spared him much suffering. "They started treating Mart's PCP with Bactrim, and he didn't respond. He started to deteriorate. The pneumonia progressed for three days. By the end of the third day, he was on oxygen and could hardly breathe. The next step was the respirator. I was on the phone to the doctor several times, telling him that treatment wasn't working and that something was going wrong—because Mart wasn't getting any better. I was getting frantic. Finally, the doctor came in—and that's when they changed him over to pentamidine [another drug commonly used to combat PCP]. As soon as they did that, he started to respond. He had twenty-one days of pentamidine, and he just gradually got better. By then, we were starting to learn that it's important to get educated about AIDS and to speak up."

Marilyn and Tim, the married New Yorkers, worked as a team with their oncologist, who diagnosed Tim's KS, and they had a very positive experience. "The first thing he told us was that, if we wanted to, we could do nothing," Marilyn says. "Tim's lesions were just on the skin, and there wasn't any danger to his life from them then. They were also only on his legs. The doctor told us that radiation was very effective against KS on the arms and legs, but really wasn't necessary now. There was also an experimental program for KS at the time, but Tim couldn't get into it because he'd had PCP before. It really helped us to be able to talk with each other, to bounce ideas around, and then to make joint decisions. It surprised us that we kept getting closer and closer.''

The Emotional Aspects

When a carepartner learns that his friend has been diagnosed with AIDS, it is without exception a shattering emotional experience. Even if you have known your friend was HIV-positive for some time, the actual diagnosis can still be overwhelming. This particular time can draw two people very close—establishing an intimacy that for all its difficulties and challenges can serve as a sustaining force throughout the entire illness.

Tom describes how he felt after he and Mart had been told that Mart had AIDS: "Within minutes after I found out, I said to myself, 'I am going to do everything I can to help Mart through this.' There wasn't any question. I didn't even consider any alternative. For me, there wasn't any alternative. It was simple: 'It's as if I've got it, too. We're in this together.' I took a vow that I was going to be a rock for Mart, to the best of my ability.''

Jack tells of his experience the day after Bruce was diagnosed in the emergency room: "For the first time ever, I saw tears run down Bruce's cheeks. You know, we don't cry down here in Texas. We don't hug, either, but who gives a shit anymore? We'd been hugging down in emergency. I said to Bruce, 'I don't want you to be afraid. I'm going to be here night and day if you want me to. We're both strong and we're both tough, and we're going to make it through this thing. I'll cover your back, and you can depend on me. God knows, you're the first man I ever really loved, and I'm not letting you go anywhere without a fight. And you can bet your ass I've never lost a fight in my life.' He smiled when I said that and pulled me to sit on the bed. 'We're a tough team,' he said, 'and I never lost a fight, either.' Then we both cried a little and sort of calmed down.''

Joan was shocked when her husband, Barry, finally spoke that day in David's hospital room, the day they learned their son had AIDS. "Barry sat there speechless for a while, then his face changed, and I thought he was going to cry. He got up and put his hand on David's shoulder. 'I'd give anything if I could stop this from happening,' he said, 'but I can't. I just want you to know that your mother and I love you. We'll take care of you. We want you to come home as soon as you can travel.' ''

Joan continues, "I knew that it was costing him to say those things. I had never heard him say 'I love you' to one of our children, and I was thinking of all our friends—at church, the bridge club, the country club. What were they going to think? It scared me to think of his golf buddies, with all their jokes about queers and how AIDS was God's lesson to all those perverts. I said to myself: 'All these years of marriage, and he's a lot braver than I thought.' "

Meredith's AIDS diagnosis came only months after Pete's death; by that time, she had moved to San Francisco with her two children. When she learned she was ill, she had no close friends—*and* she had her young boy and girl to take care of. Unlike many gay men, she had no network to turn to. Realizing that she needed help, Meredith joined a support group for women. For Meredith, her group was her carepartner. "It's a really good opportunity not only for emotional support but also physical support. It's a safe place. A place not only to be angry or fearful but also to share some of the good moments."

Although many carepartners experience a growing sense of intimacy at the time of diagnosis, others experience an almost overwhelming sense of fear and dread. "I've never taken care of a sick person before," they say, or "I've lost so many friends already, I just don't know if I can take that roller coaster again" or "I'm worried enough about my own health; will I have it in me to do what is needed?" Some people, in fact, may not be able to overcome their conflicted feelings. Sadly, they may withdraw and then disappear. But after the initial shock, most caring people find a way to handle their fears and balance their needs with those of their friend. If you are having difficulties, you may need to talk with friends, join a carepartners' group, or speak with a professional therapist.

Howard explains, "One day Alex's sister Sofia called and told him that we couldn't come to dinner that Thanksgiving. 'I'm finally pregnant after all these years of trying,' she said. 'I'm not going to take any chance with it.' Alex laughed at her. He said, 'You can't get AIDS from having dinner with someone or having them in you house.' She said, 'Well, tell that to my husband, Bob.' I only heard one end of the conversation," Howard continues, "but they started yelling at each other, and then Alex hung up. We were both very hurt, and ultimately, we didn't go. About a month later, right before Christmas, Sofia called and asked us to come to her house for the holiday. She didn't explain why she wasn't afraid anymore, but I was pleased that we hadn't lost her."

Confronting Fear

When your friend gets sick for the first time or is diagnosed with AIDS, you may well be frightened, both for your friend and for yourself. At this stage, fear is an utterly normal response. You are facing an intense and difficult situation, one that may be entirely new to you. Even if you have known other people with AIDS, each friend's illness may seem like the first time.

Try not to be afraid of your fears, which often appear more threatening than reality. "I'm afraid to talk to him about this. I'm afraid he's going to get sicker. I'm afraid we won't have enough money." As you can see, many of your fears are rooted in the *future*. Usually, you aren't afraid of what is happening *now*, because in a crisis situation, you don't have the time or the energy to focus on anything other than what you absolutely *must* focus on. That's why it's important to stay in the present (though it's also important to plan for the future).

"It took me a long time," Len says, "to figure out what was causing me such constant feelings of terror, what was keeping me on edge all day, no matter what I was doing, and up all night. I started paying close attention to the thoughts that rolled through my mind, especially when I found myself sighing or groaning under my breath. I began to see that my mind was filled with pictures—almost like subliminal flashes—of all these horrible events that might happen: Evan wasting away, suffering helplessly in a hospital bed; me in agony, alone and desperate, perhaps sick, in an empty, silent house. After a while it occurred to me: 'I'm afraid of my own thoughts.' I wasn't afraid of the situation I was in; somehow, I was handling that just fine. It was things that might happen somewhere down the road that terrified me. It never occurred to me that when I got down that proverbial road, I might be in the position to handle whatever came up."

You should work to recognize that this fear is simply fear, not a fear of real and immediate events. Fear is an emotion, not something tangible. You should try to understand your fears. Isolate them, analyze them, take them apart, and look at them piece by piece. You are not aiming to overcome fear completely—that's not possible—only to live more comfortably, and to be the best friend you can be.

Steps You Can Take

Many people have found it helpful to ask themselves a series of questions about each thing they fear. Begin with the most obvious:

- "What am I afraid of? Can I put a name on it? Can I describe it as an event or a thing?"
- "Is this fear real? Is the event imminent? Is it possible? Is it probable that this will happen?"
- "Is this fear rational? Can I do anything about it? If I can do nothing about it, can I live with it?"
- "What is really at risk here if I commit to this action?"
- "What can I do to assuage my fear today? What can I do to recognize that—at least today—I have not lost my friend?"

If you have a friend or a therapist or go to a support group, you should try to discuss your fears forthrightly. If you are apart from friends or family and don't have the funds to pay a therapist, you still aren't alone, and you don't have to carry these burdens by yourself. Turn to the mental-health and AIDS agencies in your community, which can provide many services to you at little or no cost.

Neil, a man in his thirties whose lover of six years, Ron, had recently been diagnosed, describes what he was thinking: "I can't tell him how I feel. I can't tell him that I'm terrified of this whole thing." Yet Neil was so distressed that he would periodically burst into tears and actually believe he was going crazy. His friend Melba urged him, "You must tell Ron how you feel. He knows that you're afraid. He's as afraid as you are. Is he going to leave you if he discovers you're afraid? Is he going to fall apart and be unable to cope any longer? Is he going to die if he knows you're afraid? Is he going to love you less or reject you?" In each case, Neil answered, "No, of course not." He knew that the consequences he feared most were not real; yet the fear had paralyzed him.

You will probably find that discussing your fears with your friend will open many new avenues of communication between the two of you. Open discussion should make it possible for you both to make room in the relationship for your fears. Rather than destroying the relationship, your fears can become a part of it.

Peter, a private-school teacher in his twenties, had recently been diagnosed with AIDS, and was almost immediately fired from his job. Sadly, most of Peter's friends could not deal with his illness. In fact, no one even told him that he could take legal action against the school. Instead, as he puts it, "they're all busier than I am denying that I have this illness. It's discouraging. They come visit, and they can hardly look at me. And when I mention that I see my health slipping away, they act like they want to slip away, too.

"But there's one woman who comes to see me—Diane. She's a social worker connected to the hospital, and she's really nice, and we've become attached. One day I said to her, 'You know, Diane, I'm in this situation. No one has gotten out of it alive yet.' I thought she would look away or leave, like all the rest. Instead, she said simply, 'Yes, that must be very hard for you. I'm sorry that you have this illness.' I wanted to get up and hug her. She was the first person who was there for me and could address and acknowledge my fears.''

Analyzing the Fears

Contagion

You flinch when you kiss your friend hello. You feel that your hands are contaminated when you touch anything in his hospital room or apartment. You feel uneasy about drinking from a glass he may have used, even though it has been washed. You are afraid to eat or drink in his presence. What are you afraid of? You are afraid of coming into contact with the HIV virus and being infected—even though you know you will not get AIDS by being around your friend or from his glasses, forks, toilet seats, or anything else. Documented cases of transmission of the disease by casual contact *do not exist*.

To help you overcome this fear, we suggest that you try the following: Take that glass in your hand. Examine it closely. Ask yourself what evidence you have that the virus could be on this object. Ask yourself how long the glass has been standing in the open air. Ask yourself how you think the virus is going to make its way into your bloodstream. You'll find that your fear, when analyzed this way, loses much of its power.

The Unknown

You will become more comfortable and less fearful as you become familiar with the disease and how your friend is affected by it. It is natural for you to fear what you do not know, to be uneasy around the unfamiliar.

You will probably begin to read more about AIDS and HIV disease. You will find yourself meeting other people also facing the challenge of AIDS, and it's likely you will begin talking about your feelings with these new acquaintances. Also, as time passes, most people begin to see that their friend is the same as he always was. That can be very comforting.

Linda says, "Somehow, I wasn't afraid for myself around my brother. But I found myself going crazy when he was around my

53

children. I couldn't stand to watch them kiss him or sit on his bed. And if he coughed or touched his mouth around them, it was all I could do to stop myself from running over and pulling them away. I was so ashamed, because I knew better. But I couldn't help myself.

"Then my feelings began to change. I read everything I could find. I watched those parents on TV who seemed so irrational and crazy about children with AIDS going to school. And it began to sink in. There is not one case of someone getting AIDS from being around a person with the disease. I noticed, too, that the more I was around him, the more I saw my brother, not an illness, there. After a while, he was just my sick brother, not a threat to any of us."

Death

No one gets out of this world alive, and death is the natural end of every life. Yet, as Dr. Elisabeth Kübler-Ross writes at the outset of her book *On Death and Dying*, "Death is still a fearful, frightening happening, and the fear of death is a universal fear, even if we think we have mastered it on many levels."

When a friend becomes sick with a life-threatening illness, it is part of our human makeup to become afraid—for him and ourselves. One of our most cherished beliefs—We will never die—is being challenged. It is natural for you to feel anger, confusion, guilt, and depression under these circumstances. As time passes, you will begin to sort through these confused and confusing thoughts. For now, just understand that it is okay to feel as you do.

Being a friend of someone with AIDS teaches us lessons about our own mortality, and how to make peace with it. Most likely, though, your friend is probably more afraid of death than you are. One day he may want to talk with you about this. If you can, be ready when he is. This will probably be a difficult and painful discussion.

Mary Margaret had gotten AIDS from a blood transfusion. For the past year, the seventy-five-year-old grandmother had been in and out of the hospital, her health continually declining. Yet she never seemed to notice her decline. Surprisingly, she always expected her condition to turn around. But then her condition worsened again, and she began having all sorts of nightmares, her son remembers. He says, "She would wake up in the middle of the night calling for *her* mother, who had been dead for over twenty-five years. Then she began dreaming that the hospital staff was kidnapping her and taking her away to a 'bad' hospital, where they tortured her. I knew then that she was beginning to deal with the prospect of her own death. Well, at least she was doing this in her unconscious, because when she was awake, she avoided the topic like the proverbial plague. One day she asked me what I thought all those dreams meant. 'I don't know,' I answered. 'What do you think?' And that was it, the opening. For the next hour, she spoke about her fears about dying. It was like she had to get it off her chest. And then she just stopped. It was the only time she ever attempted to talk directly about death—although the dreams continued.''

The Past

The past is the past. You can't change it, you can't erase it, you can only try to move on. You and your friend may have participated in many similar activities. Your life-styles may have been very much alike. In fact, you may be wondering why he is sick and you are not. This is commonly called survivor's guilt. You may also be worrying whether you will get sick, too.

First, if you fear that what is happening to your friend may happen to you, find out whether that fear has any basis in reality. If you learn that you have been infected with HIV, you should consult your doctor and your local AIDS education group to find out what options you have. After you have learned about all the medical choices, you may want to speak to a professional therapist or join a support group for people who have recently tested positive. (Later in this chapter, we will discuss how to find a therapist.) It will help you to talk with your friend about how you are identifying with him. Bring your fears out into the open, and discuss all the activities you shared that frighten you.

Mark and Sam solved this problem with a painful discussion. Mark says, "It got to the point that I couldn't look Sam in the face. If he caught my eye, I got uneasy and looked away. One day he said to me, 'Something's wrong here. You and I have got to talk.' I looked at him, and I wanted to cry. 'I'm making myself crazy,' I said. My feelings started to pour out. 'Every time I'm around you, I think about going to the clubs with you. I think about all the things we did together, all those things that put us at risk for getting this disease. Not just you; me, too. We did the same things, and you're sick and I'm not. I may be next. Being around you reminds me of that and scares me. Sometimes I feel guilty. Why did this happen to you and not to me?

"Sam said, 'Do you think I haven't thought of that—why I'm sick and you're not? Do you know how mad I am? I'm mad at you. Did God or somebody throw some dice, and I came up a loser and you didn't?' Then he started shaking his head. 'Goddamn it, Mark, I hate my feelings, too. I don't want you to get sick, I'm just jealous. I want to be healthy, too.' "

Helplessness

If you stay away from your friend because you feel helpless to do anything for him, you are probably trying to do the wrong things. You know you can do something for your friend by helping him to monitor his life and remain as healthy as possible. You shouldn't feel helpless, because *you can* influence the course of the disease by helping him understand his situation and by assisting him in learning more about HIV. You can also greatly influence the quality of your friend's life. You can help him to create a life that is worth living, a life that helps him to continue to fight with dignity and courage. Many people with AIDS attribute the quality of their lives to the caring friends and carepartners who stepped in and helped them.

Another way to overcome helplessness is to become involved in the fight for more AIDS funding on a local, state, or national level. Political activism, whether stuffing envelopes for an AIDS agency, researching FDA protocols, or demonstrating, is empowering, and it can help you feel stronger and more powerful.

Shortly after Peter had been fired from his teaching job, he began volunteering at a local AIDS organization, first on its telephone hot line and later as an AIDS-policy researcher. "I couldn't believe how my politicization went from zero to sixty in about three months. I look back and see that I was fired in April—and knew nothing and did nothing about my rights—and by the end of the summer I was very well versed in workplace rights, particularly the Americans with Disabilities Act. I always laughed when I heard the cliché 'Knowledge is power.' But for me, I can't tell you how true it has become. Since then, I've gotten more involved, demonstrating in Sacramento, even getting arrested in Washington. In a funny way, I feel like I've found my true course in life now. I'm even ready to sue my former employer. How's that for change?"

Three days after the actor Anthony Perkins died from AIDS, his wife and carepartner, Berry Berenson, took up the AIDS fight. Speaking with *The New York Times*, Berenson explained that Perkins's disease had been kept a secret for two years. "He simply never wanted anyone to know. He figured if anyone knew, they'd never give him work again." Berenson acknowledges that the fear of exposure was enormous. "He went twice to stay at the hospital, and we went under another name. You can't even be yourself in a situation like this. You're signing 'Mrs. Smith' or whatever," she said, near tears. "You think that this man has spent his entire life giving people so much pleasure in show business, and this is his reward. He can't even be himself at the end." When her husband died, Berenson decided the time was right to speak about the disease's devastating effects on her marriage and about the enormous problem of facing AIDS in Hollywood. "I can't play this charade," she said. "I just can't." And so Berry Berenson took her husband's secret out of the closet and joined the ranks of other celebrities fighting to bring AIDS out of the Hollywood shadows.

You have a right to be afraid when you approach your friend. Almost everyone is afraid. These fears, both rational and irrational, can become part of the relationship and help it to grow, *if* you can share them. You can say, "I'm telling you this because it's important to me that I be comfortable around you. And this fear—or at least my trying to hide it—is making me uncomfortable." Don't forget: These are extraordinary times, extraordinary circumstances. There is no rule book of dos and don'ts.

Dealing with Your Feelings

Denial

The two of you may react to the diagnosis with disbelief and denial. "No," you might say, "this can't be happening." Your friend might say, "There's some mistake. This can't be happening to me." It's quite possible that the two of you will react this way even if you already knew your friend was HIV-infected. Denial is very powerful.

It's also a way that your mind protects you from realities that could overwhelm you, realities that you are not yet ready to confront head-on. It provides you with the time you may need to get used to a situation and devise means of dealing with it. Above all, denial gives you and your friend time to work through your feelings.

You shouldn't think something is terribly wrong if you or your friend cannot accept the diagnosis at the outset. At the time of an AIDS diagnosis, denial is perfectly appropriate behavior. You and your friend will probably use denial not just immediately after the diagnosis but from time to time throughout his illness. When the situation becomes too painful or too anxiety-filled, you may find yourself talking as if your friend is not sick, acting as if the whole thing never happened—in effect, indulging yourself in an unreal world. You are using denial to cope.

Your friend is most likely experiencing the same levels of denial that you are. Be very careful and sensitive to how he is feeling at any

57

given moment. He may be able to talk about his illness only now and then, and only for a brief time, or he might overcome the denial of his illness early on. You should listen to him and follow his lead.

James and Earl, brothers less than a year apart in age, black men in their twenties, had been close friends all their lives, even leaving home and moving together to a big city after finishing high school. Since then, they've lived together most of the time. James tells this story about Earl: "For weeks while he was in the hospital and then when he came home, he never said anything about being sick. It scared me. He acted sick. He needed twelve to fourteen hours of sleep a day just to be up the other twelve. But he didn't talk about being sick. Then one day we were watching a ball game on TV, and the commercial came on. He clicked off the sound with the remote and said, 'I can count on you, can't I? You know, I mean, if this really gets bad.' I was caught off guard, and it took me a minute. I said, 'You can count on me no matter what happens.' Then he clicked the sound back on, and that was that."

Sometimes, people cannot get past denial. This is a matter that you may or may not need to confront. Many people—people with all sorts of illnesses, not just AIDS—have died still denying they were sick.

Often, people's denial influences their behavior in ways that could be perilous to themselves and to others. Here are some warning signs to look for:

- Your friend doesn't seek medical treatment or take his medicine because he doesn't believe he needs it or because he insists he is not sick.
- Your friend continues his life as if nothing has changed, indulging in behaviors that hurt his health, like getting drunk, taking drugs, and staying up all night.
- Your friend practices unsafe sex, and says he does not believe he is doing any harm.
- Your friend relies on spiritual or holistic methods to the exclusion of standard medicine.
- Your friend ignores doctors and treatments even when he is sick and aware of it.

If you notice any of these behaviors, you should think seriously about confronting your friend or getting him to seek professional help.

Rocky, who was sick, was Samantha's first "buddy." Only seventeen, Rocky had already had one case of PCP when the caseworker asked Samantha to visit. As Samantha recalls, "He never wanted to acknowledge that he was sick or that he had AIDS. After a couple of weeks, I started to get worried. I knew we were supposed to be dealing with these sorts of things, but was I supposed to bring it up? One day, weeks after that, we were talking about Rocky's childhood when he looked up at me and said, 'Do you think I'm going to get AIDS?' I didn't know how to answer that, because he had already been diagnosed. I said, 'What do you think?' And he said, 'I don't think I am.' Later, he would bring it up again and I would say, 'Weren't you in the hospital? Didn't they say something like you had AIDS?' He'd say, 'Yeah, but I don't have it anymore.' Finally, we talked about it, and after a long time he accepted that he was sick. He told me he didn't really want to be sick and he didn't want to have AIDS and he didn't want to get ugly and he didn't want to get KS."

Anger

Occasionally, you will experience moments of profound anger. You have many reasons to be angry, and you may find some of these reasons flashing through your mind at any time. "This isn't fair. How can this be happening to us? Why did his family have to act like that? Why isn't the government doing more?"

You have a right to be angry, as does your friend. From out of the blue, your lives have been interrupted, your plans changed, your futures made uncertain. And there is no focus for this anger. Are you angry at the virus? At God? At your lover? At your parents? At the world? At the doctors and nurses? At all of the above? The danger here is that you and your friend may project this anger onto the closest target—namely, each other—striking out unreasonably.

"One evening right after work, I went to see Bruce," Jack says, "and he was surly. 'Why the hell didn't you bring me something to eat?' he barked as soon as I stepped into the room. 'I just got here,' I said. 'You didn't say anything about food when I called you earlier.' He snarled and yelled at me: 'Asshole, I have to tell you everything!' I was tired. I was hot. I'd been framing a roof all day. I felt like punching him in the face, so I stepped out into the hall. The nurse came up to see me. She had heard him yell. 'He's been acting up all day,' she said. 'He even called the doctor a stupid bastard. I won't mention what he called me.'

"I went back into the room and sat down. 'Back off from me,' I said. 'I'm here, I love you. You want something? I'll go out and get it.' He just ignored me and turned on the TV. I sat and watched TV for about an hour, then I left. He was still mad when I left. The next morning, he called me at home like nothing had happened."

You should each express your anger when it is appropriate, but be careful. On the other hand, there are things that anger can be focused on in a constructive manner. ACT UP (the AIDS Coalition to Unleash Power) and other AIDS activist groups drew much of their early membership from the legions of angry young gay men and lesbians around the nation. Fed up with government bureaucracies and Red Cross–type AIDS agencies, these activists funneled their energies into political anger, often with positive results.

Writer Larry Kramer has been called "the angriest man in America." Seeing the government do so little for people with AIDS during the early part of the epidemic, Kramer founded GMHC and, afterward, ACT UP. He intended that both groups, fired by anger and commitment, would fight for the lives of people with HIV disease. Kramer has also directed his anger into other projects: his two autobiographical plays *The Normal Heart* and *The Destiny of Me*, as well as numerous essays, speeches, and, as is his style, harangues of public and private officials who he believes are not doing enough to save his brethren.

Seeking Professional Help

As we've said, an AIDS diagnosis can be devastating. There may be individuals who find during this period of crisis that their usual methods of coping and dealing with problems are not working. It's during these times, we suggest, that you and/or your friend should seek professional counseling. We have found—and we want to stress this—that the benefits of therapy can be substantial, particularly in helping you to reduce anxiety, understand your feelings, and come up with new coping strategies. There are several kinds of counseling available. Here is a partial list:

Individual Therapy

Individual therapy usually focuses on personal issues. These days, a wide array of different therapeutic approaches exists, including Freudian, Jungian, and cognitive. You may find it beneficial to choose a therapist who is familiar with and has treated people with HIV disease. More important, your therapist should be someone you feel comfortable with, someone with whom you can discuss *all* your feelings and the most intimate details of your life.

Group Therapy

This kind of therapy provides a forum for individuals to talk about common issues. Those participating share mutual support, understanding, and feedback. These groups, led by professionals, fall into two distinct categories: support groups and therapy groups. Usually, support groups help individuals deal with specific issues, such as coping with an AIDS diagnosis, how to tell family and friends about the disease, and talking about common fears. These groups provide their participants with emotional guidance and direction on resolving some of the issues raised by this disease. Therapy groups, by contrast, help individuals to understand their psychological makeup and so to effect changes in how they function. Therapy groups are particularly useful in dealing with the psychological and social conflicts relating to AIDS.

Couples or Family Counseling

This type of therapy, for two individuals—who may be partners, spouses, or a carepartner and his friend—or the larger family structure, is designed to focus on patterns of interaction within the system.

Carepartners' Groups

If you are the primary caregiver or an involved caring friend, try to locate and join a carepartners' group in your area. These groups can be a great resource. In the years that such groups exist—some go on for a long time—they accumulate, like oral history, the experiences of all the people who have ever attended them. You'll find it sustaining to be able to bring up any problem you may be facing with your friend: medical, emotional, or legal. Undoubtedly, someone in the group will have been in your situation or will know someone who has. This is the time, if you are able, to reach out and build your own support network; however uncomfortable and daunting the process may seem to you, it's worth the effort.

This is also the time to suggest to your friend that he join a group for people with AIDS, or that the two of you join a group together. Getting over the denial and finding the right group are two crucial first steps.

For many years, *Fran* and Bill ran a carepartners' group in New York. During that time they must have seen more than one hundred people, with every conceivable problem, in their group. Fran explains that this work was unlike any other she had ever done: "I began working with people with AIDS and their carepartners in 1981. This was when people were still unfamiliar with AIDS and its progression. Participants in the carepartner group were from diverse backgrounds: all ages, ethnic groups, and socioeconomic levels. They were friends, lovers, spouses, brothers, sisters, and parents of someone with AIDS. They started as strangers but in a short time became an integral part of one another's lives, creating a supportive, family-like atmosphere.

"Initially, everyone in the group was devastated by the uncertainty of the illness, his or her feelings of isolation and loneliness, and a fear of losing someone who was loved very much. For most, the group was the only place where they could vent their rage toward family and friends who were unsupportive or who had rejected them. Many of the carepartners found that they had been stigmatized because their friend's disease was sexually transmitted or because their friend's life-style was not acceptable. This increased the carepartners' sense of loneliness. The group then became the only arena where they could cry and openly express their fears, sadness, and anger without being judged.

"One example that stands out for me is when one of the group members talked about feeling overwhelmed with events in his daily life: having to conceal his lover's situation from people at work, spending every night at the hospital watching his lover deteriorate, feeling helpless and out of control and in a constant state of stress. In the group, he allowed himself to express these overwhelming feelings that he otherwise had to contain. He sobbed uncontrollably and allowed the group to hold him and be there for him and understand his intense pain. There was a real feeling of acceptance of one another and that the illness was not a punishment for one's life-style or some wrongdoing."

Tom explains one important thing he learned in his carepartners' group. "I began to realize that Mart's illness wasn't going to be all doom and gloom. When I got into my group, I began meeting men who had much longer experiences with the disease than mine, and many more ups and downs."

After Tim was diagnosed with PCP and, later, with KS, he and Marilyn didn't really know how to relate to each other. They fought. They were like two lost children, Marilyn recalls. "I had to do something, because I didn't know anything about what was going on. So I joined a group of women whose husbands or sons had AIDS. I just couldn't believe my ears. I mean, the stories these women told kept me up all night from one week to the next. And Tim and I were not getting along at all. All of a sudden he had some need to tell me everything, stories about other women, and even some men, he'd had sex with. I don't know why he thought I wanted to hear that stuff. Probably he didn't care if I wanted to hear it or not, he just wanted to talk about it. I started thinking, 'I don't want to go through this. Nothing says I have to deal with this or with Tim.' And it was then that I started thinking about leaving. I brought up how I felt in group. One woman thought I was being a selfish bitch, planning to run out on my husband when he needed me, but most of the women seemed to understand."

Linda and Rose drove seventy miles to attend a meeting of women involved in caring for someone with AIDS. Rose explains her reaction: "I'm in my sixties now, and it's hard to surprise me. But that group of women amazed me. I felt immediately that I had found kindred spirits. We are all faced with this terrible thing. My son, that woman's husband, that woman's daughter, they all had this disease. I'm not one who cries a lot, but I cried when I talked about Gary. So did Linda. We love him so much, but we were just watching him waste away in front of our eyes. They all understood. They held our hands. They made all kinds of suggestions of ways to help Gary. Then, when the meeting was over, each woman hugged all the others. We didn't go every week after that, but we went as often as we could, and everyone understood."

Choosing a Therapist

Finding the right therapist can take some effort and homework. To get a list of possible referrals, you can call your local AIDS organization or county department of mental health, or you can ask a friend or colleague to recommend someone. You will want someone who is sensitive about AIDS issues and, depending on who you are, aware of issues affecting gays, lesbians, and/or drug users.

Before you go too far, you should consider the financial element in choosing a therapist. How much does he charge? Will your insurance pay any of it? Does the therapist set fees on a sliding scale? After answering these questions, you may decide that a clinic setting is more affordable; generally, clinics set fees based on what clients are able to pay.

Many people like to shop around a little before they choose a therapist. They may see two or three therapists for an initial consultation to see how they feel about each. After each consultation, you will want to ask some questions of yourself: How comfortable did I feel talking with the therapist? Did he seem to understand my concerns? Is he sensitive and well versed in the issues that I will be discussing? Did he provide me with enough feedback? If your gut tells you that a particular therapist isn't right, trust your judgment and keep looking.

Before making your final decision, ask the therapist about his academic credentials. A therapist should have at least one of the following: a master's degree in social work, counseling, psychology, or nursing, a doctoral degree in any of those fields, or a medical degree with a specialization in psychiatry.

There are many reasons for you both to maintain hope in the face of AIDS. Advances are being made on the medical front, people with HIV disease are living longer and better lives, and many organizations now exist to assist your friend with almost any kind of AIDS-related problem. How your friend chooses to live with HIV disease will determine a great deal. Does he see himself as a victim or a warrior? Is he seeking out the appropriate medical information and getting the best care? There *are* choices to be made at every juncture. And that's where you come in: to provide information, guidance, a shoulder to cry on, support, love, whatever he may need that you have to give. Your job, putting it simply, is to sustain his challenge of the disease.

4

HIV DISEASE: SYMPTOMS AND TREATMENTS

Although most people refer to "AIDS" when they have a friend who is sick with HIV, AIDS, it bears repeating, is one stage—the most advanced stage—of what is now called HIV disease. HIV disease is often called a "spectrum" illness, with each stage being defined by specific infections and symptoms, or the lack of them. The first stage is primary infection, which results in an individual's initial HIV infection—the state of being seropositive. From this point, infected people usually progress to more serious stages of infection, with increasing symptoms and a continued weakening of the immune system. These other stages can be difficult to define, owing to the vagaries of HIV and the different ways an individual can slow the progression of the disease (through, for example, certain medical treatments).

How You Can Help Your Friend

At some point in your friend's illness, you will begin a crash course, either together or individually, in infectious diseases and treatments. Gradually, the two of you will start to understand what specific symptoms mean, what side effects are possible when your friend starts a new treatment, and what questions to ask the doctor along the way.

Throughout this process, you should keep your friend informed of all that you are learning, always helping him to be as much a participant in his medical care as he wishes to be. You will find that some people want to know everything: every choice, every upside, every downside. *In fact, nothing in these pages is meant to be interpreted in any way that disempowers an infected individual from taking complete control of his health and health-care decisions. The active involvement of your friend in all decisions affecting his well-being is, when feasible, always preferable.*

However, this book is for you—the carepartner—and describes the roles and duties you can perform for your friend. You may find that your friend wants to know nothing, that he can comfortably leave all the questions about treatment to you, to his family, or to his doctor. Sometimes your friend may even vacillate: at one point, he will want to know everything; at another, he may want to know nothing.

You should periodically ask your friend how informed he wants to be at that specific time. He doesn't need to know everything. He needs to know only what he wants to know. He may want to know just the name of his current condition or infection, how it's to be treated, and what discomfort he can expect. He may not want to know the percentage of people who recover from this particular illness and the percentage who do not, or what side effects the treatments may cause. Keep listening to your friend; sometimes, he may not know what he wants. At those times, you, his other friends, and his doctor will need to rely on your best collective judgment to make certain decisions.

There are two simple and important rules to follow: *Let your friend take the lead in being responsible for himself and his medical choices. And, when necessary, play backup to him.*

It can be difficult to know precisely when to step into a particular situation. If your friend is monitoring his health, seeking out new information, and following his doctor's orders, the role you play can be diminished. But if denial overtakes him or if he becomes too ill to do certain things, then it *may* be an appropriate time to work with him in safeguarding his health. If your friend starts to run a fever, take his temperature regularly. If he gets a new rash, develops a cough, stops eating for a day or two, or has night sweats, advise him to call his doctor. Your early vigilance can be very helpful, and most likely it will save your friend discomfort, pain, and needless anxiety. If treated early, most infections are less severe and more likely to respond to treatment. Still, and this is an important caveat: your friend's life is his own. There may be times when you feel he is making the wrong choice or further damaging his health; there may, in fact, be times when you simply will need to let your friend take full responsibility for his actions.

Before you go any further in this chapter, here is *an important caution*: The sheer number of infections and conditions listed here may overwhelm you. Be sure to take deep breaths as you read, and remember that your friend may not develop most of the diseases outlined here. This chapter describes a lot of symptoms; your friend won't have them all, and you shouldn't drive yourself nuts anticipating every one. As with all aspects of HIV disease, you've got to take the medical story one day and one problem at a time.

How to Fight HIV

No matter where your friend is in the progression of the disease, he should begin to think about treatment strategies. The primary debate among doctors and researchers now concerns the time at which treatment should begin. Your friend will have to make informed decisions about this question. Many doctors have used the "if it ain't broke, don't fix it" rationale to argue in favor of treating the symptoms and infections of HIV disease only as they appear; they maintain that it's easier for people to take action when they are faced with a visible illness, and that the use of potentially toxic drugs should be put off for as long as possible. The downside to this approach is that the disease can progress quite far before symptoms show up, at which point fewer options for treatment may exist and those that do may be less effective.

Increasing numbers of doctors and researchers, however, are stressing that the immune system begins to "break" at the time of primary infection, and not when a disease like *Pneumocystis* pneumonia or Kaposi's sarcoma is diagnosed. It is crucial, they argue, for you to monitor your immune system to know where you stand. In that way, early treatment can take place, which may well be the key to slowing the devastation of HIV. Still, many individuals who feel well find it difficult to begin a course of treatment based primarily on laboratory test results; moreover, sometimes antiviral drugs can make them feel sick.

The conventional wisdom today argues in favor of the second approach, usually called early intervention. Project Inform, a San Francisco–based HIV-education agency, explains its philosophy this way:

Because HIV infection can be a life-and-death matter, it is critical to take a preventative approach. This makes it possible to:

- use treatments at the stage in which they are most effective,
- head off serious opportunistic infections and the further damage they do to the immune system,
- slow the spread and reproduction of the virus.

Treatment Strategies

There are five generally recognized types of intervention against HIV. Many researchers believe that all are useful, but that no single strategy is itself sufficient. Project Inform has listed the five interventions:

1. *General Health Maintenance*: This includes proper nutrition, adequate rest, exercise, and fresh air, and avoidance of alcohol, smoking, drugs, and unnecessary stress. By itself, good health maintenance won't prevent the progression of HIV, but a good defense against disease relies on a solid foundation.

2. *Holistic therapies*: These include stress reduction, massage, visualization, yoga and relaxation techniques, psychological and spiritual support, and natural medicines. Many of these therapies can help your friend to cope with certain symptoms of illness and side effects from drugs, and, generally, to keep his sanity. Again, taken alone, holistic therapies won't solve the entire problem; they are best seen as complements rather than alternatives to medical treatment.

3. *Antiviral medicines*: HIV attacks and disrupts the immune system. Medicines exist that can help attack the virus and slow down its work. The best known antivirals are AZT, ddI, and ddC—all now approved by the Food and Drug Administration to fight HIV disease. At various stages of disease, these drugs have been shown to slow progress of the virus, especially in combination with one another and other medications.

4. *Immune-modulating medicines*: Because the body's immune system is weakened by HIV, it makes sense to seek out medicines that would help boost the system or correct the underlying deficiencies. Some pharmaceutical products

have shown a limited ability to influence the immune system, and some natural products have a long anecdotal history of helping. Although taking these medicines may seem a commonsense approach, science has not yet found truly feasible ways to bolster the immune system. Trentol, Tagamet, and Naltrexona are being studied as immune modulators.

5. *Preventative treatment*: Many infections, such as *Pneumocystis* pneumonia, are so common that they can be expected to occur when a person's T-cell count falls below 200. Careful and timely use of Bactrim can prevent most cases of PCP. New prophylactic treatments are becoming available for other infections as well—though none combat HIV itself.

As is the case with many diseases, common sense goes a long way in fighting AIDS. Don't put all your eggs in one basket. Find out as much information as you can for your friend. As Project Inform states: "The key to successful intervention is comprehensive inclusion—doing all the things that make sense. The biggest mistake we can make is to dogmatically choose one approach over the others. HIV is not a political debate or opinion—it is a life-threatening illness. It makes no sense to bet your life on any single philosophy of medicine."

How Laboratory Testing Can Help

Recently, tests have been developed to help determine the relative strength of the immune system, which reflects the progress and severity of the disease. Your friend should have his doctor perform these tests on a regular basis. These tests include:

• *The T-cell test,* which is considered a fairly accurate gauge of the immune system. As the actual number of these cells falls, the body slowly loses its ability to fight infections. Certain infections become likely below specific counts. Generally, T-cell counts under 500 are cause for concern; a count under 200 indicates a high likelihood of developing PCP or another opportunistic infection. The CDC recently revised its guidelines to include T-cell counts of less than 200 as an AIDS diagnosis. Your friend should know that T-cell counts can vary widely—even during the course of a day. Doctors look at overall trends, not individual readings, as the best indicator of the health of one's immune system. To reduce variability in T-cell testing, test at a consistent time of day, use the same lab, and test when you are feeling well (not when fighting an infection, for instance). T-cell testing should be repeated every three to six months.

- *The P24 antigen test,* which measures the level of a particular protein produced in the core of HIV. The presence in the blood of the P24 antigen, naturally foreign to the body, can indicate that the virus is reproducing rapidly. A positive or high P24 antigen level is a warning of further disease progression.
- *The P24 antibody test,* which measures the level of protective antibodies to the P24 antigen. High levels of the P24 antibody indicate that the immune system is functioning and that the virus is being attacked by the body. A drop in the P24 antibody level is a predictor of a rise in the P24 antigen, which indicates further damage to the immune system.
- *The Beta-2 microglobulin test,* which measures a tiny blood protein known as Beta-2. Beta-2 is released as cells die from infection. This test, too, is an indicator of disease progression.

No single test will provide an accurate picture of the state of your friend's immune system. Taken together, some researchers believe, they hold the key to understanding and monitoring an individual's health status. Experts hope that these tests will provide guidance about what treatments to use, when best to begin them, and how to evaluate their efficacy. Many of these tests are still new; their accuracy and significance are still a matter of debate. Over time, it is expected, these and other tests will become the standard tools for monitoring and managing HIV infection.

Antiviral Treatments for HIV

The science of HIV and AIDS is evolving at a fast pace. Any information you receive regarding specific diseases and treatments should always be double-checked with an AIDS-informed doctor and an AIDS hot line. Treatments become outdated; new ones appear suddenly. Later in this section, you will find the names of particular

Government-Approved Therapies

Twelve years into the epidemic, the FDA has approved three drugs to treat HIV infection: AZT, ddI, and ddC. Of the three, AZT is the most widely used and best known, and is considered the cornerstone of anti-HIV treatment. After four years of testing, AZT's value has been repeatedly demonstrated for people with AIDS and for many HIV-infected people without symptoms. AZT works by slowing the reproduction of HIV; thus, along with ddI and ddC, it actually treats the underlying HIV infection. Specifically, AZT stops or slows the production of an enzyme that HIV needs to reproduce itself. When this enzyme is suppressed, the virus has a harder time infecting new cells, and when it can't infect new cells, it stops reproducing and growing.

Although AZT clearly has helped many people, the drug is not a cure for HIV disease, and its toxic side effects limit its usefulness for some people. Moreover, its effectiveness diminishes with time, although its value is thought to be longer lasting in HIV-positive individuals without symptoms.

The primary side effects associated with AZT are anemia and suppressed white blood counts, both probably due to the drug's toxicity to bone marrow. Recent studies indicate that providing the drug earlier in the course of HIV disease and at a lower dosage can substantially reduce these side effects.

Both ddI and ddC are antiviral drugs, similar to AZT, that also slow reproduction of HIV, lessening its damaging effect. ddI has been shown to be more effective than AZT in certain clinical trials; however, the principal advantage of ddI over AZT is that it has different and generally lesser toxicities, and causes less pain and/or numbness in the extremities. Unfortunately, one of its side effects, pancreatitis (inflammation of the pancreas), can, in rare instances, be fatal. Use of this drug, like all others, requires extremely careful monitoring.

Recently, the FDA approved ddC *in combination with AZT* for individuals who cannot tolerate AZT by itself. Scientists believe that the greatest benefit from ddC may come from combining it with AZT. Side effects of ddC are similar to those of ddI, except that there have been no reported cases of pancreatitis.

At the moment, these are the only government-approved drugs to fight HIV. Other potentially effective treatments are in various stages of development and testing, and are available only to those individuals enrolled in experimental trials. (For example, D4T, another antiviral, appears to be very promising at this writing, having boosted

CD4 levels by as much as 25 percent for up to two years in both Phase 1 and Phase 2 trials. CD8 expansion or infusion is another experimental treatment being used—with apparent success—to slow and stop the spread of Kaposi's sarcoma. Similarly, scientists are studying compounds that block the growth of blood vessels as possible treatments for KS and cancer. These drugs are known as angiogenesis inhibitors.)

Combination Therapy

Researchers and practitioners have come to believe that combining drug therapies will produce the greatest benefits for people with HIV disease. A treatment strategy that combines AZT with ddC, or AZT with ddI and another antiviral drug, will probably slow reproduction of HIV for a longer time than any one drug alone. Combination therapy also reduces the likelihood that HIV will develop a resistance to any one drug. You and your friend should speak to a doctor and an AIDS hot line to get the most up-to-date information about fighting HIV.

Common Opportunistic Diseases

Pneumocystis Carinii Pneumonia

Known as PCP, this is the most common life-threatening HIV-associated infection. Almost 70 percent of people with AIDS will develop PCP at some point. It is present at diagnosis in about 60 percent of people with AIDS. PCP is a protozoan infection of the lungs with symptoms similar to other pneumonias: high fevers, shortness of breath, and, in this case, a dry cough. Weight loss, night sweats, and fatigue are also associated with PCP.

With the newer, more sensitive laboratory techniques, PCP can usually be diagnosed from an examination of coughed-up sputum. Otherwise, a definitive diagnosis can be made only by finding the organism in bronchial secretions or lung tissues through the use of a bronchoscopy or by sputum induction, in which a scope is passed into the bronchial tree while a patient is under anesthesia. Chest X-rays, gallium scans, white blood counts, and measurement of arterial blood gases can together determine a PCP diagnosis.

First-line treatments include trimethoprim-sulfamethoxazole (also known by its brand names, Bactrim and Septra); intravenous pentamidine; dapsone, with or without trimetrexate; and primaquine with clindamycin. Corticosteroids might be suggested in moderate to severe cases. While these treatments are often successful in combating PCP, they may cause allergic or other toxic reactions. None of these drugs treats the underlying HIV infection or immune deficiency.

Bactrim and Septra are also being employed as highly effective means of preventing the onset of PCP or a recurrence of symptoms. Many doctors recommend these medications and, as a third option, aerosolized pentamidine, to their patients who have already had PCP and/or whose total T-cell count is below 300.

Candida

Candida, commonly called thrush, is a fungal infection that is seen in about 45 percent of people with AIDS. It appears as a whitish coating on the tongue, in the mouth, and also in the esophagus. Thrush can cause significant pain and can make swallowing difficult; among women, it can result in vaginal burning and itching. Thrush is usually not life-threatening, but it can be very uncomfortable.

For candida in the mouth or vagina, diagnosis is made by a visual exam and a smear and culture. In the esophagus, the infection is usually treated presumptively (that is, before actual diagnosis), and then confirmed by a biopsy culture.

Most of the time, thrush is not difficult to control with the use of fluconazole or nystatin, as well as clotrimazole troches and creams. The troche, a large tablet that is dissolved in the mouth, simply kills the fungus. However, as soon as treatment ends, thrush usually returns, so the use of a daily troche is recommended. Nystatin, another antifungal drug, is commonly called "swish and swallow" because it's used like a mouthwash and then swallowed. Nystatin is very effective, with few side effects. Other treatments include ketoconazole and itraconazole. Although treatment is usually quite successful, some doctors prefer to treat prophylactically with fluconazole. And it is recommended that individuals who have had thrush continue to take one troche a day.

Common Viral Infections

Cytomegalovirus (CMV)

CMV is a common infection among people with HIV disease who have low T-cell counts. The virus is frequently found in gay men, and when HIV is not present, it's usually harmless. Its exact role in the development of AIDS is not entirely understood, but it is known that CMV infection has a negative effect on the immune system and therefore could be one of the factors influencing the onset of more serious symptoms. Cytomegalovirus can appear in the eyes (CMV retinitis), lungs (CMV pneumonitis), brain (CMV cerebritis), or colon (CMV colitis), or it may attack other organs, including the trachea or the liver. CMV retinitis usually starts with blurry vision and can lead to blindness if it's not caught in time. Altogether, CMV is the primary cause of death in 10 percent of all AIDS patients.

To diagnose CMV retinitis, an Amsler Grid (a kind of eye chart) test can be administered to check for early vision loss, followed by an eye examination during which the pupils are dilated. For other types of CMV, diagnosis is made through a biopsy and endoscopy (a tube inserted into the rectal or throat canal). Ganciclovir and foscarnet are the drugs of choice, administered either orally, intravenously, or by injection into the eye. The most serious drawback to ganciclovir is that it cannot be administered to people taking AZT, because both drugs reduce the white blood count. Other side effects of ganciclovir include disorientation, rashes, blood clots, nausea, and vomiting. Foscarnet does not suppress the production of white blood cells and therefore can be used in conjunction with AZT. Decreased kidney function is the primary side effect associated with foscarnet.

Herpes Simplex and Zoster (Shingles)

Herpes simplex virus is found in nearly all people with HIV disease, and it is the cause of many problems. This is the same virus that can cause sores around the mouth and genital areas of people who are not HIV infected. Among those who are HIV-positive, the virus is persistent and often painful. Herpes simplex is very contagious, regardless of a person's HIV status. It is not advisable to kiss a person who has herpes sores on the mouth or lips.

Herpes zoster, commonly called shingles, is a form of chicken pox caused by the zoster varicella virus. This virus is present in nerve cells and expresses itself by traveling down a nerve root. Infections can appear as patches of raised red bumps on the skin of the legs and buttocks, or of the arms and back, following the path of a large nerve root. The rash is frequently preceded by a sensation of burning, tingling, or pain. These bumps can turn into painful, itching sores, and they may erupt simultaneously in several places on the body. Often, these outbreaks are accompanied by fevers and malaise.

For both herpes simplex and herpes zoster, diagnosis is made with a visual exam, tissue biopsy, and culture. Herpes simplex and herpes zoster are treated with oral or intravenous acyclovir, which is usually highly effective. Herpes sores can be treated with Zovirax, the trade name for acyclovir.

Brain and Central Nervous System Problems

Three main problems can affect the central nervous system of persons with AIDS. All can cause behavioral and mental problems. Your friend may begin to lose muscular coordination, withdraw socially, or show other signs of physical and mental impairment. These diseases can be among the most difficult for the two of you to deal with, because they may alter your friend's personality.

Cryptococcal Meningitis

This disease, a fungal or yeast infection, most commonly appears in HIV-infected people as an inflammation of the brain. It can also cause lymphadenopathy (swollen lymph glands), endocarditis (inflammation of the lining and valves of the heart), a rare form of pneumonia that mimics PCP, and skin ulcers. The symptoms of cryptococcal meningitis include mild to severe headaches, intermittent fevers, progressive malaise, nausea, fatigue, and an altered mental state. In rare instances, seizures may occur.

Doctors test for the cryptococcal antigen by analyzing a blood sample, cerebral spinal fluid, and urine or other bodily fluids. If a patient exhibits neurological symptoms, a CT scan or MRI scan should be performed, followed by a lumbar puncture (spinal tap). Cryptococcal meningitis is usually treated first with amphotericin B, with or without flucytosine. Amphotericin B is highly toxic, and as a result, it must be slowly dripped into the body intravenously for eight hours each day. The side effects of amphotericin B can include nausea, vomiting, loss of appetite (and consequent loss of weight), fever, severe chills, and cramps. This medication can also cause the hands to shake, or result in blurred or double vision. No drug can totally suppress cryptococcal meningitis; relapse is common, so continuing treatment is almost always necessary.

Toxoplasmosis

Toxoplasma gondii, or "toxo," is another parasitic infection that attacks people with HIV infection. It usually invades the nervous system, especially the brain, resulting in seizures, high fevers, and a decreasing level of consciousness. Delusional behaviors, paralysis on one side of the body, and severe headaches that do not respond to painkillers are also associated with toxo.

Toxoplasmosis used to be one of the most frightening and life-threatening HIV-related infections because continued infection could lead to immobility and loss of speech. New treatments, usually pyrimethamine in combination with sulfadiazine and/or clindamycin, have been shown to be highly effective. Sometimes, this disease can be treated at home. Unfortunately, someone with toxo requires maintenance treatment because the infection usually reappears as soon as the therapy stops. Many doctors will keep a patient with toxo on a low dosage of treatment as a protection against recurrence. Bactrim and Septra are currently being used prophylactically *on a test basis* against toxoplasmosis.

Sulfadiazine and pyrimethamine are toxic drugs with strong side effects, but since toxo is life-threatening, no choice exists except to continue treatment. Among the most common side effects are loss of appetite (and related weight loss), nausea and vomiting, mouth and tongue pain, and anemia. Either drug may cause hair loss, decreased hearing, diarrhea, sensitivity to light, and kidney damage. These drugs also take their toll on the bone marrow (which manufactures blood cells) and hence can further depress the immune system. When a patient does not respond to treatment, a physician may order CT and MRI scans and, rarely, a brain biopsy to learn more.

AIDS Dementia

Also called HIV encephalopathy, AIDS-dementia syndrome, or AIDS-dementia complex, "AIDS dementia" is an imprecise term used by doctors and researchers that is associated with the following symptoms and conditions: auditory, visual, and other sensory disturbances, muscular impairment, personality changes, memory and judgment difficulties, and/or a severe loss of intellectual, social, or occupational abilities. "AIDS dementia" is a loaded term that frightens many people, often unnecessarily. Experts believe that there are multiple possible causes for dementia as well as different degrees of dementia, from mild to severe. As many as two thirds of people with AIDS are thought to have dementia at some time during their illness; it is also believed that otherwise healthy HIV-infected individuals may experience mild dementia.

True dementia can be difficult to diagnose because few doctors have the opportunity to rule out all the possible psychological variables present, such as depression and anxiety. In other words, "dementia" has become a catchall term for a variety of neurological, psychological, and other organic problems that may not actually constitute true dementia. If your friend is exhibiting some of the symptoms, assist him in getting the most accurate diagnosis of his condition; an accurate diagnosis is the only path to helpful treatment.

Of all the many manifestations of HIV, mental impairment, however treatable, can be one of the most difficult for the carepartner or caring friend. There may be times when you feel you are no longer in the company of your friend, but attending a child or someone who is rapidly losing his mind. It can take great love, compassion, and patience to be with someone who is enduring mental problems and personality changes.

It is now understood that there are many causes and kinds of dementia. If a dementia is caused by a drug, the course of the disease may be changed by altering the medication regime. If a dementia is caused by an infection, treatment of that infection may improve your friend's condition. And if the dementia is psychological in nature, the underlying conditions may be addressed through psychotherapy and/or appropriate medication. When all other possible diagnoses have been investigated and ruled out, a diagnosis of true AIDS dementia can be considered. For many years, the prevailing view was that nothing could be done for dementia. Recent reports indicate, however, that some success has been obtained with AZT as well as with methylphenidate and dextroamphetamine. Early-stage studies also suggest that peptide T may be an effective treatment. The difficulty with dementia lies in finding drugs that can be absorbed by the brain from the blood system. Scientists have long been plagued by the difficulty of finding medications that can cross the blood-brain barrier, which is crucial to the successful treatment of many brain disorders.

Bacterial Infections

Mycobacterium Avium Complex

Known as MAI or MAC, *Mycobacterium avium* intracellular infections can appear in various organs and in the blood. These bacteria are found in nearly half of the people with HIV infection, although they do not cause symptoms or disease in everyone. When they do cause illness, the following are likely symptoms: diarrhea and intestinal pain, persistent high fevers, weight loss, night sweats, weakness, dizziness, nausea, enlarged lymph glands (frequently on only one side of the body), and an enlarged liver and spleen.

Any of these symptoms can alert you to the possibility of MAI, but this disease is difficult to diagnose. A doctor may suspect MAI because of elevated liver functions or through a biopsy of a swollen lymph node. It can also be detected through blood, tissue, or bone-marrow cultures. Because of the inability of any single test to accurately isolate and identify MAI, several tests may have to be done in conjunction with one another. As a result, some physicians decide to treat MAI presumptively (prior to a definitive diagnosis).

Although there is no standard approved therapy, MAI is usually treated with combinations of anti-malaria and anti-tuberculosis drugs including rifampin, ethambutol, clofazimine, amikacin, and isoniazid, as well as with rifabutin, azithromycin, and clarithromycin. Since these drugs are rarely used alone, it's difficult to ascertain the particular side effects of each. Generally, however, multidrug treatments are likely to cause problems for people because of the possibility of cumulative side effects. Anti-MAI regimes are commonly continued for many months, especially when they are shown to be working. Ethambutol, azithromycin, and clarithromycin are frequently prescribed prophylactically.

Mycobacterium Tuberculosis

Tuberculosis is a highly communicable disease that is often seen among HIV-infected individuals. In recent years, TB has become epidemic in many cities, particularly New York, Newark, and Miami, where the disease has become rampant among people who use intravenous drugs. TB is caused by the bacterium *Mycobacterium tuberculosis*. As with HIV, infection with TB is lifelong.

The TB organism can cause disease in every organ of the body, but the most common site is the lungs. To infect other people, an individual must have active, untreated TB in his lungs; transmission may then occur as a result of sneezing, coughing, or even talking, as infectious particles become airborne and find their way into the lungs of a healthy person. Because TB is so contagious, you should take special precautions, such as wearing a face mask during each visit with your friend and washing your hands thoroughly afterward, if you know that he has active TB. You should also be tested, at least annually, with a simple diagnostic skin test, called the PPD, to learn whether you have been infected.

TB symptoms generally include coughing, weight loss, night sweats, fatigue, fever, and swollen lymph nodes. When a PPD is positive, it will result in a raised bump greater than 5 millimeters in diameter. (Sometimes among people with HIV, the PPD reads negative even when TB infection is present. Doctors may prescribe a follow-up test to make sure the diagnosis is correct.) Everyone infected with HIV should regularly be tested for TB. People with a positive PPD should then be evaluated to determine whether their infection is active or latent; this is done with a chest X ray, a physical examination, a sputum smear and culture, and blood, urine, lymph-node, bone-marrow, or liver cultures.

If there is no evidence of active infection, isoniazid, which is a highly effective means of preventing active disease, is generally prescribed for one year. In cases of active infection, HIV-infected individuals should be put on the standard drug treatment: isoniazid and rifampin for twelve months (with ethambutol and/or cyclosporine being added if the strain of TB seems resistant to standard drugs). Individuals with an active infection are contagious only before treatment and during the first two weeks of treatment. During those times, they should *scrupulously* avoid crowds and public places.

Cancers

People with HIV disease often suffer from various cancers—two in particular are much more common in people with HIV disease than among the general population.

Kaposi's Sarcoma

KS, as this disease is known, is a cancer of the small blood vessels of the body, and it usually first appears as red blotches on the skin; in time, these turn into purplish red lesions that are hard to the touch and are often raised above the level of the surrounding skin. KS lesions, as the blotches are called, usually show up initially on the arms or legs, but they can spread to the chest, back, face, and neck. They can also develop in the mouth and throat, where they can become obstructive and thus more dangerous. Eventually, they may appear in internal organs such as the intestines, colon, or lungs. KS is not a leading cause of death among people with HIV disease, but it is the second most common disease (after PCP) that warrants an AIDS diagnosis. Unlike other cancers, KS does not spread from one locale to another; each lesion appears without connection to the others, which means that removal of the first lesion, or several lesions, is not a useful therapy to prevent the spread of the disease.

Diagnosis of KS requires a tissue biopsy for confirmation. After they get one KS lesion, some patients go a long time without the appearance of additional lesions, while in others the disease can progress rapidly. Generally, the strength of the underlying immune system is key to how well a person with KS will fare. Prior or concurrent opportunistic infections, anemia, fevers, night sweats, and weight loss are more important predictive indicators for survival than the number of KS lesions.

In the early stages of KS, many patients forgo any treatment for their lesions, focusing instead on systemic treatments such as AZT to slow the reproduction of the virus. Later on, after the disease has progressed, radiation can reduce the number of lesions in a particular area, such as the feet or the throat or the mouth, where they may be interfering with walking or eating. KS is very sensitive to radiation therapy, and sometimes a single large dose will prove highly effective. KS is often responsive to a variety of treatments, including various types of chemotherapy, radiation, and cryotherapy (liquid nitrogen). The most common chemotherapy agents are vincristine, bleomycin, vinblastine, and VP-16. Currently being studied for effectiveness are drugs such as alpha- and gamma-interferon and interleukin-2, and combinations such as alpha-interferon and AZT.

All chemotherapies produce side effects. Your friend may experience nausea, vomiting, and extreme fatigue after each administration. Chemotherapies are also immunosuppressive, which means they act to weaken the immune system; this may hasten the onset of other infections and weaken the body in general.

Many people with KS feel "marked" by their lesions. Removal of lesions can provide significant psychological reassurance, even if such a procedure is not medically warranted.

Lymphomas

Lymphomas are cancers of the lymph nodes. Among people with HIV disease, lymphoma has the ability to spread rapidly to sites outside the lymph nodes, such as the bone marrow and the central nervous system. The type of lymphoma found most often in people with HIV infection is called high-grade, B-cell, non-Hodgkin's lymphoma.

The response of patients with lymphoma to various chemotherapies has been relatively poor; only about one third to one half show any improvement. Furthermore, the relapse rate has been high, and people on chemotherapy are, as we have stated, more susceptible to other opportunistic infections. Many of the drugs used against lymphomas are prescribed in various combinations; they include cyclophosphamide, bleomycin, doxorubicin, vincristine sulfate, prednisone, and, sometimes, methotrexate. All chemotherapy agents are highly toxic and can cause nausea, vomiting, weight loss, hair loss, fatigue, low white blood count, mouth ulcers, and kidney problems.

Other Physical Conditions

In addition to the above-mentioned primary diseases your friend might encounter, other conditions are common among people with advanced HIV disease.

Diarrhea

People with HIV disease often suffer from diarrhea, which can result from one or more of many possible causes. Two bacteria, salmonella and shigella, can infect the intestines and colon, and both can cause severe diarrhea. Both can be treated with ampicillin and trimethoprim-sulfamethoxazole, but these drugs' side effects can include rashes, fever, nausea, vomiting, and weight loss. Salmonella can also be treated with milk, which has a high level of antibodies against these infections. Diarrhea is a common and difficult problem, and it must be dealt with promptly.

Wasting Syndrome

When associated with HIV infection or parasites but not with other infections or cancers, diarrhea can often lead to what is commonly called "wasting syndrome." Careful and systematic evaluation can, in many cases, uncover a treatable infection. Even a badly "wasted" patient can regain weight if the underlying infection is diagnosed and then treated.

Cryptosporidiosis

If your friend is suffering from a severe, watery diarrhea that does not respond to any of the known treatments, the problem may be cryptosporidiosis (or "crypto"), a disease caused by a small parasite that results in chronic, watery diarrhea in people with HIV infection, usually accompanied by rapid dehydration and wasting. Anything that a patient tries to eat or drink simply passes through his system. There is no established medical treatment for crypto; the current treatment is mainly to keep the patient hydrated by intravenous infusion of liquids. A feeding tube can also prolong a person's life. Researchers are currently experimenting with several drugs—including azithromycin, letrazuril, and paromomycin—to combat this infection. Crypto is no longer considered as untreatable as it once was.

If your friend gets crypto, you should, as always, use sanitary precautions (i.e., wear latex gloves) when dealing with his excretions, since an HIV-negative person can contract crypto (but again *not* HIV) from contact with excreta; this can cause severe diarrhea for about a week.

Fevers

Many people with AIDS run almost constant low-grade fevers that "spike," or shoot up, to 102, 103, or sometimes even 104 degrees. People often forget that fevers are the body's way of combating illness; fevers are also an indication that something is wrong; your friend should contact his doctor as soon as possible if a fever begins to spike. Often, your friend will be told that there is no particular reason, other than his underlying condition, for the fever. In cases such as these, the doctor may prescribe analgesics such as acetaminophen (Tylenol) or ibuprofen (Advil) (aspirin would upset the stomach). Analgesics control fevers and reduce body pains. When your friend is experiencing fevers, he may often find that they are accompanied by night sweats, which serve to release excess heat. When a fever breaks, the heat that has built up in the body may be dissipated by sweating. When the fever disappears; the night sweats also tend to cease, although this is not always the case.

Rashes

Your friend will probably suffer from different kinds of rashes, which are common among those with HIV disease. Many of these conditions cause mostly cosmetic problems, while others can be more painful or serious, requiring the attention of a doctor. In fact, your friend should always see a doctor when he has a skin condition, because an underlying immune deficiency can make even the simplest skin disorder difficult to treat.

Sometimes, rashes can be caused by allergic reactions to pre-scribed treatments. In these cases, the rash may abate if the treat-ment is changed or the dose lowered. Other disorders, such as herpes zoster and simplex, are easily recognizable by a doctor, and the treatment is standard. Still other conditions may be more diffi-cult to control. Molluscum contagiosum is a skin condition caused by the poxvirus. In people with HIV infection, the molluscum le-sions are difficult to contain and may be very uncomfortable and disfiguring. They generally appear as small white bumps with or without a red rim and a central indentation. These lesions are es-pecially hard to control when they appear on the face, where they are easily spread by shaving or scratching. Treatments include freez-ing the lesions, excising them surgically, or using chemicals to re-move them.

Among people with compromised immune systems, ordinary warts, which are easily controlled in healthy individuals, may be difficult to treat, especially genital warts. Weekly treatments with various acids and a drug called podophylin resin are usually pre-scribed, although alpha-interferon has recently been licensed as a new treatment. All warts should be treated immediately by a doctor. Aggressive treatment is necessary to prevent them from spreading.

Seborrheic dermatitis is one of the most common skin rashes among people with HIV and is frequently one of the first visible signs of infection. This rash, which is typically red, has been de-scribed as a "greasy scale." Seborrhea usually appears around the eyebrows and the hairline, the sides of the nose, or on the cheeks, chin, chest, and scalp. This condition may be difficult to control in some individuals, but has been shown to respond to steroid treat-ments and antifungal creams.

Psoriasis is another common skin disorder among people with HIV infection. People who have never had psoriasis may discover a rash of raised bumps, while those with a previous history often find their condition worsened as a result of HIV infection. Typical lesions are red, frequently covered with a thick silvery scale. Diagnosis should be made by a doctor; treatments are varied and depend on the severity of the disease.

Other usual fungal infections are generally exacerbated in people with HIV. These include jock itch and athlete's foot, which can generally be treated with antifungal creams such as Lotrimin or Mycelex. Sometimes a virus or fungus gets into the fingernails or toenails, causing these to become disfigured, either in shape or color (a toenail could turn white, for example) or both. Pigment and texture losses seem to be linked with chronic illness and inadequate nutrition. These conditions should be discussed with a doctor on a case-by-case basis.

A final word about all skin disorders: Be alert to new outbreaks. Your friend should talk to a doctor immediately about any new symptoms, because infections can spread quickly and become difficult to treat.

Bedsores

People who spend long periods of time in bed develop bedsores, which form at pressure points, spots where the weight of the body puts pressure on the skin, limiting the flow of blood to the skin. Bedsores usually occur on the buttocks, shoulder blades, heels, arms, hips, chest, or knees—whatever part of the body the person lies on the most.

If your friend is in the hospital or confined to his bed at home and you see that he is developing bedsores—usually noticeable as red areas on the skin—you should see that he is turned more frequently so that the pressure does not build up on one spot or area. Frequently, nurses will institute a turning regime that should help to minimize discomfort from bedsores. It also helps to massage the reddened areas lightly to get the blood circulating again.

A word to the wise: Bedsores are better prevented than cured. They are difficult to get rid of and can become a constant source of infection and irritation. In addition to regular turning, use a sheepskin or foam-rubber pad designed to help redistribute the weight of a pressure point over a greater area. "Egg crate" mattresses are another boon in preventing these sores. You may also have to put pads in between your friend's knees and under his heels and elbows.

Special Concerns About Women and HIV

Currently, there are nearly 30,000 women who have been diagnosed with AIDS in this country, or about 13 percent of all reported cases. Eighty percent of women with HIV are either black or Hispanic; 80 percent are also of childbearing age. Generally, HIV infection progresses similarly in women as in men. Like men, women are frequently diagnosed with potentially life-threatening HIV-related diseases, including PCP, MAC, and toxo. Still, there are some important differences. The most common early symptoms in women are usually gynecological complications, such as chronic vaginal yeast infections, genital or anal warts, pelvic inflammatory disease, and herpes simplex. Women also experience many of the same early symptoms as men do: fevers, night sweats, coughing, and weight loss. Curiously, Kaposi's sarcoma, common in gay and bisexual men with HIV, is rarely found in women in the United States. Only in late 1992 did the CDC finally expand its definition of AIDS to include gynecological symptoms such as invasive cervical cancer.

In short, AIDS is different for women than it is for men. The de facto exclusion of many women from official CDC lists has had severe repercussions on these women with HIV. For years, women have been denied government disability benefits because many of their specific diseases did not meet the CDC definition. Women with AIDS have also tended to be poor, with less access to decent medical care. Frequently, as a result, they learn of their primary infection only when they begin to have clinical symptoms, which can be very late in the progress of the disease.

Following are the diseases specific to women with HIV:

Yeast Infections (Vulvovaginal Candidiasis)

More than one third of women with HIV infection develop chronic yeast infections, which may cause severe itching and burning, and vaginal odor and discharge. These infections are caused by an increased growth of yeast in the vagina, resulting from immune suppression. Treatment includes antifungal agents such as intravaginal miconazole or clotrimazole and ketaconazole and fluconazole taken orally. As the immune system falters, yeast infections may also appear—with more serious consequences—in the mouth, throat, and esophagus.

Human Papillomavirus and Cervical Cancer

The human papillomavirus (HPV) causes the development of anal and genital warts, which may result in abnormal Pap smear readings, cervical warts, and, in some cases, cancer-causing tissue growths. Recent studies show that HPV is not unusually frequent in women with HIV infection but that it does produce in these women severer and more frequent occurrences of disease than it does in uninfected women. Anal or genital warts are generally red and spiked and are usually found in the moist areas of the anus or vagina. They are not difficult to recognize and are usually treated with acetic acid, by freezing them off, with laser therapy, or by surgical removal. Frequent recurrences of warts, especially after sustained treatment, may indicate as-yet-undiagnosed HIV infection in women.

Pelvic Inflammatory Disease

Known as PID, this disease is thought to be caused by sexually transmitted organisms, particularly chlamydia. PID is a painful inflammation of the upper genital tract; infections in the fallopian tubes or the ovaries may also occur. Symptoms include abnormal vaginal bleeding, unusually painful and difficult menstruation, infertility, and pregnancies that occur outside the uterus (usually in the fallopian tubes). Some reports suggest that PID is especially common and severe in women with HIV. Diagnosis of PID is extremely difficult because there is no single diagnostic test. If a woman suspects she has PID, she should consult a doctor. Treatment includes standard antibiotics such as azithromycin.

Problems of Pregnancy

Pregnancy does not appear to accelerate a woman's HIV infection. However, pregnancy raises some fundamental questions for infected women and their partners. Women with HIV infection must expect health problems down the road that would severely impact anyone's ability to raise a child. Moreover, about one quarter of babies born to HIV-infected women are also infected, and approximately one third of those will develop a serious HIV-related illness within the first eighteen months of life. Many of those die within that same period. If your friend is pregnant or is considering pregnancy, you can help by being a nonbiased sounding board, providing information, and following up with referrals to appropriate doctors or clinics. The decision whether or not to have a child when HIV-infected is one of the most difficult any woman can face. As a friend, you may be much needed.

Experimental Drugs and Treatment Programs

For years, people with HIV disease and their advocates have been urging the federal government to expedite approval of new medicines because of the life-threatening nature of AIDS. In this country, all drugs must be approved for human use by the Food and Drug Administration. The FDA has been under immense pressure to speed up its process; at the current rate, approval of a new drug usually takes at least ten years because of the controlled nature of the studies as well as the typical delays of bureaucracies. For those with a potentially fatal illness that has no known cure, this length of time is unacceptable.

Before a new drug is made available to the public, the FDA attempts to ensure that it is effective against the condition it is prescribed for, and that it does not have side effects that outweigh its benefits. To assure that these minimum standards are adhered to, the agency requires that all new drugs be put through a series of tests and trials. Early trials of a drug are "dose escalation" studies, which involve small numbers of people who are given different doses of the same drug to determine the most effective and safe levels.

Once the proper dosage is established, researchers begin longer clinical trials. There are two kinds of clinical trials. The first is a *controlled experiment*, which separates subjects into two groups, one of which receives the drug under investigation while the other receives a placebo (a substance that contains no active ingredients). The latter group, called a control group, provides a comparison with people in the former, or experimental, group. In most cases, subjects are assigned randomly to one group or the other. If the study is "blind," the subjects do not know which group they are in. In a "double-blind" study, the doctors monitoring the experiment don't know which group their subjects are in, either.

In an *uncontrolled experiment*, only a single group exists—and everyone in the group is receiving the same drug. An open trial is an uncontrolled experiment that does not place any limits on the subjects' use of other medications and treatments. Uncontrolled experiments have resulted from pressure put on the government by people with AIDS and AIDS advocates who believe that it is unconscionable to deprive individuals of promising treatments when the alternative is frequently greater ill health, if not death. The establishment of uncontrolled experiments is one of the most important AIDS-advocacy victories of the recent past, and pressure must continue to be placed on all government agencies to speed up the process.

The FDA has established three phases for all new drugs. Phase I, the safety study, investigates the potential danger in humans; such studies are usually very small in scale. Phase II trials seek to determine whether a drug actually works (its efficacy) and what, if any, short-term side effects can be expected. Phase III studies look for long-term side effects, further investigate the effectiveness of the drug, and help determine the appropriate dosage.

Getting into a Treatment Program

If your friend wants to learn about or participate in the drug experiments currently being conducted, the first step is to ask a doctor and call an AIDS hot line. Many doctors involved in AIDS treatment are also involved in research or drug trials as well. If your doctor is not helpful, then you should consider contacting the hospital where your friend was treated or your local AIDS organization (listed in Appendix C).

The federal government has also designated many institutions as research centers for HIV/AIDS clinical trials. Among these are Memorial Sloan-Kettering Cancer Center and New York University Hospital in New York City; Harvard University in Cambridge, Massachusetts; Johns Hopkins University in Baltimore; Stanford University in Palo Alto, California; the University of Miami in Coral Gables, Florida; the University of Pittsburgh; the University of Rochester in upstate New York; the University of Southern California in Los Angeles; the University of Texas at Austin; the University of Washington in Seattle; and the University of California campuses at Los Angeles, San Diego, and San Francisco. For more information about AIDS/HIV clinical trials conducted by the National Institutes of Health and FDA-approved efficacy trials, call 800-TRIALS-A (800-874-2572).

If you are unable to get into an FDA-sponsored trial, there *are* other avenues. You may want to contact the Community Research Initiative (CRIA) in New York City or Project Inform in San Francisco. These community-based organizations, along with a network of others in different cities, organize and conduct clinical trials, which are not government sponsored. These trials, known as "parallel track," are instituted when a drug goes into Phase III or widespread testing. The drug companies themselves often provide subjects in these trials with free medications. Doctors can refer potential subjects to such programs.

If you are unable to participate in *any* clinical trial, it is still possible to obtain experimental drugs. You should speak to your doctor about applying for access to certain drugs that have been classified as "investigational new drugs" and are being dispensed on a "compassionate use" basis, or you may want to contact a "buyers' club"—an informal underground network—which can provide your friend with unapproved medications.

Unapproved and Alternative Therapies

Some people with AIDS are willing to try almost anything that may help them, including drugs not approved for human use by the FDA as well as alternative treatment approaches like holistic remedies, stress reduction, and special diets. Unfortunately, over the years many highly touted unofficial drugs and other treatments have in the end proved ineffective, sometimes very expensive, and at times harmful. On the other hand, some drugs that were unofficially available at a relatively early stage, such as ddI and ddC, were later shown to be highly effective. Similarly, alternative treatment strategies exist that many claim have made a positive difference. What to do? Our best advice: Get the most information you can from the most reliable sources. Talk to your doctor. Talk with your friends. Talk with your local AIDS organization. As Project Inform states: "In the end, any therapy is only deemed worthy if it presents credible evidence that it can help people, and the test of this is ultimately one of science. We do no one any good, and generate considerable harm, if we abandon science altogether."

If your friend does decide to go ahead with an unapproved drug, the following minimum precautions should be undertaken:

- *Discuss the therapy with a doctor.* Try to arrange with the doctor for your friend to have periodic blood tests, so that you can see what, if anything, the drug is doing. At the very least, you should make sure that no harm will come as a result of its usage.
- *Purchase the drug from a reliable source,* such as a known buyers' club.
- *Get the dosage right.* If two are good, four are not twice as good. An overdose can be poisonous.
- *Call the doctor immediately* if your friend's health starts to change for the worse. Stop his taking the drug.

It needs to be emphasized that there are sometimes serious risks in taking an unapproved drug, and we are in no way advocating that people do this. But we certainly understand why some people would choose to go this route.

As for alternative therapies, Project Inform has categorized them as follows:

- unlicensed pharmaceutical products and nonstandard uses of approved drugs
- natural products, like herbs and vitamins, and nutritional therapies (including special diets)
- special medicine systems like homeopathy or Chinese medicine
- spiritual remedies, including visualization techniques, self-help religions, and spiritual healers

In considering a nonmedical therapy, you and your friend must ask many of the same questions you have asked about established and experimental drug therapies. What are the potential results? What are the side effects? How have people evaluated the results? What have been the proven effects? Will a nonmedical therapy conflict with any other treatment you are taking?

In addition, you will want to ask other questions: How much does it cost? Who is making money from it? Who recommends such a course of action, and who warns against it? In many cases, your doctor may not be enthusiastic about these alternative treatments. Bear that in mind as you go to other sources, like your local AIDS agency or Project Inform in San Francisco, to find out more. Most likely, you will find little hard information and almost no scientific data on such treatments. Nevertheless, many people with AIDS believe that their quality of life has been enhanced by holistic or spiritual practices and beliefs. They may be correct. But remember: Alternative therapies that circumvent medical treatments may cause harm to your friend—in fact, if they are used instead of some standard treatments, they could diminish his chances for longer-term survival.

Knowledge Is Power

The amount of available medical information about AIDS is staggering and continues to expand. You can be of the greatest assistance to your friend in helping locate information so that he can make his treatment decisions intelligently. Remember, to fight AIDS successfully, knowledge is power. Do your homework.

5

GETTING YOUR HOUSE IN ORDER: DEALING WITH LEGAL AND FINANCIAL MATTERS

As the second decade of the AIDS epidemic unfolds, so, too, does HIV and AIDS law grow and evolve. People with AIDS now have recourse to a great many legal protections. Moreover, there are numerous entitlement programs on the federal, state, and local levels, including Social Security Disability Insurance, Supplemental Security Income, and Medicaid. Safeguards include antidiscrimination protections covering your job and home, and privacy protections regarding HIV status. In this chapter, four major areas will be examined: (1) the private financial and legal planning an individual should undertake, (2) the steps a parent should take to protect his or her children, (3) government benefit and entitlement programs, and (4) the laws that protect a person with HIV disease or AIDS from discrimination.

The best time to begin talking about the many legal and financial issues that your friend will face is when he is relatively well. Even though both of you may want to put off dealing with the practical preparations for future illness and possible death, neither of you will want to face them only in the midst of a crisis, when it may be too late. For instance, you do not want your friend to be hospitalized for a severe infection only to discover *then* that you have no say in his health care. Nor do you want to learn that his parents are going to inherit the house the two of you paid for together and have lived in for ten years because the deed is in his name only, and you never got around to changing it.

Understanding the law can be challenging, and dealing with bureaucracies can be frustrating. Take your time, ask questions, and, when necessary, get assistance from a legal aid society, your local AIDS organization, or the appropriate governmental office. And as we have said previously: *Take what you need from the information in this chapter as you need it, scrutinizing the rest only when circumstances require you to.*

A word of warning: Laws and government programs are generally based on the notion that they apply equally to *everyone.* If you or your friend does not follow the rules—for whatever reasons, whether through ignorance, illness, or civil disobedience—you will severely limit your chances of prevailing in a given situation. Of course, if others, such as the government, do not follow the required procedures, you—as the injured party—will usually have some legal remedy. In other words, know the rules—and play by them—when it comes to dealing with all your financial and legal planning.

Personal Planning: Legal and Financial

Someone with HIV disease must confront a host of legal and financial matters, including health insurance, living wills, powers of attorney, planning for the future of any children, dispersal of property, and funeral arrangements. Some are tasks the law requires you to perform; others are simply advisable. Many people have found it helpful to go to a large AIDS agency that will "case manage" all these duties for them. Only when that is impossible should an individual work with more than one AIDS agency; the more players, the more complicated the entire process can become. Many have found that retaining a lawyer who specializes in AIDS work is a convenient and efficient—although sometimes more expensive—approach to the maze of legal and financial issues and problems.

Health Insurance

The issue of health insurance cannot be ignored or sidestepped by either you or your sick friend. If your friend currently has health insurance, make sure he hangs on to it. Impress on him, if necessary, the importance of paying his premiums on time and familiarizing himself with all his policy's provisions. It's also a good idea for your friend to review his health-insurance policy with his doctor so that both fully understand what limitations exist in his coverage.

Until recently, health insurance could not be canceled because an individual contracted AIDS (or any other illness). A late 1992 court decision did, however, allow an employer to do just that, despite the catastrophic consequences, because that employer provided its own insurance and did not go through an insurance company (such "self-insured" plans are often outside the bounds of federal and state regulation). That decision may be altered by an act of Congress, but does, in any case, demonstrate how anyone with insurance must be fully aware of his policy, its protections, and its pitfalls.

Insurers have always had the right to cancel a policy for nonpayment. They may also be able to rescind a policy if they learn that application materials were incomplete or contained "a material misrepresentation" about an individual's health. In addition, some policies come up for renewal from time to time, and the insurance company does maintain the right not to renew a policy at that time.

If your friend does not have health insurance, he should do his best to get it. Unfortunately, many insurance companies will not cover someone who they know has HIV disease—and to camouflage one's health status could only lead to more difficulties. On the other hand, some AIDS advocates suggest that if a person is HIV-positive *and healthy*—and if few people know of his health status—he can probably purchase insurance. If your friend faces this situation, think about it carefully. He may succeed and all will be fine, or he could be accused of misrepresenting the truth and the policy could be canceled, leaving him with no coverage at the least opportune time.

There are other options. Many Americans receive health coverage through their employer; health insurance is usually part of the benefits package that comes with most full-time positions. Most employers have group coverage for their workers; usually anyone working for the company is automatically covered. Maintaining a full-time job is probably the easiest way to get health insurance, and in all likelihood, an employer-sponsored policy is the most comprehensive one likely to be found. Increasingly, however, employees are being asked to pay for a portion of their benefits, including health care.

Some Blue Cross/Blue Shield programs have an open enrollment policy, in which everyone who applies is accepted—under certain conditions. If this is the case in your area, your friend should sign up immediately. Remember: There is no way to know when he may have to visit a doctor or be hospitalized, and the most catastrophic bills, sometimes running at the rate of thousands of dollars a day, will be those from the hospital. It may seem expensive to purchase health insurance now, but the alternative could be financially devastating.

Another way to get health insurance is by joining a group with health coverage. This can be a professional organization, an alumni group, a church, or a union. All options should be explored aggressively. Some people with HIV have even found that it makes sense for them to change jobs in order to obtain a solid health insurance plan. For others, changing jobs could result in losing valuable coverage. Certainly, if your friend is covered by his job or another group, he should obtain a copy of his policy—which he has a legal right to see—and study it. He should understand the preexisting-condition clause, the maximum lifetime benefit, and what conditions are covered, partially covered, or not covered at all.

In many states, a prospective insurer can ask to be provided with the results of a recent HIV antibody test. If your friend knows he is HIV-positive, he should withdraw the application, *because it will be rejected.* Worse, the insurer could share this information with other health-insurance carriers.

Whatever you do, don't let your friend delay. Start looking today. You might also call a local AIDS organization to get help in answering difficult questions and to learn the name of an insurance broker who is familiar with the problems of obtaining insurance for people with HIV disease.

Health insurance usually has two separate components: hospitalization and medical insurance. The first pays for all hospital bills; the second for doctors' bills. Some health insurers pay up to 80 percent of doctors' charges, while others will pay only a percentage of what they deem to be a customary fee. Most health-insurance policies do not cover routine dental work, elective surgery, or eyeglasses.

If your friend has health insurance through his job, he may have many questions and concerns that can cause him anxiety. He may be worried that his employer will learn of his HIV disease or AIDS diagnosis through the insurance forms he submits. He should know that *any information garnered from insurance forms must be kept confidential by those who receive it.* If any actions are taken against your friend by his employer as a result of information received by a breach of confidentiality, your friend could legitimately claim to be a victim of discrimination.

Leaving one's job can also be of great concern when it comes to dealing with health insurance. A federal law called COBRA entitles individuals who are no longer working to continue group coverage if the previous employer has twenty or more employees. To take advantage of COBRA, an individual must pay the monthly premium plus a small administrative fee. COBRA coverage lasts for eighteen months after employment is ended. Upon leaving a job, an individual should declare in writing to his employer that he wants to take advantage of the COBRA provisions. If your friend meets the Social Security definition of "disabled" at the time he leaves his job, he can maintain his health coverage for an additional eleven months—for a total of twenty-nine months—at which point Medicare kicks in.

If your friend is eligible only for the eighteen-month period, he should be aware that many states require health insurers to provide for a conversion to an individual health plan at the end of the COBRA coverage. This coverage, however, when available, will in almost all cases be inferior to your friend's group plan and substantially more costly.

COBRA does not apply to life or disability insurance. In some states, like New York, an individual can convert a group life-insurance policy into an individual one, paying the premiums directly. If a person is disabled, he may be able to continue his group life insurance at no cost when he leaves his job. It is not possible to continue job-sponsored disability insurance after terminating employment.

Joining a health-maintenance organization, or HMO, is another way to get medical care at reasonable costs, although these organizations are not established in all areas of the country and may be unwilling to accept individuals with HIV disease. When you belong to an HMO, you must use its facilities and doctors for your medical care, or pay for care yourself. It is important for you to learn what kind of expertise a particular HMO has in dealing with AIDS patients. If a group is incapable of dealing with AIDS or is not known to be sensitive to the needs of AIDS patients, perhaps you and your friend should keep shopping around.

Disability Insurance

The time may come when your friend realizes he can no longer perform the functions of his job, or that work is taking too much of a toll on him. Even before this juncture, he should think about his future. If he is unable to work, what kind of disability benefits—job-related and otherwise—is he eligible for? How does he proceed?

Generally, employers have three kinds of plans to pay employees who are unable to work: sick leave, private disability, and government disability. Your friend will need to find out what his employer's coverage is so that he can maximize those benefit programs. Many companies have private disability-insurance plans that supplement the government disability payments to maintain a disabled person's income at up to 75 percent of what it was when he was working.

In New York State, for instance, if an individual becomes disabled while employed, he is entitled to six months of short-term disability. (Check with your local AIDS agency to learn the policy in your state.) If he is covered by a long-term disability plan, either through his employer or a private policy, payments under that plan will usually commence at the end of a six-month waiting period. Most long-term policies require that an individual be employed for a minimum period of time to qualify.

A Living Will and Medical Power of Attorney

Your friend may want to draw up what is called a living will, a document that describes what he wants to happen to him under a variety of life-threatening medical situations in the event that he is not able to do so at the time. It's also a way for you, the carepartner, to know precisely how to act in certain circumstances.

In a living will, your friend can state exactly what treatments he may or may not want. He could explain, for example, that he would not want to be kept alive on a respirator if his condition was considered terminal or if he was not expected to regain consciousness after a defined period of time.

Your friend can also execute a document that explains what his intentions are and *authorizes someone else* to represent his desires and to make medical decisions for him in the event he is unable to do so. This is called a medical power of attorney. This document can also grant a designated caregiver all hospital visitation rights and access to medical records. Since many hospitals allow only the closest biological relatives to visit and have access to medical records, these are key provisions.

In most states, neither a living will nor a medical power of attorney is a legally binding document that doctors and hospitals *must* honor. In our experience, however, it is rare that a problem arises when a lover or friend participates in important medical decisions once that wish has been formally communicated to the physician and other hospital staff, or that doctors will deliberately disregard a patient's directives. Before a life-threatening situation develops, your friend's doctor should be given a copy of his living will and/or a medical power of attorney. Be sure that the necessary papers are put into his medical chart—early on—in the event that other medical personnel are unexpectedly called upon to treat your friend. (You should also keep a copy in case your friend is taken to a new hospital and is unable to express his wishes, or for any other unforeseeable situation.) You may also want to talk to your friend about having a "Do Not Resuscitate" (DNR) order placed in his chart if he has been very ill for a long time. This means that if his heart or breathing stops, he is not to be given cardiopulmonary resuscitation to get them started again.

These topics may be difficult for you to raise and discuss with your sick friend. On the other hand, such dilemmas and options may already be on his mind. Give him time and the opportunity for counseling, if he wants it, to decide how much, if any, extraordinary treatment he may wish to undergo in the later stages of his illness. You can both be assured that if he is ever in need of artificial means to stay alive, and is conscious at the time, he will be asked again about such treatments, regardless of whether or not he has executed a living will.

If your friend is wary of such a document, or won't draw one up, make sure that you and he and anyone else who would have a say in the matter—his parents, for example—understand his wishes and know how to act on them. While it is best that a living will be drawn up by an attorney, it can be done between yourselves, if necessary.

Power of Attorney

Power-of-attorney papers authorize one person to act on legal and financial matters in the name of another. Your friend (the grantor) can appoint someone else to manage and make decisions regarding all his legal and financial affairs, or he can appoint different people for each area. The person so designated is authorized to deal with both everyday matters as well as significant decisions. An individual with power of attorney in financial matters can write checks, pay bills, terminate a lease, and sell assets. A so-called durable power of attorney allows the designated individual to act even when the grantor is extremely ill, in a coma, or in some other way incapacitated and unable to act for himself. The power of attorney goes into effect as soon as it is signed. Your friend should take great care in choosing the individual who will be responsible for safeguarding his possessions and well-being.

Having a power of attorney can become particularly important if your friend has been in conflict with his family and serious decisions need to be made when he is unable to participate in the decision-making process. Under these circumstances, the person granted power of attorney should, however, try to consult family members if they have indicated that they want to be involved.

A power of attorney has no validity once a person has died. Then, an individual's executor, as named in his will, is entrusted with carrying out the deceased's wishes.

Buying Out Life Insurance

For the last several years, it has become possible for a person with AIDS to collect on his life-insurance policy in advance of his death. To do this, he must have held an individual life-insurance policy for a minimum of two years, his life expectancy must be estimated at eighteen months or less, and the face value of his policy must be at least fifty-thousand dollars (these criteria may be negotiable). The policyholder then assigns ownership of his insurance to one of the several companies that have been set up expressly for this purpose, and names it as beneficiary (he will also have to secure legal consent from his life-insurance company and his previously named beneficiaries). The assigned company then pays between 60 and 75 percent of the face value of the policy *at that time*. For individuals who are worried about their present financial situation, this may be a viable option.

Last Will and Testament

Lawyers have been telling us for years that everybody should write a will, but not surprisingly, many people still do not have any kind of last will and testament. The AIDS epidemic has underscored just how little protection American laws accord those who are not in traditionally defined relationships. Without properly executed legal documents, many legitimate survivors may not be recognized by the law, by blood relatives, or by society when it comes to the distribution of property and to decisions about funerals and other postmortem arrangements. A lover or friend may receive nothing, regardless of the duration of the relationship. A favorite charity will be bypassed even if the person who dies had told others that he wanted his property to go to that organization.

Under the laws of intestate succession, the details of which vary from state to state, if your friend dies without a spouse or children, his property passes to his closest living blood relatives: parents are first, then siblings, then nieces and nephews. This type of distribution would occur even if one had never met the particular relative or if there were bad feelings between them. In some cases, the state becomes the beneficiary of the estate. If a will is not executed properly, family members may more easily challenge its provisions. The lesson is quite clear: Do it and do it right.

Gay men and lesbians, people living together who are not married, and others who maintain very close friendships have a special need to write wills to make sure their loved ones are included. If your friend with AIDS dies without a will, it is extremely likely that complications will arise. A will is the best way for a person with AIDS to protect himself and to control the distribution of his property. Lovers should be especially certain to draw up wills together, so that no matter what happens, each has taken care of the other.

In a will, your friend can do as he pleases with his property. He can leave his assets to a favorite charity, or he can divide them among family and friends. Your friend can leave instructions about how his debts are to be paid; he can even name the people to whom he wants to leave nothing.

Many people don't realize this, but a will can also be used to express many other wishes. For instance, your friend can leave instructions about whether he wants a funeral or a memorial service, and whether he wants to be buried or cremated. He can specify where he wants to be buried, and what provisions he has made for this. Your friend should, of course, make his intentions known to those close to him and let them know where the document can be readily found upon his death. It may even be a good idea for you or another close friend to keep a copy of the will in your possession.

Each person drawing up a will should name someone to carry out its provisions. This person is called the executor and is responsible for probating the will in court. All this means is that the executor— who need not be a lawyer—must take the will to the appropriate court and file it. The court will oversee the proper execution of the will if there are challenges to its terms. The executor will also have to deal with hospitals, doctors, insurance companies, and property distribution at the appropriate time. There is no reason why the primary beneficiary of the will cannot be the executor.

In almost all cases, a lawyer should draw up a will. There are standard-form wills that can be purchased in stationery and office-supply stores, filled out, and made legal by signing before a notary public and witnesses, but do remember that the law has strict guidelines about how wills must be drawn up and executed. If these guidelines are not followed exactly; then the will may not be valid, and it becomes easier for others to challenge.

To draw up a will, your friend will need four things:

- a precise idea of what he hopes to accomplish in the will
- the names and addresses of his beneficiaries and his executor, and substitutes for all of them
- the names and addresses of all his family members, even if they are not mentioned in the will
- a written description of what his property consists of and where it is located

If your friend cannot afford to pay a lawyer, many AIDS and legal-aid agencies can provide free legal assistance.

Your friend should know that he can always draw up a new will, revoking any previous ones. He can also make an amendment, called a codicil, to an existing will. To do either of these, however, he needs to work with a lawyer to make sure that all legal guidelines are followed. For instance, your friend cannot change his will simply by writing or typing changes on it after it has been signed. In fact, any change could void the original signed will.

If your friend refuses for whatever reason to have a will drawn up, the best you can do is to raise the topic periodically. Explain to him that the reason to make a will is not that he is feeling sick or may die, but that it is the *practical* thing to do to protect his property, his friends, and his family. Having a legally executed will, you can tell him, should decrease his anxiety about what could happen to his possessions and about the fulfillment of any personal wishes. You might also suggest to him that the two of you draw up your wills simultaneously—that may make the task seem less daunting.

Property Outside the Will

If you and your friend own property jointly, like a co-op or a house, a car, a bank account, an insurance policy, or a pension plan, any of which may not be mentioned in either person's will, you should attend to these assets legally, assuring that the property will pass smoothly to the appropriate person. If you and your friend own real estate jointly, make sure that the deed describes you as joint tenants with a right of survivorship. Make sure that your bank accounts are held jointly, or change them to trust accounts. Each of you can name the other as the beneficiary of any insurance policies without stating this in a will.

These precautions are especially important should a relative of your friend's not recognize your relationship and challenge the will. Even when the will is executed properly, a challenge can cause months of distress and delay. According to the law, property held outside the will can be passed from one person to the other, so this passage is less likely to be challenged—even if someone were to attempt to break the will.

Funeral Arrangements

Your friend may have some very definite ideas about what he wants to happen after his death, from his preference for burial or cremation to how he wants to be memorialized. If he wants to discuss these matters at any point during his illness, allow him to do so.

Many people with AIDS have planned their own memorial services as a last chance to share with friends and family the poems, the writings, and the music that they particularly loved and that they want remembered in association with them. They may want their service to be a reflection of what they had achieved in their personal relationships or what they accomplished in their professional lives.

You, as a carepartner, should also do some planning of your own. Which funeral homes in your community will handle the remains of someone who has died from AIDS? You may also want to make a mental plan of what things you would need to get done in the event of your friend's death, from making a list of people to be contacted to handling your friend's financial obligations.

You may have great difficulty discussing these issues with your friend, but you should try to at an appropriate time. They are topics you can bring up gently and drop if your friend shows signs of agitation, anger, or resistance. But once you have planted the seed, you may get your friend thinking about the vital plans he has to make. He may even appreciate the amount of control he can feel about how he can resolve his own life. If you feel comfortable doing so, you should also try to ascertain the wishes of other significant people in your friend's life, such as his parents or siblings. They, too, may have definite ideas about what they want to see done, such as burial in a family plot. All of this can be very delicate and takes good sense, good timing, and diplomacy.

Children: How Best to Protect Them

If your friend is HIV-positive and has children (and the other parent is unable or unwilling to step in), you should encourage him or her to begin thinking about the long-term care of the children. This can be a most painful and devastating subject of conversation, and we suggest that you speak up early, and at a time when your friend is prepared to deal with the ramifications of the disease on the future of the family.

There are several options available to a parent who wants to make provisions for offspring. These include choosing a legal guardian, giving the children up for adoption, placing the children in foster care, and making a temporary care and custody document. We will discuss each of these options in detail. (All of these options preclude the involvement of the other parent.)

Guardianship

If your friend can no longer care for his or her children, the other parent usually gets custody. If that option is not possible or if your friend does not want the children to be placed with the other parent, then it is important to name someone else to take care of them. Such a person is the "proposed guardian"; only a court can make a final determination about guardianship. This is a difficult subject, but your friend should put his or her wishes in writing as soon as possible to prevent disagreement later about who will care for the children.

Your friend should be certain that the proposed guardian can and wants to take care of the children. Whenever possible, an alternate guardian should be chosen in the event the proposed guardian cannot fulfill his or her obligation or the court does not approve the selection.

Your friend may choose to elect a guardian if he or she has reached a point where he can no longer properly care for the children. If approved by the court, this guardian would remain the children's legal guardian upon the death of your friend.

Adoption

There are some crucial differences among adoption, guardianship, and custody. The people who adopt a child become his or her parents for the rest of their lives. The biological parent loses parental rights in an adoption. Guardianship or custody is less final and can be changed by a court order.

Adoption gives new parents all the rights previously held by the birth parents: the right to custody of the child and to decide where the child goes to school, the child's religion, and the kind of medical care the child will receive. Arranging for the adoption of the children may give your friend a certain peace of mind that the

102

children's future is secure. On the other hand, he or she may not be ready to give up being a parent.

If your friend is considering adoption as an alternative, he or she should try to get the help of a lawyer to ensure that his or her wishes are met in the court process.

Foster Care

When children are placed in foster care, they become the custody of a city or county agency. Your friend should think very carefully before exercising this option, because he or she could lose a lot more control over the children than by choosing a custodian or guardian. The children could also be permanently lost to the parent and all blood relatives if they remain in foster care for a long time, especially if there is no regular contact between parent and children.

Children are placed in foster care when the parent or guardian signs a voluntary-placement agreement with the local agency. They can be placed for a specific time—for instance, until the parent gets out of the hospital—or without a limit. Your friend should speak with a lawyer before signing a voluntary-placement agreement.

Many problems may be engendered by placing children in foster care. A government agency may interfere with your friend's relationship with his or her children. It can be difficult to get children back from foster care, especially if your friend has not seen them regularly. If possible, it is best to avoid placing children in foster care.

Temporary Care and Custody

A time may arise when your friend needs to have someone else take temporary care of the children because he or she is in the hospital or is too sick. A relative, carepartner, or other reliable friend can be given short-term oversight duties through a temporary care and custody document, which is required only if the children need medical care or to be enrolled in school and your friend is unable to fulfill these responsibilities. This document will not prevent the children's other parent from trying to get custody, nor is it a recognized legal document. To execute such an arrangement, your friend needs to put in writing the name of the person being asked to take care of the children and what your friend wants that person to be able to do; then he must sign and date the document in front of a notary public and a witness. A lawyer need not be involved in this process. You may want to call an AIDS or legal organization to see if they have any sample temporary care and custody documents.

Government Benefits: How to Manage the System

Many government benefit programs, running the gamut from Social Security Disability to the Food Stamps program to the AZT Drug Assistance Program, serve people with HIV disease and AIDS. These programs are designed to be a safety net for those in need. Many people with AIDS—unable to work, and without savings—have come to depend on government entitlement programs to make ends meet.

Be forewarned: Dealing with the government can be daunting. Your friend will encounter long lines, unclear application materials, overworked bureaucrats, and a host of other roadblocks. Be prepared. Phone ahead to see if an appointment is necessary. Provide as much documentation as you can with your application. Follow the rules—even if you don't understand the logic behind them. If possible, always try to have an AIDS or benefits counseling agency help you and/or your friend.

Social Security Benefits

The federal Social Security Administration runs two programs providing separate but related disability benefit programs: Social Security Disability Insurance (SSDI) and Supplemental Security Income (SSI). To be eligible for either, an individual must be disabled—not able to work—according to federal definitions. The Social Security Administration defines *disability* as any physical or mental medical condition that prevents or is expected to prevent an individual from working for twelve months or more, or that will result in death. This definition generally includes individuals with an AIDS diagnosis; however, the Social Security Administration will evaluate individuals with other stages of disabling HIV disease on a case-by-case basis to determine eligibility. If your friend is unable to work because of his HIV condition, he will need to work with a doctor to document his disability claim. According to the California State Legal Services Association,

> It is not enough to show you are unable to perform the duties of the job for which you have been trained. *You must*

be unable to perform any job [emphasis added]. This means that if you are no longer able to perform your job as an astronaut, but you are physically able to work as a ticket-taker, you are *not* disabled under the Social Security Administration definition of disability.

The Social Security Administration has developed a list of HIV-related physical and mental conditions it uses to determine an individual's disability. Some of the conditions are considered sufficient to warrant an automatic disability classification. These include, but are not limited to, the following: *Pneumocystis carinii* pneumonia, toxoplasmosis, HIV encephalopathy (dementia), and HIV wasting syndrome. According to Paul DiDonato, an attorney with the AIDS Legal Referral Panel in San Francisco, "Documenting one of these conditions is the quickest and easiest way to receive Social Security benefits."

Further down on the agency's list are HIV-related conditions that require proof of disability (beyond the mere presence of the condition itself) before a person is deemed eligible for benefits. With the presumption of HIV infection, these include lymphadenopathy (swollen lymph glands), repeated fungal, viral, or bacterial infections, fatigue, wasting, night sweats, memory impairment, and depression. To establish eligibility on the basis of any one of these conditions, the Social Security Administration looks at severity, duration, frequency, resistance to treatment, or demonstrated impairment. Determination is made on a case-by-case basis.

Along with proving he is disabled according to the government definition, *an individual must show that he has paid into the Social Security system to qualify for SSDI or has a financial need based on limited resources to qualify for SSI.*

Individuals should apply for SSDI as soon as they become disabled, because the Social Security Administration does not pay benefits until five months from the time disability was claimed. At that time, however, the agency may determine that an individual is eligible for retroactive payments. The monthly SSDI check will depend on several factors, including previous earnings, age at the onset of disability, and the date of disability. The average benefit is about six hundred dollars a month. Many people with AIDS are eligible for SSDI if they have had some sort of work history. SSDI recipients also receive Medicare medical coverage, but only after twenty-four months on the SSDI program.

If someone has never worked, or has worked for less time than is required to qualify for SSDI, he should apply for SSI. This program usually assists needy people sixty-five years or older, but it also serves those who are blind or *disabled* regardless of age. To determine eligibility for SSI, the Social Security Administration uses the same criteria as for the SSDI program.

Before the government gives anyone SSI, it wants to ascertain that the individual is in fact poor and in need. The Social Security Administration will want to know the applicant's income, defined as "anything received that can be used to meet the needs of food, clothing, or shelter." Generally, to be eligible, your friend cannot have assets exceeding $2,000. Included in his assets are bank accounts, cash, stocks and bonds, antiques—actually, anything of any material value. His monthly income must generally be below $500; any car he owns must be valued at less than $4,500, unless it is used for medical purposes or "essential daily activities." If he owns his own home, he may keep that, regardless of its value. If your friend has transferred any of his assets to another person in the two years prior to applying for SSI, he could be disqualified. If your friend qualifies for SSI, he will usually also qualify for food stamps, as the requirements are much the same.

As with SSDI, SSI benefits should be applied for immediately when your friend becomes disabled. The agency has established an expedited process by which SSI payments can be sent out within days of application if the medical records proving disability are in order. In any case, these benefits are retroactive to the date of application. The maximum monthly SSI payment varies from state to state; in California, it is currently about six hundred dollars.

It is possible for some individuals to receive both SSDI and SSI benefits, but this is rare because all SSDI income is counted against SSI income and resource limitations still apply. Both programs offer incentives so that an individual can test his ability to work without losing benefits if he recovers from a serious bout of illness. Restrictions do exist, so it is a good idea to check with your local AIDS organization benefits program or the Social Security Administration office in your area.

Medicaid

Medicaid is one of the federal government's two major health-insurance programs (the other is Medicare, for which one becomes eligible by working in jobs covered by Social Security). Medicaid is designed for individuals whose incomes and assets put them below the poverty line in their state or whose incomes fall to the poverty level through *incurred* but not necessarily paid medical bills. (Individuals who might otherwise be ineligible for Medicaid because they earn too much can still qualify if their monthly income less the amount of their medical bills equals a figure below the poverty line.) In most cases, individuals eligible for SSI or Aid to Families with Dependent Children (discussed below) are automatically eligible for Medicaid. Most people with AIDS qualify because they are considered disabled according to the Social Security definition. Still others—those with limited incomes as well as those with symptomatic HIV disease but not full-blown AIDS—will be considered on a case-by-case basis. Under some circumstances, people receiving SSDI payments can also receive Medicaid, especially during the twenty-nine-month period when someone is on SSDI and waiting for Medicare to kick in.

Once an individual is approved, Medicaid will help pay for (1) inpatient and outpatient hospital care, (2) doctors' services, (3) diagnostic tests, (4) skilled nursing care, (5) home health visits, (6) hospice care, and other medical services. Each month your friend will receive a book of coupons that he can utilize for the above-mentioned services. Your friend should know, however, that while Medicaid is a comprehensive medical program, it does not cover unconventional medical treatments such as a macrobiotic diet, chiropractic treatments, acupuncture, herbology, and most other holistic approaches to medicine.

Food Stamps

The Food Stamps program is a federally funded state-run welfare program to help needy individuals to buy food. People on SSDI or SSI generally receive larger allowances than others do. To qualify for food stamps, an individual cannot have assets of more than $2,000 or a gross monthly income in excess of $648. The government doesn't count as an asset a disabled person's car (unless its worth exceeds $4,500) or his home, no matter what its value. It also doesn't count his burial plot, household and personal belongings, and tools or machinery he needs to earn a living.

Each month, food-stamp recipients must go to a designated site to exchange their monthly Authorization to Participate form for the stamps, which can be used to buy food but not alcohol, cleaning products, toilet paper, tobacco, or pet food. The average monthly food-stamp allocation is approximately $100. (If an individual qualifies for SSI and food stamps, he also qualifies for Medicaid, which will pay for hospital costs, long-term care, hospice care, medical costs, and prescription medicines.)

General Assistance

If your friend with AIDS is truly in financial need, and is waiting for SSDI or SSI payments to begin or cannot receive SSDI or SSI, he may qualify for general assistance (commonly known as welfare). This federal entitlement program is administered on a local (state and county) level; as a result, the size of payments, eligibility requirements, income restrictions, asset restrictions, and a variety of other conditions will vary from place to place.

Generally, though, a very strict limit exists on an applicant's resources, whether cash, savings accounts, or anything else usually counted as an asset. Under the terms of this program, an individual may own an automobile, but only one of a limited value. While payments vary, recipients can expect to receive between $200 and $250 each month, which is intended to cover all basic needs, including rent, food, clothing, electricity, telephone, and nonprescription drugs. An individual automatically becomes eligible for food stamps and Medicaid when he qualifies for general assistance.

Other Federal Benefit Programs

Aid to Families with Dependent Children (AFDC) is a federal-state welfare program that makes payments to low-income families with children in which the parent is single, unemployed, or disabled. A parent with AIDS who has a child under the age of eighteen living at home is eligible for AFDC.

AZT Drug Assistance, a federally funded, state-administered program, subsidizes the high cost of AZT and other FDA-approved drugs for HIV disease. In 1989, 6,500 individuals received nearly $20 million worth of AZT and other drugs through this program.

The Department of Veterans Affairs, a federal agency, provides support and medical care to disabled (and other) veterans and their dependents.

For more information on any of these government programs, contact your local AIDS agency as a first step, or call one of the national AIDS hot lines and ask for the name of the appropriate government agency.

Other Sources of Financial Help

Your friend may be able to get some financial aid from a local AIDS agency or a local church with an AIDS program. Some hospitals also provide assistance programs for those in need.

Making your way through the maze of government programs can be trying and time-consuming. If you can find a social worker or benefits counselor to help you and your friend, take advantage of the situation. Also, try calling your local AIDS agency to see if it has benefits counselors; many agencies do have both paid and volunteer counselors.

Discrimination: Protection Under the Law

During the course of the AIDS epidemic, an increasing number of laws have been enacted that protect people with AIDS and HIV disease from various kinds of discrimination in the areas of employment, housing, schools, and health care. Still, not all areas are covered—for example, as we discussed earlier, a recent court decision allowed an employer to terminate a health-insurance policy for an employee diagnosed with AIDS. Moreover, the law cannot and does not always prevent discriminatory actions from occurring, even when they are blatantly illegal. It's important that you and your friend understand what protections exist and that they exist in an imperfect world.

The cornerstone of federal protection is the Americans with Disabilities Act (ADA), a major piece of civil rights legislation enacted in 1990 that protects people with many kinds of disabilities, including all forms of HIV disease, from discrimination in most settings, including their place of employment, the school they attend, the hospital they're being treated in, and in most places where business is conducted or services are provided. "Disability," as understood here, is a legal term intended to establish a person's basis for antidiscrimination protection. It is a very broad definition, and it is *not* the same definition of "disability" used to establish eligibility for government benefit programs.

Effective July 1992, the ADA prohibited any business with more than twenty-five employees from discriminating against people with HIV disease. Starting in July 1994, the law extends to businesses that employ more than fifteen people. In many states, there are already local laws that give additional protections to people with HIV disease, usually by covering employers with even fewer employees than the ADA requires.

The ADA provides many specific protections to people with HIV disease. For instance, an employer cannot refuse to hire an individual because he is HIV-positive or has AIDS. Nor can a person be fired because of his health status. An employer is not allowed to use the possibility that a person may become too sick to work in the future as an excuse for not hiring—or for firing—him now. The ADA also requires an employer to make "reasonable accommodations" for people with HIV disease. According to the American Civil Liberties Union (ACLU) AIDS Project, "the employer has a responsibility to make changes in a job that will help the person perform the job adequately. This could include establishing flexible work schedules and allowing a person time off for medical treatment. The bottom line is that an employer cannot treat a person with HIV disease differently in the terms of employment simply because of HIV disease."

Besides employers, many others are also prohibited from discriminating against people with HIV disease, including doctors, dentists, pharmacists, hotels, restaurants, movie theaters, health spas, bakeries, banks, travel services, museums, parks, schools, homeless shelters, adoption agencies and programs, and any place that provides social services. In other words, according to the ACLU, "all of these businesses and service providers may not discriminate against you in providing goods and services because you are regarded as having HIV disease, or because you associate with a person with HIV disease."

If you believe that either you or your friend has been discriminated against because of HIV status, you should speak to a representative of your local AIDS agency to see how the ADA or other federal, state, or local laws protect you and what you can do to assert your rights. You can also call the local legal-aid society or one of the national AIDS legal and civil rights organizations.

Tenant's Rights

It is illegal for landlords to discriminate on the basis of a person's HIV status. The federal Fair Housing Act, as amended by Congress in 1989, prohibits discrimination against people with HIV disease in the sale or rental of private housing.

Your friend cannot, for example, be evicted from his apartment because of his health status—no matter the number of units in the building—as long as the rent continues to be paid. However, if your friend's apartment is not rent-controlled or rent-stabilized, the landlord could attempt to evict him once the lease period is over. The eviction process is usually a lengthy one, and your friend would be able to stay in the apartment for the duration of the proceedings.

If you and your friend live together in a rented apartment and have done so for many years, either of you should be able to stay on if the other dies—even if you aren't both on the lease. In some cases, this may mean signing a new lease at a higher rent or paying a finder's fee to the landlord to defray some of the losses he's incurred by not renting to a new tenant. You should know, however, that you cannot *force* a landlord to put an additional name on a lease. In cities like New York, you should not expect to keep an apartment beyond the death of the original tenant unless your name is on the lease. In cities with higher vacancy rates, you may have more options. Check with your local AIDS organization or the agency dealing with rental-housing advocacy in your area.

No matter where you live, if you receive correspondence from the landlord, especially legal documents, deal with them immediately. Although the legal process is usually long and encumbered, local legislation may give landlords a particular advantage or shortcut, so it is advisable to do your homework promptly.

In most areas, if your friend falls behind in the rent, the landlord must give him written or verbal notice demanding payment. After that, the landlord must deliver a Nonpayment Petition, which initiates court action and requires your friend to go to housing court to file a response. After the papers have been filed, unless a settlement is reached, both parties will have to appear in court to argue the merits of the case before a judge. A health disability is not a defense for nonpayment of rent.

In many areas, it is *not* advisable for your friend to tell the landlord or any other tenants about his condition. This is taking an unnecessary risk that could leave him open to harassment.

If your friend is the roommate of a leaseholder and is asked by his roommate to leave, he must be given thirty days' notice. If your friend refuses because he is too ill, does not have the energy to look for another apartment, or for any other reason, the leaseholder must go to court and get an eviction order. Your friend's belongings cannot simply be put out in the street.

Workplace Discrimination

As stated previously, the Americans with Disabilities Act prohibits discrimination against people with HIV disease (other laws, such as Section 504 of the Rehabilitation Act, provide additional protections). Under the terms of the ADA, as long as your friend is capable of performing his job, he cannot be fired. It is also illegal for an employer to fire an individual because he is believed to be at a high risk of contracting AIDS—that is, because he is gay or an intravenous drug user—or is believed, mistakenly, to have HIV. In New York City, San Francisco, Minneapolis, and many other cities, it is illegal to discriminate on the basis of sexual orientation.

Many individuals at risk for AIDS are fearful that an employer or a prospective employer will require an HIV test. Because it is illegal for an employer to treat an individual differently as a result of an HIV test, in almost all cases it is unlawful to require someone to take the test in the first place. It is also usually illegal for an employer to obtain information about an individual's HIV status.

Another concern to those with HIV disease is their potential inability to do their job in the way they are accustomed to. As the disease progresses, it may become more difficult to keep the same arduous hours or to exert the same physical labor, or to travel on a moment's notice for a sales call. If an employer is already aware of your friend's condition, it may be worthwhile for your friend to approach his company's personnel director and explain that in light of his disability he requires a more flexible work schedule and/or less strenuous work activity. The ADA requires the employer to do all it can to "reasonably accommodate" a disabled individual. If your friend works for a large corporation and asks to work from 10:00 A.M. to 4:00 P.M. instead of 9:00 A.M. to 5:00 P.M., that request would likely be deemed reasonable. If he is one of only three partners in a law firm and asks to be switched to a position with different responsibilities, this request could easily be considered unreasonable since a small firm might be unable to respond to such a request. In short, explains a GMHC legal publication, "you can ask that adjustments be made, but they must be within reason."

Other Protections

Businesses and service providers may not discriminate against people with HIV disease, people who are thought to have HIV disease, or people who associate with someone with HIV disease. Restaurants may not refuse to serve someone with HIV, nor can a doctor or a dentist refuse treatment to an individual with HIV disease.

If you believe that you or your friend has been discriminated against on the basis of HIV status, you should speak with a representative from your local AIDS agency or a trustworthy legal clinic, or with a lawyer well versed in AIDS law. The AIDS Legal Referral Panel in San Francisco and the Lambda Legal Defense Fund in New York and Los Angeles are two nationally recognized organizations that can help you free of charge.

Confidentiality

Your friend's health status is considered a private matter, and many protections exist to safeguard his privacy. "Confidentiality" is the term used to describe these privacy protections. Some examples include the following. If your friend is admitted to a hospital, he cannot be tested for HIV antibodies unless he gives written consent before blood is drawn; the same holds true for insurance companies. Under most circumstances, an employer is not permitted to review insurance claims to learn about an individual's health; if such an action occurs and your friend's employment is adversely affected, he could file suit for unlawful discrimination. By and large, doctors and other health-care professionals can pass on information about you only if you have signed a release form for that specific individual or medical facility (they can, however, give the information to insurance companies for reimbursement and to others providing health care to you).

The laws regarding confidentiality are strict, especially regarding HIV-related information; if your friend feels that his privacy has been violated, you or he should seek additional information and expertise from a legal organization.

Know Your Rights

There is obviously much to do and much to plan for in terms of your friend's financial and legal rights and responsibilities. Regarding financial planning, the best approach is to start early, act promptly, and play by the rules. In terms of the law, it pays to know your rights, to demand them, and—when necessary—to know where to seek legal advice.

6

LIVING WITH AIDS: YOUR RELATIONSHIP CHANGES

The months after the diagnosis and, if it occurs, your friend's first hospitalization can be an extremely difficult time for a carepartner or friend of someone with AIDS. Even if there is a lull after the crisis, everything will seem to have changed. For some, there will be a great number of things to deal with right away; for others, anxiety and concern will become even more paramount.

During this time, you should expect vast changes in your relationship with your friend. Perhaps the relationship will grow deeper, more intimate, and more loving; perhaps it will become very tense, filled with anger and resentment. It may even end. You will find yourself asking: What are the things I can do that can make a difference?

After the diagnosis and initial treatment, your friend may feel better than he has for many months. Although he may feel weak, get tired easily, and need several weeks to rest and regain his strength, after a while he may feel well enough to continue his life as before his diagnosis. If that is the case with your friend, you should support him in as many ways as you can, both emotionally and practically. You can do everything from encouraging your friend to talk about his feelings and fears to helping out with some of the regular chores and household duties.

When Your Friend Returns to Work

After their first crisis, many people may, in effect, deny their illnesses. They go back to work all revved up. They plan to resume their lives as if nothing had happened. You may see your friend driving himself as hard as he did before he became ill. He may get up early, go to the gym, drive to work, stay late, eat dinner, then go out to a movie. For someone who is a homemaker, the impulse may be to take total care of the children and perform all the household responsibilities at the same pace as before. For some people, this kind of activity should pose no problems; for others, it could be harmful. Your friend should listen to his body, so as not to push too far too fast.

In making the myriad decisions that are necessary at this juncture, your friend should rely on the opinions of his doctor and other informed people. For your own part, try not to let your friend overdo things. After being sick, he may not want to acknowledge that he tires more easily, doesn't sleep well, is distracted by the changes in his life, or runs occasional fevers in the afternoon or night. If he pushes too hard, he could develop additional symptoms and complications. On the other hand, you must remember that it is his life and that he bears ultimate responsibility for all his actions and decisions.

After his first hospitalization, Mart talked incessantly about returning to the business he owned. "I tried to go back to work earlier than I was ready to," he recalls, "and it actually took another month before I could really go back. Even though my office is only five blocks away, I found that I got exhausted just walking that distance. There are times, even now, when I get tired, and it upsets me that I don't have enough energy to do all the things that I've done in the past."

Jeffrey remembers his anxiety when his lover, Paul, was ready to go back to work. "He told the doctor he was feeling better and that he wanted to go back to the office. Still, he asked his boss to reduce his work load, and his boss agreed, keeping Paul at his regular salary. We both thought the company seemed very generous at the time.

"Paul was there, it turned out, exactly two weeks. At the end of the first week, he started getting these horrible, horrible headaches. They would start at two o'clock in the afternoon, and by five he couldn't sit up. He had to get out and lie down somewhere. But, curiously, the headaches would go away at night; he'd wake up each morning and feel fine. It wasn't long before the headaches started happening earlier and earlier in the day. He went to the doctor, who thought it was just a case of nerves. After another week of this we were worried, big time. 'Could he be sick again?' So we went to the hospital. It turns out he had cryptococcal meningitis.''

After Meredith's first bout with PCP, she returned home weak, but still, she had a house to run and two young children to care for. She tried to do it all as she had before but soon found herself getting sicker and sicker. Not long after, she was hospitalized again. "It's very difficult for me to take care of me," she says. "I feel guilty about it. It's just like this last period when I had to take some time off from the kids because of a combination of events: stress, an infection, and a terrible skin rash. I felt so guilty about taking care of me and not taking care of the kids the way I'd like to, the way I used to." Eventually, Meredith took the wrenching step of asking some friends to formally adopt her little girl and boy.

Others have returned to work, cutting back their schedules, arranging for somewhat lighter responsibilities or working at home, either permanently or at least some of the time. Depending on your friend's health and his employer's flexibility, there are many options. If your friend feels that his employer will be sympathetic, he might initiate a conversation about part-time work, job sharing, flexible hours, or some other more convenient—and healthful—arrangement. There may also come a time when your friend will consider going on disability, which can be psychologically difficult but also a way for him to revise and renew his life.

Stephen had been out sick from his job as a radio producer for nearly two months when he called his boss and told her that he was ready to come back to work. "I was really nervous the day I called because I knew I was well enough to work a half day, but not the whole day. So I told my executive producer exactly what was up. She asked me what I wanted to do. I said, 'I'd like to be able to work mornings and take on half my usual number of shows. She listened and then said, 'I'll get back to you in a couple of days. I'll see what I can do.' Two days later she called and said I should report the following Monday. 'We're glad you'll be back and that we can make use of your talents,' she added. I've been working half days for a while, and so far it's working out fine for everybody."

"Of course," Jack says, "Bruce didn't tell anyone at work why he was out, except that he was sick. So when he came out of the hospital and went back to work, people were really surprised when they saw him. He had lost twenty-five pounds. The worst part was that he needed a strong back and strong arms to do the work he did. He was staying with me at that time, and the first two days he came home he just fell into bed and didn't get up until the next morning. He didn't even eat dinner. I was going crazy. It took his boss about two days to figure out how weak Bruce was, so then he decided to have him drive the truck and work as a flagman. That was certainly less taxing. And it worked for nearly a year. Bruce got stronger over time, and we adjusted, slowly but surely.''

If at any point you find your friend is pushing himself too hard, speak with him gently but firmly. He may, after all, be overcompensating, trying to cram as much as he can into the time he feels he has left. At this point, he may feel a strong need to accomplish something, to leave his mark on the world. When he is feeling well, his denial may be too strong to allow him to hear anything about his illness. The safest thing to do, if you are monitoring his daily activities, is to slow him down as much as you can. This won't always be easy. It might not always work. You can try to do this by finding activities for the two of you that are relaxing and require a minimum of physical effort on his part. Seek out particularly interesting shows on TV (if that's possible!), or rent some of his favorite movies. Invite a friend or two for dinner. Plan some weekends away. Also, if your friend has children and another parent is not involved in their upbringing, this would be a good time to ask your friend whether you should assume more of the day-to-day responsibility of caring for them—and explaining to them what is happening.

When Your Friend Decides to Stay at Home

Sometimes people will find that they can't return to work or manage a household. They simply may not have the strength, the concentration, or the desire. Nor do they feel that they want to try some new, less demanding kind of work.

Even when it's financially feasible, coming home to stay can be a particularly difficult problem for a person with AIDS or HIV disease. Some people are very good at taking care of themselves and keeping themselves occupied. They may develop a productive schedule: doing volunteer work (an AIDS agency could be a good place to start), visiting friends regularly, joining a social club or bridge club. For those with a positive attitude, many outlets are available. But others may not know what to do with themselves. Some people become bored, depressed, and angry. Whatever your friend does, his daily routine is going to be part of *your* daily routine, too. And you will have to help him if his behavior begins to affect your relationship.

How You Can Help

You can choose what kind of friend you want to be. For instance, you may decide to make an occasional phone call, perhaps just once a week, to inquire about your friend's health and well-being. Or you may choose to do the marketing and household cleanup or to baby-sit on a regular basis. Or you might decide to become an integral part of your friend's support system—even becoming his carepartner. The decision is for the two of you to make as circumstances warrant; the nature of your role will evolve in surprising and often positive ways.

If you do choose to become a part of your friend's support system, you may find yourself increasingly involved in his life, becoming one of the people he counts on to be there. As time goes on, you will probably experience more intense and dramatic emotions than you've yet encountered. This can be very painful and unsettling. At the same time, you may also find yourself growing closer to your friend, which can be very rewarding. You will also come to know yourself better, realizing more of your strengths and limitations. Most of all, you may learn more about love and what it means to care for someone through sickness as well as health.

Be Consistent

Whatever you decide, be consistent. Don't call your friend and say "I'll be over Saturday," then call Saturday morning and say you can't make it. Don't disappoint him by making promises and then not coming through. Often, people do not mean to be cruel or to hurt their friend. They simply do not know their limits, so, unfortunately, they make promises they can't keep. Before you make a commitment to your friend, be sure yourself that you are willing to stick with it and that you will make the time.

Joan and Barry had very mixed feelings while visiting their son David after he became ill. Joan explains, "Barry had to go back home to take care of the business, do the payroll, that sort of thing. But I stayed on to take care of David. I thought that as soon as he was well, I would take him home with me. But two days after Barry left, he called David's apartment. 'We can't bring David here,' he said. 'We'll have to make some other arrangements.' I said, 'What are you talking about? You told him that you wanted to bring him home.' Barry sounded so angry. 'It's impossible. I got carried away when I was there. We won't be able to live in this town. We won't have a

118

friend. I wouldn't be surprised if we got put out of business.' I said, 'What are you talking about?' Barry said, 'I told Charlie [his best friend], and he said to me, "If you bring David home, you might as well begin packing. AIDS is worse than leprosy. No one will come to your house, or even sit by you in church. They'd be afraid you'd give them the disease." '

"And then Barry said to me, 'Can't you see the word spreading around that you can get AIDS from getting your clothes cleaned at Barry and Joan's?' I was screaming: '*You* call him during the day, and *you* tell him. I won't do it. This wouldn't be nearly as bad if you hadn't opened your big mouth in the first place.' Somehow I had known from the beginning that we weren't going to be able to take David home."

Len remembers a similarly disappointing experience. "When Evan was in the hospital for the first time, Claire, a friend he had known since grammar school, came by and brought a little plant. I wanted Evan and Claire to have time to visit, so I left and went to the gym. When I got back, Evan was all excited. He told me that Claire was coming back on Sunday with all the people from their home-town who lived nearby, and they were going to have a little reunion. Five or six people were going to come. So on Sunday morning, Evan got up and showered and shaved, and I came to make his room neat and stay with him until Claire and her friends arrived. To make a long story short, I went to the gym, and when I came back at about five in the afternoon, no one had arrived. And no one ever did. *She* didn't even bother to call him and tell him she wasn't coming. I felt so bad for him, I could hardly contain myself. He just lay there sort of stunned and very hurt. Fortunately, neither of us has ever seen that woman again."

Stay Involved

Call. Visit. Let your friend know that you'd like to be part of his life, and that you want to help in any way you can. Show him some signs of affection; give him a hug or a kiss. Be gentle and open around him. In short, create a feeling of warmth when you visit.

Sam's friend Mark remembers how Zak, another friend of Sam's, always managed to say just the right thing. "Zak came by to see Sam about twice a week. I was there a few times when Zak arrived, and it struck me how well he knew how to deal with Sam. He'd come in and hug him and take a long look at him, and whatever was going on, he'd notice, no matter what it was, even if it was just that Sam seemed more animated or had more energy that day. He'd say something like, 'Your mustache looks good trimmed that way.' Sam loved his visits. And I knew that when Zak was coming, I should leave. Sam always made sure he looked his best when Zak was coming.''

No matter how ill your friend is, you should remember that he's still the same person he always was, only now the circumstances of his life are quite different. From time to time, you may worry about what to say or that you have said something upsetting to your friend. Usually, you can figure out what's easy to talk about with your friend, staying away from the more painful topics. But if you blunder—as we all do from time to time—the best thing to do is to clear it up at that moment. Don't let it hang in the air, and don't let it make you feel bad later. Often, a blooper can be an occasion for closeness or even humor. "You know," you might say, "I don't mean to say things like that. I seem to stumble into them. Sometimes I'm just nervous. Forgive me if I'm an idiot once in a while."

Stephen had been undergoing chemotherapy for about six weeks for an AIDS-related condition. At that point, he hadn't yet told everyone where he worked about his diagnosis. He recalls that one day as he was buying a cappuccino at a sidewalk café, a colleague came up and made a joke about his thinning hair. "Hey, Stephen," he shouted, "it looks like you're getting bald in a hurry." "What could I say?" Stephen remembers. "I was incredibly sensitive about having lost half my hair. I was sure this guy didn't know what was going on with me. Anyway, two days later he comes up to me in the office with the most pained expression. 'Stephen, I really didn't know. I can't believe I said something so awful. I apologize from the bottom of my heart.' And you know, that made it okay."

Sometimes, though, a price must be paid, particularly if what is said truly hurts. Joan remembers David's reaction to her husband's phone call telling him he couldn't come home. "I was in the room when he finally got through. I watched David's face, and it turned to a sort of shocked disbelief. 'Business reasons,' David repeated. 'People aren't as understanding in small towns. Yes, yes, I understand. I understand.' Finally, he hung up and looked at me. 'You knew that call was coming?' he asked. I admitted that I did. I told him that we would see to it that he got the finest care, and that he didn't have to worry about anything.''

Joan says she really didn't know what to say. "It was a truly awful moment," she recalls. "How could I make it better? Then David said, 'Would you mind leaving and maybe coming back this evening?

I have some things to do.' I said, 'Are you angry?' He answered, 'I don't know. I don't know what I expected from you and Dad. I'm disappointed, I guess.'

"When I got back that evening, there was a man in David's room, fortyish, very trim, like an athlete. David said, 'This is my friend Don. He came down from San Francisco a little while ago. I'm going to stay in his house up there. I can get the help I need in San Francisco. Right now, though, I am going to need some money to move out of my apartment.' I said, 'Anything, anything you need.' He just looked at me and said, 'Sure. Anything.' "

Help Run the House

If your friend lives alone, or has children and is solely responsible for the household, you may be able to make a sizable contribution by helping maintain the home or simply keeping the routine intact. Because people have a lot of pride about this sort of thing, be sure not to interfere without asking. Here are some specific ways you might help:

- Clean the apartment some weekend. Help with the wash, care for the children, walk or groom the pets, take out the trash. Whatever you do, though, don't just charge in and run things. Always ask how you can help.
- Go grocery shopping for your friend with a list he's prepared.
- Agree to take your friend to the doctor or for his treatments.
- Cook food that you can leave with your friend so that he'll have something to eat for several days.

When Meredith would go into the hospital, her friend Judy took in the two children. "It just started very impromptu," Judy recalls. "She was in a jam one day, so I said I would take them. It was only for five days. We all got along fine, and I could see that it took a huge worry off of Meredith's shoulders. So one thing led to another, and I began to take the kids whenever she needed to be hospitalized."

Patricia had worked for her boss, Ron, for almost three years when he was diagnosed with PCP, practically out of the blue. As word of his illness spread through the office, Patricia decided to organize a "support team," a group of Ron's friends and co-workers who would each take care of him one evening a week. "First, I talked with Ron about my plans," she says. "After he gave me the green light, I invited everyone over to his apartment to talk about how they could help. It was amazing. We made up a chart, with each day of the week on it for a month at a time, and then we all signed up for shifts. I had Tuesday dinners. We were lucky that Ron had such a solid group of friends who really cared and were willing to give of their time. And do you know what? Just about everyone kept to their assignment. And when they couldn't, they would arrange for a substitute."

Plan Activities

If you can arrange it, and if your friend is able, plan to go out together. Go for walks, to restaurants, movies, plays, concerts, church—anywhere he wants to go. If you can take an afternoon off, you might plan a drive to the country or a long lunch. You could arrange a small dinner, inviting your friend's closest buddies or family members. If you're no Julia Child, you can always call for take-out Chinese or a pizza.

When you plan an activity, be sensitive to how much energy your friend has. *Let him make the decisions about what you will be doing and where you will be going.* Give your friend every opportunity to make his own decisions.

Stephen remembers when he had been recently released from the hospital after having PCP. Still very tired, he had been at home for a week and was developing an acute case of cabin fever. His best friend, Martha, could see both sides of the problem; he was not strong enough to go out for an evening, and yet he couldn't stand to spend another minute looking at the ceiling over his bed. She asked him what he wanted to do. "I'd just like to get out for two hours," Stephen told her. So Martha called up another friend and asked if he would drive them to the movies on Saturday afternoon. He agreed. "It was perfect," Stephen says. "Martha told me about the plans on Wednesday, so it really gave me something to look forward to. It also made me comfortable to know that Christo was going to drive and that we were going to a matinée. No crowds. No waiting." Saturday came, and they were off. "It was just what I needed. We left at twelve-thirty, and we were back by three. But, you know, it was the first regular thing I had done in weeks. I was out with two of my best friends. I sat in the balcony like I always did, and the movie was a distraction. I had told Martha, 'No movies with hospital scenes!' Sure, I was tired when I got home, but I was so thankful to Martha and Christo."

122

Do "Nothing" Together

Sometimes your friend may just want you to sit quietly with him, to be with him. If you find yourself spending an evening this way, you can be silent, you can read quietly, you can watch television, rent a movie, discuss politics and people, dish your friends, or discuss anything else going on. Every moment does not have to be jam-packed. The point is simply to be there.

Linda describes her brother Gary's visits from his lover, Bob. "Gary looked forward all week to Bob's visits. On Friday he was all excited, and then on Monday he was glum. It always amazed me when I was around those two. They were so much like any other couple I knew. Sometimes when Gary felt good, they'd go out to dinner or a movie, and sometimes they'd just sit and watch TV or read, or Bob would tell Gary about his job or how things were going in the city. Bob came faithfully every weekend, even when Gary had to go into the hospital. I think Bob's visits helped Gary to fight."

By observing these visits, Rose, Gary and Linda's stepmother, grew to understand Gary and Bob's relationship in a new light. "All my life I had seen men together: my father and his friends, my brothers, my sons and my husband, and their friends. I thought I had seen men as close as they could be to each other. I remember how they were together during the war, when they didn't know if they'd ever see each other again. But this was different. Gary and Bob were closer than any men I had ever seen. At first, I didn't know what to make of it, and I asked Linda. She said, 'Ma, look at them. They're a couple.' So I just started looking at them as a couple, and I saw that they were just like any other very close couple. They loved each other. They looked out for each other. They were so strongly tied together that it amazed me. They never let anything interfere with the time they had together. Once I understood that, I was more comfortable around them. I thought, 'This man makes my son happy. So what else matters to me?' "

Plan for the Future

At the end of each visit, try to plan your next. This gives your friend a sense of continuity. But be sure to call before you arrive the next time. You never know how your friend might feel that day. He may not be able to see you, or he may want some time to himself. If both of you decide to skip a visit, try to plan a time for another visit right away, or promise to call back the next day. In this way, your friend feels secure that you will be around soon.

These are just a few of the many things you might do to improve your friend's quality of life. Surely you can think of others. All it takes is imagination, good intentions, and good sense.

Dealing with Your Friend's Emotions

When Your Friend Is Angry

From time to time, you may arrive and find your friend greatly distressed, crying, angry, or close to despair. When this happens, try not to run away. Instead, ask him to try to explain how he's feeling or why he's upset (he may not know, however). Or you may decide just to hold him and have a good cry together. Be as comforting as you can. If you feel he needs additional support, contact an appropriate support group or AIDS hot line, or seek out individual psychotherapy for him. It's certainly possible that your friend may need more help that you are capable of supplying. Even if you love him, he may need someone who can provide the kind of counseling you don't have the training to provide.

If your friend is angry because he is sick, allow him his anger. You can say, "You have every right to be angry. There is no logic or reason for why this is happening." At the same time, do not let him blame himself. If he says, for instance, "If only I hadn't had sex with Tony" or "I was such a fool to shoot up with those guys," you could reply: "You did what you knew to do at the time. Lots of people did. Having this disease has nothing to do with who you are."

If your friend is angry with you and seems to be picking on you when you are visiting, try to stay calm. He would not be doing this to you if he did not feel comfortable enough with you to share his anger. Often, we lash out at those closest to us. Try to remember that. If he attacks you personally, allow yourself to feel your emotions and, in return, allow yourself to react to his anger. If you feel too uncomfortable with the situation, you can always leave for a while. In such a circumstance, you could say: "I don't love you any less because you're angry with me, but I can't be here right now. I'll come back later after I've taken a walk and cleared my head."

"I was always there for him," Jack explains, "but Bruce had this need to beat up on me. I'd come home and he'd start in. 'You're late tonight. Don't tell me about traffic again. Did you bring the food I wanted?' It wasn't like he couldn't have done for himself most of the things he told me to do. He just needed somebody to beat up on, and I was there. A couple of times, our friend Sal was there, and he said that Bruce would be laughing and having a great time right up until I'd walk into the house. Then he'd turn surly. I guess he knew for sure I wasn't walking out on him. So why not beat up on the one you know'll be back?''

Mark got rough treatment more than once from Sam. "I remember one day, I came over to his apartment after work, and he was really in a mood. 'Why do you keep coming to see me?' he asked. 'You think you're some sort of Florence Nightingale, taking pity on the poor AIDS victim? Then what do you do, go home and dislocate your shoulder patting yourself on the back? Go around bragging about what a good guy you are?' I was so surprised, I didn't know what to say, but I remembered that the hospital psychologist had told me he might do this. I said, 'I do it because I love you and you need me. I want you to love me and be willing to do the same thing for me when I need you.' That sort of got to him, because his face softened, and he said, 'I know you love me. I'm just so frustrated sometimes, I think I'm going crazy.' "

When Your Friend Needs to Talk

There will be times when your friend wants to talk about what is happening to him. Be willing to talk about the illness or whatever else in on his mind. If he has recently gotten sick again, ask him if he wants to talk about it. He may have a need to express his fear of what is happening. Whatever else you do, listen. Listen carefully. Don't try to change the subject. Ask questions that will help your friend clarify what he's thinking.

If your friend starts to talk about his fear of death, the possibility of his death, or the sense that he may be dying, be very careful. Try to help him maintain both his sense of reality and his sense of hope. Stay rooted in the facts about his condition as you know them. Don't let things get too far ahead. Try to avoid all the "what if"s.

Still, don't confuse him with denial of his condition. If the situation is not good, don't camouflage it with statements like "Things aren't that bad. You're just down today. You'll be up and around in no time." Nor, however, should you depress him with doom and gloom. Don't say to him, "Yes, it is true that people in your condition seldom recover. The end can come rapidly." Instead, you should acknowledge his condition. "Yes, you do seem weaker today, and you do seem to have a very clear picture of your condition and what that means." This will help him to maintain his connection to reality and what's really happening. And if you're honest with him, he can be honest with you.

Keep in mind that your friend may be asking you, albeit indirectly, to gird for the challenge of the disease. Always listen, but don't let a downward spiral get out of control. At the right time, a loving "Snap out of it!" can go a long way.

Almost as soon as Ron's support group was in place, his health worsened, and his dementia came on full force. "There were days when he was really on another planet," Patricia says. "Sometimes he'd ask the same questions, but I could tell there was no point in explaining everything. Other days"—Patricia smiles—"he'd have all his wits about him. He'd be asking a lot of questions about his condition, his next appointments, what his prognosis was. On those days, I would talk to him as honestly as I knew. I think he appreciated that."

Remember, too, that your friend may have seen and known other people with AIDS. He may have known people who have died. Based on his experience with others, he may try to judge where *he* is in the progression of the disease. When he gets more than one opportunistic infection at a time, when he cannot stop his weight loss, when his herpes won't go away—any one of these may be a sign to him that the disease is progressing, that he is on the same train as his friends. *Your role here is to let him know that the disease does not follow one track. Someone else's experience cannot be piggybacked onto his.* Tell him again that you love him, listen to him, and assure him that you will be there. Offer him all the hope that you can by helping him keep open the possibility of some improved treatments, if not a cure. This does not mean that you should lie; it means that you should share hope that something good and unforeseen might happen.

When Your Friend Can't Live Alone Anymore

Some carepartners and caring friends already live with their friend when the diagnosis is made. Many, however, live apart, and this can present problems. Eventually, it may become obvious that your friend is not going to be able to take care of himself. It might be that he simply does not have the strength, or that he becomes ill more quickly than expected, or that working takes all the energy he has. To commute or help someone in this situation can be very trying for you. You may find yourself trying to run two lives: yours and his.

You may decide to move in with your friend or to move him into your home. Decisions like these are not to be taken lightly; living with a person with AIDS means living the illness day in and day out, with all the accompanying ups and downs, traumas and responsibilities. But to live together can vastly simplify the job of getting things done and providing care.

Michael describes how he felt right before his friend Joe moved in with him. "All of a sudden it dawned on me that I had someone seriously sick moving into my house, and what I envisioned was that he was going to be an invalid and need to be taken care of, that he'd really be weak and would have to be waited on and attended to. That seemed like an awful lot to do. Worse, my place was a wreck! So I just sort of got manic and tore the whole apartment apart and put it back together. Twenty-four hours later, he moved in and we began."

Jeffrey and Paul also decided they would live together in Jeffrey's apartment because life had become too complicated for them now that Paul couldn't take care of himself. Jeffrey says, "When we were still in our own places, there were a couple of times when I'd be getting ready to go out, and he'd call and say he wasn't feeling well. 'Could you come over?' And so I'd drop everything and run out there. And it's not like he lived right around the corner. Or there were times when he would tell me what he was eating, and I'd realize that he wasn't really eating anything good for him. So we both sort of decided together that he should live here."

"When Bruce came out of the hospital the first time, he came to stay at my house," Jack recalls. "We didn't really have a good sense about what the disease meant. We thought that when he went back to work, he would start staying at his place. But when he did go back to work, we realized he couldn't live alone. He sure couldn't work and take care of a place. We had only been going together for a little over a year and a half when he got sick, and I wasn't used to having anyone around all the time, but I didn't see any other choice. I loved him. That was a cinch. I just hoped that the love was strong enough to survive living with him! He was such a slob."

Joan and her husband, Barry, had made a different choice. "After David moved in with Don in San Francisco, he seemed much happier," Joan explains. "I'd call him and he sounded so, I guess, content. Once he said to me, 'Don has been wonderful to me. I mean, I've only known him for three years, and he came through like *that* for me. People accept me here. I have another friend who comes to see me every day. They don't make me feel crummy or like I did something really awful to get sick.'"

The decision to live together is an important one, one that you should discuss thoroughly beforehand. At the outset, you could ask each other, "What are you most fearful of? How will living together help? How could it hurt?'' Always keep the lines of communication open, and respect each other's need for privacy.

When Things Go from Bad to Worse

As a carepartner or a caring friend, you will most likely find that the longer you are with your friend, the more effort you'll be making in the relationship. Because your friend may not be feeling well from time to time, can tire easily, and is sometimes less physically able to take care of himself, he may be unable to do many of the duties he could previously. Suddenly it's only you who cooks, washes dishes, cleans, shops, takes care of the children, mows the lawn, pays the bills. He simply doesn't have the physical energy to do the things he did before.

Jack was very angry when he found himself picking up after Bruce, who was home all day. "At first, I thought he was just depressed or just taking advantage. We were always neat people. I mean, we didn't just take off our clothes and leave them there on the floor. And we never expected one of us to clean up after the other. But he started to leave glasses and dishes on the counter, and his clothes on the floor. He didn't clean up after himself. So that led to some pretty serious arguments. I didn't feel like having to move his stuff from the bathroom sink when I wanted to shave, and the bedroom looked like a hamper. So I griped and griped about it. One day he started to shake, and his face got all twisted up like he was going to cry, and he said to me, 'I can't do it anymore. I hardly have the energy to get up to go to the bathroom. It tires me out just to get my lunch out of the refrigerator. Please do those things for me.' Once he said that, I started paying more attention to him. He really was exhausted all the time. Actually, it took me about five minutes to stick his dishes in the dishwasher and pick up his clothes. It wasn't any trouble once I understood what was happening.''

Changing Sex Habits

For *some* people with AIDS, once they have been sick or hospitalized, they lose much of their interest in sex. The sexual element may begin to decrease even before the person is formally diagnosed. Learning that you are HIV-infected can take its toll. If you are in a sexual relationship with your friend, this, too, can become a source of tension.

Jack's adjustment to Bruce's loss of interest in sex was painful. "At first, before he really got sick, he used to say that he didn't feel like

128

it, or he was too tired, or he had a headache, just like you see in the movies. I couldn't understand why he was losing interest. We're both athletic, and that's what our lovemaking was like. So I never had any sense that he wasn't happy with it. But when Bruce started developing symptoms, Dr. Bill told us that losing interest in sex was a common problem. Sounds terrible, but it was a relief. Somehow it was easier to know that he lost interest because of the disease and not because he didn't find me appealing anymore."

Mirabel and Luis found that her HIV infection had a profound impact on their intimacy. "After I developed AIDS, we were both in denial," she recalls. "Our sexual relationship remained pretty much the same, but then it 'dulled out' somewhat. And then I got pregnant." Mirabel's pregnancy set off a crisis for the newlyweds. After much professional counseling and talking with each other, they agreed to abort the fetus. "Luis was devastated when we decided to have the abortion. This was his child. I already had six; he hadn't had any. Prior to the abortion he would lay next to me and caress my belly for hours. He'd talk to the baby inside of me. This brought us much closer."

Paul speaks about his sexual relationship with Jeffrey in the months after Paul became ill. He says, "My sex drive is zilch. That would have been a real big concern a few years ago. But frankly, sex is not that important anymore. It doesn't bother me. What bothers me is, am I satisfying Jeffrey? Are the things we're able to do satisfying to him?"

If you and your friend have a sexual relationship, you should discuss it. You may have no idea how much you resent the disappearance of sex unless you talk about it, and your partner may have no idea how guilty he feels unless, he, too, can talk about it. Sex plays an important role in most intimate relationships, so when it disappears, adjustments are necessary. Try to make these adjustments together, not separately. Keep communicating about this issue. As you go along, you may discover that you and your friend make love in different ways, without sex; you may become much more affectionate, loving, considerate, and, yes, intimate. Bear in mind that for some, the fear of maintaining sexual relations with an infected partner is part of a broader intimacy issue that will necessitate talking about many of the other fears faced by carepartners who are also lovers.

Still, if your lovemaking diminishes or ceases altogether, you may find yourself frustrated, with no outlet for your sexual energy. This is a common and difficult problem for carepartners and their friends who are involved sexually, a problem that is solved differently by each couple. On the one hand, you may feel you need or want a sex partner, particularly in these very stressful times. On the other hand, you may feel your friend will be hurt if you should find one. Further, what kinds of complications might arise if you were to find another partner and then begin to fall in love with that person? This issue is very complex, and some carepartners find that the increased intimacy of the relationship, without sex, somehow keeps those needs under control. Others do not. If you are not able to feel comfortable with your decisions—either individually or as a couple—you may want to talk with a therapist, separately or together. Knowing your own needs as well as the needs of your partner is paramount. Communication is the key.

Picking Up the Financial Burden

At some point, your friend may be unable to continue working and drawing a salary. Although he may become eligible for government assistance, more of the financial burden of the relationship may fall to you. Not only will you have to do more work in the relationship, but now you may also have to pay the bills, make the rent or mortgage payment, buy all the groceries, arrange and pay for child care, and even pay doctors' and other medical bills. This can be a heavy financial burden, especially if you and your friend do not have many resources. Be sure that you and your friend look into all the benefit and entitlement programs due a person with a permanent disability according to local, state, and federal law. Such programs can provide much-needed assistance, but in all likelihood they will not fully replace lost income. (These programs were discussed in Chapter 5.)

Finances, like all other intimate matters, should be discussed with your friend. More than likely, he feels guilty about not being able to do his part financially in the relationship. You may also feel resentful. Talk about it. You should also discuss your feelings about this matter with your friends, or with a therapist or support group.

Dealing with Special Tensions

Many other problems can cause tension as the disease takes its toll on the body. There are two problems—not unique to HIV disease or AIDS—that nearly every person who has dealt with an ill friend talks about as special areas of strain: the eating habits of the sick person and the difficulty of hospital stays.

Changes in Eating Habits

Often, people with AIDS have poor appetites. Moreover, some of the drugs administered to them can destroy what appetite they had in the first place. So you may go to the hospital day after day to find that your friend has not eaten, will not eat the food you brought (although he asked you to bring it), and, as a consequence, is losing weight fast.

Not surprisingly, you may feel, "I have no control over this disease. About the only way I can help him fight it is to get him to eat. Otherwise I am helpless." Some carepartners get obsessive about their friend's eating habits and find it hard to understand why someone so ill just won't force the food down. Your concern can actually add to the problems that already exist.

First, you must accept that your friend's loss of appetite is part of his disease. He has stopped eating not because he doesn't want to eat, but because he can't eat, because food may be repulsive to him, because it may be painful to chew, swallow, or digest.

Several remedies exist. At home, prepare his favorite foods. Experiment with new things. Try foods that he liked when he was a child. Often, this works. Try to have the food readily available for him to eat, whether he eats it or not. You need to do this at least partly for yourself, so that you can feel you are doing all you can. Sure, insist that he eat. But at the point where he begins to get prickly, stop insisting. He is not going to feel better—and neither are you—if he tries to eat because you are yelling at him. The tension may be a bigger problem than the eating.

When he's in the hospital, bring him the food he asks for, if you can afford to do it. If you find that you are wasting food this way (and your resources), you might try saying, 'All right, I'll get a big roast beef sandwich, and we can share it. We'll eat together." Have the sandwich cut into quarters, and eat part of it as your lunch or dinner. You can do this with many foods, and it will make you less apprehensive about wasting food and money. In addition, ask a doctor about medications that decrease nausea and increase appetite. Finally, you can request a nutritional evaluation by your friend's doctor or hospital staff to determine whether nutritional supplements would be beneficial.

"Bruce never paid much attention to what he was eating before he got sick," Jack recalls. "Put a steak and a baked potato in front of him, and he was a happy man. But after he got sick, all that changed. He started looking at food and smelling it. He got to be a real picky eater. In the hospital he'd complain that the food wasn't fit for hogs, and then I'd bring him some good stuff, like a turkey sandwich with corn-bread stuffing, and he'd say how great it looked. He'd smell it, but he wouldn't eat it. I used to say to him, 'Bruce, eat, man! That's what we can do to beat this thing.' But he'd just look away and tell me he'd get to it later. But he never did.''

Long Hospital Stays

Your friend's stays in the hospital can strain you to the breaking point. Not only do you have to go on with your life—get up, go to work, manage the household, pay the bills, take the kids to school, to the doctor, wherever—but now you have to make trips to the hospital, watch over your friend's treatment, see to his comfort, bring him food if he cannot tolerate hospital meals day after day, and sit with him to keep him company. You may find your life to be one continuous chore, a mad rush just to get done all the things that need to be accomplished every single day.

What if you have to work late, or you have other pressing commitments? Then you might find your day stretching from six in the morning until eleven or twelve in the evening. And you won't have had a moment to yourself. You may discover that you wish to and can arrange to sleep in the hospital because this will allow you more time with your friend and will help you slow down by eliminating some trips you were making from home to the hospital.

Jennifer, a housewife with two small children, was astounded at the pressure her husband Alex's hospitalizations put on her schedule and sanity. A typical day found her going back and forth to the hospital at least twice, tending to her sons, preparing dinner, and relaying news as well as comfort to her parents and her in-laws. "I felt that I had no choice but to practically live wherever my husband was. I had child care that I was having to hire as much as ten hours a day. Most days, I'd go to the hospital until three P.M.; I'd come home, see my kids, fix dinner, get another baby-sitter, and then go back to the hospital. I was always an emotional wreck. I'd hate to tell you how many speeding tickets I got during this time.''

Taking Care of Yourself

During these times, you may find that you need help, on both a practical and an emotional level. This could include help cleaning your home, making lunch on a very busy day, or taking your friend to the doctor when you're busy; you may also need a person to confide in about your own pain, fears, and needs. Many people, unfortunately, find it more difficult to ask for help for themselves than for a loved one. It's also easy at a time like this to get so wrapped up in the caretaking role that you forget about your own needs. You should try not to let that happen. Take some time for yourself every day—even if it's only a quick cup of coffee, a workout, or a phone conversation with a good friend. *Your needs are as important as your friend's.* And if you don't take care of yourself, it's possible you won't be able to go the full distance for your friend.

This is a time when your mutual friends can make a big difference just by showing up to do simple tasks. Sometimes, people might not be calling because they think you have the situation totally under control or because they are fearful. To get past this, just call and ask whether friends can do whatever it is you need that day. Be polite. Be direct.

As Alex's illness progressed, Jennifer says, "I made a point of calling up my best friend at least once a day just to chat, just to get everything out of my head. After he had been sick for many months, I also realized that I had to take care of myself and my life. Even though I felt guilty being away from the hospital, I would try to go to an aerobics class twice a week. You know, it was only an hour, but it made my body feel good, it reduced my stress, and it gave me some time to myself. I really needed those things, and what's amazing is that I didn't know it until I started."

Remember that one of your greatest gifts to your friend is your continued good health and sanity. Without doubt, you and your friend must now deal with *all* your emotions if you are to keep the kind of physical and emotional balance you need. Those emotions will grow increasingly intense for your friend because his self-image and level of self-esteem are constantly under attack, and for you because you are now carrying heavy responsibilities and concerns, many of which are new to you.

7

HELPING TWO PEOPLE TO COPE: DEALING WITH YOUR EMOTIONS

As you continue to look after your friend or partner, visit the hospital, do more at home, take care of the children, pick up the financial end of the relationship, manage your job, and cope with your own fears, you may, like many others, find yourself wearing down and burning out. Don't be surprised if you become moody, distracted, depressed, easy to anger, and, from time to time, close to tears. Your friend's condition is beginning to take its toll on you. People may begin to ask if anything is wrong. You may want to answer, "*Everything* is wrong, but I can't tell you anything about it." Or you may find yourself wanting to talk openly and honestly with friends or family.

The intensity of your emotions may overwhelm you sometimes. Suddenly you may find yourself lashing out at a store clerk who is keeping you waiting. Or you may discover that you have little or no patience at work. "Just get it done," you snarl. You may even find yourself yelling at your sick friend: "Why don't you eat? You're making me crazy." As the disease comes to dominate your life, you may find yourself knocked off balance, overflowing with emotion.

Hugh tells of a particularly difficult time he and John experienced as John grew more ill: "Life turned into a nightmare. I had to get up in the morning and give him his special foods—something to put bacteria back in his stomach. As soon as I'd wake up, we'd fight. Once, I was so angry I threw my beeper at him. Of course I missed, but it busted anyway. Talk about making life difficult. I had one of those 'antique' answering machines, and without a beeper, I had to go to my apartment to get messages. On any given day, I'd start off at his apartment, then go to mine, go shopping all over the place to get the right foods, and then head off to work."

For Jennifer, Alex's continued deterioration seemed to bring out her worst personality traits. "I had a really hard time with the odor that Alex's body emanated. The cancer in his mouth was just such a horror. It became a symbol to me of his dying, and so I became a bit of a harpy about it. Like, 'Here, have some chewing gum' or 'Here, take some mouthwash.' I became hysterical about it. Soon after, Alex told his father that I had been ragging on him, and his father came in one night and was just screaming at me right in the hospital room. I thought I was going to go over the edge. I started smoking cigarettes again, after being six years without one. I took tranquilizers during the day and sleeping pills at night. I had to *be* so goddamn much."

Jack remembers how he reacted during a period when Bruce was very sick. As it happened, the event that set Jack off had nothing whatsoever to do with his lover. "It was as if the pitch of my emotions became higher and higher, and I didn't notice it until I got into a real jam," Jack says.

"Several months before, I had stopped driving on the freeways because I'd learned that I just couldn't deal with that. One morning, a delivery truck was blocking all but one lane of the street I traveled on to get to work when suddenly the car in front of me stopped and blocked the only open lane. I blew my horn. He got out and looked at his tire. So I got out and asked him what was going on. He said he was going to have to change his tire. 'Look up the street,' I said. Cars were backing up for blocks. My blood was boiling, and I wanted to stomp his stupid ass into the pavement. After all, he could have pulled up in front of the truck. But then I kind of flipped. *All* the anger in me came charging through. I went over to the guy and grabbed him by the shirt and kept banging him against his car. I couldn't believe it was me doing this. Finally, I got over it and drove around him to work. The whole day, I felt like I was walking on eggshells. I was so mad. I had never seen so much violence and craziness in me. It scared the hell out of me."

How to Deal with Denial and Pain

The longer it has been since your friend first became sick, the more likely it is you will see him getting sicker. It may be months; it may be years. The fact of AIDS as a progressive illness will begin to feel real to you and weigh on you: "This person I love is really sick. This could be a terminal illness."

The more this reality intrudes on you, the more anxious you may become. You won't want to think about it. But you'll have no choice. The situation can overwhelm you without notice. You may feel yourself wanting to cry in the middle of a business meeting, on the bus, or in a restaurant. You may find that it's getting harder to protect yourself from the disease by denying its existence. Denial is no longer working for you.

All this is intensely painful. You have to expect pain and not be afraid to hurt. You shouldn't be afraid to talk about your pain and your fears—and don't be ashamed to cry if that's how you are feeling. Some carepartners have a friend they can cry with. Others cry with a family member. Some cry on their own.

Marilyn talks about Tim's denial of his illness: "Sometimes I thought Tim was losing his mind. He would sit there in his hospital bed, telling me about all the great things we were going to do as soon as he got out, and I knew we weren't going to do any of them. He had already lost thirty pounds, and he was really weak. I'd ask the doctor what was wrong with him, why he was talking that way, and he'd tell me that Tim just couldn't face his illness. But Tim was just making it harder on me. I couldn't sit there making plans with him. I didn't even want to be sitting there after a while. I could see it happening. I knew it was real. I kept thinking, 'Why do I have to go through this?' "

Linda and Rose cried often as Gary's condition worsened. "We seemed to be carrying the heaviest burden of Gary's illness," Linda explains. "After a while, we began to talk about the fact that he was just getting sicker and sicker. Every time something happened to him, he would get better after a while, but he was always weaker than before. One day, we went to lunch so that we could talk, and after lunch, while sitting in the car, we just cried and cried. That day, we both admitted that we thought Gary might die. It was almost too painful to bear. I kept thinking about him when he was a little boy. He was just so cute and curious about everything. I can't imagine what my mother was thinking."

Rose, too, recalled that afternoon with Linda. "We got dressed up so we could treat ourselves to a really nice lunch, and then we spent the whole time trying not to cry. I kept thinking that this couldn't be happening in my family. It all wasn't real. Here I was with my lovely daughter in this beautiful restaurant, and outside the weather was cold and clear. But back at my house was this terrible problem. This disaster was happening in my family. I had to admit it: My son is dying. My child is dying. I can see it happening. I see it every day, and there's nothing I can do about it. Sometimes I want to take him in my lap like I did when he was a little boy and he was hurting. I want to rock him back and forth and make him better.''

When Anger Replaces Denial

As your denial of your friend's disease wears thin, it may be replaced with anger. This is often the case. Anger is one of the emotions that the two of you are going to face as you come to terms with what is happening in your life together. At this point, you are clearly beginning to confront the reality of the illness, even if you only sometimes consider what the ultimate outcome might be. You will probably see that your earlier astonishment and disbelief regarding your friend's illness may now be replaced with a question: ''Why is this happening to us?'' That there is no logical answer to this question provokes anger. Focusing your anger is your greatest challenge now. And for just about everyone, there's a hell of a lot to be angry about:

You May Be Angry at the Disease. ''Why did it have to strike here? Where did this nightmare come from? How can we stand having the lives of these young people cut down like this?''

You May Be Angry at Government Leaders. ''Why did the government let this problem reach this magnitude before trying to do anything about it? Are they telling us everything they know? Is there a policy in this country that says it's okay to kill off all the drug users and gay men?''

You May Be Angry at the News Media. ''Why do they describe AIDS as 'fatal' or refer to 'AIDS victims'? Don't they realize that many of the people diagnosed with AIDS are still alive? Don't they realize that people with AIDS listen to the news and are hurt by what they hear? Don't they realize that people with HIV disease are fighting for their lives every day?''

You May Be Angry at Your Families. ''Why do they have to be so narrow-minded? Why can't I be comfortable telling them about what I am going through? Would my brother have this fear of telling our parents if his wife had some life-threatening disease?''

You May Be Angry at Your Friends. "I can't believe that the people I've told have run away. Why do *I* have to confront this, and my friends *don't?* Why can't I tell all my friends about something that they might have to face, too?"

You May Be Angry at People in General. "Look at them, doing their silly, selfish things. How can they be worried about their problems—kids, work, finances—at a time like this? They don't have the problems I do."

You May Be Angry at God or at Your House of Worship. "How could a good God let this happen? How can so many religious organizations continue to condemn relationships like ours when there is such love and concern? How dare anyone even think, much less say in public, that this disease is the wrath of God visited on us? How can they possibly know anything about love and mercy and compassion—about God—and still say those things?"

You May Be Angry at The Medical Profession. "Why don't they show more concern for us? Why haven't they found a cure for this thing? Why don't they speed up drug trials? You can bet they'd be working twenty-four hours a day if the risk groups were Girl Scouts and U.S. senators."

You May Be Angry at Your Friend. "How did he get this? Look at all the responsibilities I'm carrying, and all he does is make more and more demands."

And You May Be Angry at Yourself. "Could I have done more for my friend? And what about my life and my feelings? Don't they count?"

Jack began to see his anger clearly, especially when Bruce was very sick. "I'm pissed about so many things, I can hardly get them on one list. I'm pissed at Bruce because he's such an asshole sometimes and so unfair with me. I'm pissed that this thing's been around for over a decade now, and there still is no cure. And I'm pissed at some of our friends who just didn't want to hear about it. I'm just pissed in general. Why us? Why him and why me? Why did I spend all these years looking for a man to love, then fall in love with a man who had this damned rotten disease?"

You and your friend have many reasons to be angry at this time. It's okay to be angry. But it's also important not to let anger get out of control, or to lash out and hurt people who may mean well. Start to pay attention to each and every thing that makes you angry, and ask yourself a few questions. "What actually happened here? Is this really what I'm angry about? Would I ordinarily be angry about this? Can I control this anger by expressing it rationally or by talking about it? If a particular situation is always going to provoke anger, can I avoid it?"

But don't think that you are going to eliminate anger from your life. If you look back, you will probably see you always had a little anger in you; anger is an understandable part of everyday life. AIDS can intensify those feelings—sometimes enormously. Your goal, when you examine your anger, is to understand it, to express it appropriately, to incorporate it into your daily functioning, and to know when to reach out for support.

Jack describes his anger as a boiling caldron. "I would boil over at the drop of a pin. No one was safe, not a little old lady on the street, not a burly sanitation worker. I had such a need to strike out in any and every direction. The newspaper enraged me, seeing the president on TV enraged me, even people who pulled away from a red light too slowly set me off. One day I was griping about every and any thing to Bruce when he told me to come lie next to him on the bed. Next thing I knew, he put his arm around me like he was trying to protect me, and I put my head on his chest. I remember thinking how skinny his arm was and how strong it used to be. 'Slow down, baby,' he said. 'Don't be so mad. I'm here, you know. I can help you be strong.' When he said that, I started to cry, and I cried for a long time. All the time, Bruce sort of rocked me. When I finished, though, I felt so much calmer. I actually felt stronger. Sick as he was, he knew how to do that for me.

"As time passed, I started trying to take control of my anger. When I needed to be somewhere, I made up my mind ahead of time that I was going to leave fifteen minutes early or be fifteen minutes late so that traffic wouldn't make me crazy and angry. I avoided banks, stores, pharmacies, when I knew they would be crowded. I guess what I'm saying is that I started removing a lot of the occasions for outbursts of anger from my life—the underlying causes."

As your balloon of denial deflates, you are likely to begin experiencing a whole new set of emotions, many of them disquieting. Be prepared.

Fear

Many find that the fears they began to experience as their friend first became sick remain present, coming to the surface from time to time. The fears may be more or less intense as circumstances change, but they will always be there, and they can disturb you night and day. These are some of the fears you may find yourself confronting:

You May Be Afraid of Getting Sick. "Have I also been infected? There's no denying it now. I see how it's working. I could easily be next."

You May Be Afraid That Your Life Is Being Consumed by This Illness. "My friend is so sick. It seems *everyone* I know is sick."

You May Be Afraid of Being Abandoned. "What if I get sick? Will anyone be there to take care of me when I need it? Who will take care of my children? What will my life be like if I lose my friend?"

You May Be Afraid of the Unknown. "What is going to happen next? Is my friend going to get better again? How will the illness change him? Will I be able to be there for the relationship?"

Mark's fears became more focused the longer he took care of his friend Sam. "I kept thinking that I had always been the one to have little affairs, but never to let anybody get me into a relationship. I didn't want to be tied down. After a while, taking care of Sam, I started wishing I had gotten into a relationship. I ran through my mind the different men who had wanted me, or who said they had fallen in love with me. And I'd think, 'Wouldn't it be nice to know he was there for me, and that he'd take care of me if something happened to me?' And of course I realized that I didn't feel like I had anyone in the world I could count on except Sam, and he was sick. Sometimes I'd have this little film clip in my mind, about being alone and sick in my apartment and looking at the telephone sitting there next to the bed on a table, but having no one to call and ask for help. It was terrifying, so I'd put it out of my mind immediately. But it was there."

Guilt

You may feel guilty about being angry at your friend. After all, here is someone you love, and you find yourself angry at the demands he makes. You know he is sick, yet you resent that you have to do so much in the relationship. You may also feel guilty that your friend is sick and you're not, that more than likely you will outlive him. This is called "survivor's guilt." You may find yourself asking, "Why should I survive and not him?" Unfortunately, there is no answer to such a question.

Not surprisingly, you may also feel that you should not be feeling the way you do—that, too, may be a source of your guilt. "Everything I've ever heard since I was a child tells me that I should be happily doing these things for my sick friend, but instead I'm angry and resentful. Maybe I'm not a good person."

Joan explains how she and Barry felt about guilt when it came to their son David. "We know that there's this idea that parents should do anything for their children, and in a lot of ways we feel that, too. But this situation was different. We've provided him with everything he's asked for, and we've visited him twice in San Francisco. I don't think we could have been asked to do more. But do I feel guilty? Yes, of course. What mother wouldn't? He's my son. I feel that in some way, what happened is my fault.''

How to Respond to Your Friend's Feelings

One of the most difficult aspects of being a carepartner or caring friend is dealing with your friend's feelings and emotions. At some point, many people with AIDS experience almost overwhelming emotions and mood swings. One moment they feel hopeful; the next they're desperate. At different times, they may be filled with anger at the injustice of their situation, guilty that they got the disease at all, depressed because they feel helpless to change what is happening, fearful of what the future may hold—or improbably joyful about some treatment or medical advance. Nor can they always control these emotions, which may be as new and unnerving to them as they are to you. You have to try to help your friend learn to deal with his feelings. You also have to learn to deal with them yourself.

No matter how long he may have been infected, when your friend begins to get sick consistently or regularly, the disease really begins to hit home, even if all the ramifications aren't immediately apparent. Before his diagnosis or before he became sick, your friend may have been an active, ambitious person, in control of his life, respected at work and in his community, and loved by friends and family. Undoubtedly, he saw himself as a person with a future.

Now your friend may see himself as a social outcast. He may be unable to support himself because he is too ill to work, and all his dreams and plans may seem impossible to obtain. He may feel that he is looked down upon or, worse, that he is feared and despised as a source of contagion by the very people who should be supporting him. He may also feel that he has been abandoned by friends and family when he needs them the most. He may feel helpless to control the course of the disease or, for that matter, any aspect of his life. He may be afraid doctors will not consult him about medical problems, or that you may not talk to him about problems at home, or that his friends and family may not talk to him about their lives or about what is happening to him. He may be afraid of pain and dying. All this dislocation, these feelings of exclusion, can be terrifying beyond reason or understanding.

And you may well bear the brunt of all this. You, the carepartner or friend, the person who is there the most, are the one who must go through these mood swings with your sick friend. You might walk into his apartment one evening to be confronted by a whole day's frustrations he has felt. You may walk into his hospital room feeling great, and within five minutes feel that he has wrung you out emotionally, beaten you up, and pushed you to the verge of tears. This may not be his conscious intention, but he is making you deal with his feelings and emotions at a time when you might be finding it difficult to deal with your own—and you may be doing the same to him.

Still, you can help your friend to retain his self-worth and a sense that his life still possesses hope and meaning. To do this will require work, love, understanding, and patience with him and with yourself.

But first, a caution: You are not a therapist. You cannot and should not attempt to be one. The incredibly complex problems that may underlie your friend's feelings—and your own—may not be solvable by anyone—not therapist, priest, minister, or philosopher. There are no answers to questions like "Why did this happen to me? How can a good God let this happen? What does the future hold?" And it is no consolation to tell someone tortured by these questions, "God works in mysterious ways" or "This plague has been sent to purify us." Better no answers than these.

If your friend is suffering emotionally, try to get him into a therapy group so that he can talk with other people who share his problems. If no group exists in your area, then try to find a therapist or a counselor—someone he can trust—who has worked with people with AIDS.

What About Your Needs?

At some point, you will have to stop, take stock, and make sure you are paying attention to yourself. Too much is happening inside you now not to. Taking care of your friend is perhaps the biggest challenge you've ever undertaken. How are you going to sustain yourself through this time? What are your needs? How will you express them. How are you going to fulfill them? You should ask, and begin to answer, these questions now.

Every carepartner reaches this point. When you do, you should shift the focus away from your friend and focus on yourself. You have to make yourself more comfortable. Still, it may be very difficult for you to sit down at this point and figure out what your needs are. You have to ascertain what you can do to lessen the tension and the anxiety you feel and to make sure you have the support you require. Obviously, a great deal of your feelings and anxiety may arise from the feelings you have for your friend.

Take Action

Without a doubt, the two of you will need to reduce your emotional burdens. You will probably need to try new ways of thinking, new ways of looking at life. An extraordinary situation requires extraordinary approaches. We recommend the following four steps: **Divide Big Problems into Smaller Ones:** The first step is to start learning about the philosophy of "one day at a time." This idea was first developed by members of Alcoholics Anonymous, and it has helped hundreds of thousands of people cope with problems that they thought were unsolvable. It's a way of dividing big problems into small, manageable parts, ones you can begin to handle on a daily basis. When a person first stops drinking, the craving for alcohol may be nearly overwhelming, and the thought that this is what life is going to be from now on is very depressing. So Alcoholics Anonymous tells its members: "You can put up with this for one day. You can put up with anything for one day." The organization sets up support systems so that there is always someone to call when things get tough. As so many recovering alcoholics can attest, this formula for dealing with big problems has been enormously successful.

The Alcoholics Anonymous philosophy means this: Solve the problems you have today. Don't worry about problems you may have in six months. Whenever something demands your attention or is on your mind, ask this important question:"What can I do about this *today*?" If the answer is "Nothing," try to put that problem out of your mind. This is not to say that you should not deal with problems that are coming up in the future. Of course, you must. But it is pointless to worry about a future problem if you can take no action today to begin solving it.

Tom and Mart used this philosophy to deal with Mart's illness. Tom says, "Mart had been going to A.A. for about a year, so he had already internalized the idea of 'one day at a time.' That really helped me get turned around, too. While he was in the hospital, I was being driven crazy by ideas of what we'd do if this or that happened. What about the business? What are we going to do if . . . ? How are we going to . . . ? I just stopped that. I started saying, 'Let's get through this. Let's get through that. Just take things as they come.' And the A.A. philosophy helped me to do that. We've been doing it ever since."

Mart says, "I also feel that if it weren't for A.A., this illness would have been much more difficult for me. A.A. gave me a certain discipline. If I had come down with AIDS and I had been drinking, I would have made a mess of myself. In the hospital, I started praying. Although I've never been very religious, I would pray to my Higher Power. I started thanking my Higher Power for having had another day. At the end of my prayer, I would always pray for a cure, and I would thank God for the day and for Tom. I still do that every day."

You Make the Rules: The second step involves a new understanding of your situation. When your friend was diagnosed, the rules changed. Since that time he cannot, and should not, judge himself by what people who are not ill are doing. Nor should he judge himself in the same terms that he used to. People with AIDS are—and should think of themselves as—in a category that sets them free from the rules and conditions of everyday life. No one can tell your friend what he should or should not do with his life, what he should try to accomplish. That is entirely up to him. So you and your friend are free to make the rules yourself. Try not to be weighed down with what could have been. No amount of "what ifs" and "if onlys" is going to change one moment of your lives, or enrich you in any way.

The important question is: What, under the present circumstances, can you do to make your lives richer, happier, more fulfilled? When you start to think this way, when you start to look around you, you will discover that the world is filled with opportunities, with choices to make life better.

Improve Your Quality of Life: The third thing we recommend that you do is to make the best of your lives. No one can guarantee that your friend will be alive tomorrow, a week from now, a year from now. Neither do *you* have any such assurance. But what you do with today, and especially how you feel about it, is under your control. You can allow yourself to become miserable and depressed, or you can decide to work actively against depression, choosing to do the things that will make you both feel better. As people continue to live longer with HIV disease, more options—and more time—become available. That can mean everything from doing a bang-up job at work to volunteering to help others in need to taking that long-awaited vacation, even reading Proust from cover to cover (in French, of course). The point is to talk together and decide what it is you want to do. We are each alive until we die, and you and your friend should approach life that way.

For Mirabel, it would have been easy to become mired in the disease and its despair. Instead, she recalls, "I decided to fight it.

After being rejected from a support group because I wasn't sick enough, I started my own group for women. Of course, what the group that rejected me meant was that I had an AIDS-related condition, particular to women, that wasn't yet recognized by the CDC and others. So I started this group that eventually became six women meeting at my house once a week. I tell you, it was fantastic. Even though our backgrounds were entirely different, I felt—maybe for the first time in my life—that I belonged somewhere." Mirabel's attitude toward life in general also began to change. "I appreciate life more now," she says. "There was a time when I didn't care about anything. I hardly felt anything. Nowadays, I love to walk in the rain, lay on the grass, just watch the birds fly by. Every second that goes by matters to me now. Every day, I want to do something."

Set Goals: Always try to have something in the near future to look forward to, even if it's just a little thing: a nice dinner, a friend's visit, or a racy novel. Try to have more than one thing to look forward to, so that when one goal is accomplished, there are others. This way, when the present moment becomes painful or boring or depressing, your mind can move ahead to a future situation where the discomfort is gone. Often, this makes the present more bearable. And it helps the present to pass.

After Mary Margaret had been hospitalized for several weeks, she came to realize that because her son and grandchildren all visited together, she might not have any visitors for quite a stretch. "I hated to ask people to make 'appointments,' but it really helped me to look forward to a visit. I would get myself prepared mentally—which I liked. But I knew if my whole family came on Saturday, I might not have another visitor until Wednesday or Thursday. That was hard. Eventually, my family started to organize when they visited me, and that helped me to look forward to all their visits. It seems so simple in retrospect: All I had to do was talk about what I needed. But I'll tell you, it was hard to do at the time."

Your friend must take as much control over his emotions and feelings as he can. You, too, must do this. You do not have to be passive victims of depression, helplessness, or hopelessness. You can be active creators of happiness, control, hope, and love—on a daily basis. Just recognize the limits, as they change, and work within them.

But if you or your friend don't always feel in control, if you're just too depressed sometimes, that's all right, too. Let's face it, some days are like that. One way or another, the moment will pass. The worst possible day will end at midnight, just like all the others. Learn what you can from the day, and move on. If it's okay to be brave and

145

courageous and to make the best of it sometimes, then it's okay not to be brave and courageous and not to make the best of it sometimes, too. You make the rules, so you decide what's okay.

What If You Need to End the Relationship?

Some caring friends and carepartners decide at a certain point during their friend's illness that they can't go on, that they are simply not capable of dealing with the relationship, and that they are doing themselves and their friend more harm than good. This is an extremely difficult decision to make, and it should be made together.

If instead of feeling closer to your friend and he to you you feel alienated from each other, then the disease has become a wedge between you. If you have stopped telling each other how you feel, or what you need, or if you never started this process of communication, then your relationship is in trouble. If you are both angry and resentful and constantly questioning what you are doing together, then it may well be that you should not be together. This can happen to lovers and spouses as well as to friends. In each case, the decision to end a relationship should be taken very seriously.

Jerry and Arnold had seemed like a solid couple, especially during the first months of Jerry's illness. Then, Jerry recalls, during a trip to London, something happened to them both. "It was like Arnold found out that there was a huge and exciting world of nonsick people out there, and he didn't need to have me and AIDS in it at all. He got a lot of attention in London. And since I had gotten sick, we hadn't been going out much at home. So all of a sudden, when we got back, we were fighting. We weren't talking. He would go out and not come back until the next morning. I just couldn't take it. Finally, I said to him: 'Are you staying with me because you'd feel like a rat leaving me while I'm sick?' He just looked at me for a minute, almost as if he didn't understand what I was talking about.'I don't love you anymore,' he said. 'It's that more than anything else. I haven't let your sickness get in our way before, but I don't want to be with you anymore.'

"That was kind of how it ended. I was terrified for a while about being sick and alone, and I cried out of loneliness for weeks. But I've found lots of support, and my friends have been wonderful, and, best of all, my health seems to have withstood the breakup."

Lulu and *Christopher* met the first day they started graduate school in Berkeley. "Even though I was gay and she was straight, it was

146

almost like love at first sight," Christopher recalls. Over the next six years, they became best friends. "After we'd known each other for four years, I got very sick, and Lulu was there for me one hundred percent, if not more. I couldn't have asked for a better, more comforting friend. But two years later, after I learned I had AIDS, something went wrong. Lulu just shut down. That was for about six months. Then, one day, she just cut me off. She refused to talk, see me, or answer my letters. All I could ever figure out was that my disease had just pushed her over the edge. People often talk about friends like they're expendable. Well, they're not. I was crushed, I missed her tremendously, and I was extremely angry at her at the same time. At the very least, I wish we could have spoken our minds."

Before you make any decisions about ending your relationship, take all the necessary steps. Do everything you can, and involve your friend in every step.

- Try to have a therapist or counselor mediate the problems between you.
- Tell your friend your problems.
- State how you feel clearly and without fear of hurting your friend. He must know how you feel; you have to trust that he will not fall apart upon hearing it. Telling him is ultimately more productive than faking it.
- Demand that your friend tell you how he feels and what his issues are. Be prepared to be hurt. He may see what you're doing in an entirely different light than you do. What you think is generous, loving behavior he may see as selfish, inconsiderate, and demeaning.

If after doing everything you can to salvage the relationship you decide that you cannot go on, and especially if your friend agrees, then you should end the relationship. Understand clearly that your friends and family, your therapy group, even your therapist, may feel a need for you to stay in the relationship and may exert great pressure on you to remain. But only you and your friend know what you should do and what's best for the relationship.

Charles Dickens wrote in his opening to *A Tale of Two Cities*: "It was the best of times, it was the worst of times. . . ." As your friend's illness progresses, you will feel both the best and the worst. The key to a continued healthy and fulfilling relationship, whether platonic or amorous, is talking, sharing, and loving. Without a doubt, your friend's illness will cause you pain and hurt. But you can also expect that it will enrich you in ways you never could have imagined.

147

8

GETTING THE HELP YOU NEED

Taking care of your friend who has AIDS is not something you will be able to do entirely by yourself. You will need to determine those things you can control and those you cannot, those things *you* can do for him and those you cannot. *At different times, you are going to need help. This chapter will help you find it.*

Although you may spend great amounts of time with your friend, you may still wind up feeling lonely and abandoned. Large parts of what used to constitute your relationship are now gone. Even though a new and different relationship is forming between the two of you, you may still feel alone; you may feel as if you are carrying the whole burden. You may feel that the friend you had before the illness is now gone, and that you are just now learning who this new person is. You may crave assurance that you are doing the right things, that someone, somewhere, recognizes what you are doing. You may need to feel that someone is looking out for you, that someone will be there for you when you need a friend or if you should get sick or simply too tired or overwhelmed. Above all, you will need support, and this is something you can control—by reaching out.

Many people find it difficult to vent their true feelings. You may feel a need to express your sadness, anger, or fear, or your amazement at all the changes occurring in both your lives. Unfortunately,

148

friends and family may be willing to listen to only so much. What's on your mind may simply make them uncomfortable. In many circumstances, this is something you and your friend can control by reaching out to the right people.

Arnold, whose lover had had AIDS for several years, describes the reactions he got from his family when he tried to talk about his feelings: "For a while, I was so confused, I didn't know who to talk to. I'd call my mother or my sister and try to talk to them. But after a few times, I realized from their reactions that I was just causing them pain, and I wasn't feeling any better myself. I knew I had to find someone else to talk to. Even my friends didn't want to hear about it. Eventually, I got help. I was put in touch with a volunteer from our local AIDS agency, and we used to talk for hours."

For a carepartner or friend, reaching out is very important. Many times, what you cannot do or bear alone you *can* do or bear with help. There are many people who are willing to help you; you just have to find them. Many communities now have organizations devoted entirely to helping people with AIDS and their friends and families. The first place to start is also the closest: your friend with AIDS.

How to Reach Out to Your Friend with AIDS

You may feel that you spend all your waking hours, outside work, caring for your friend and his needs, and that you seldom pay much attention to yourself or your needs. Neglecting your needs can cause you to feel resentful, depressed, even angry. The first person you should talk to about these feelings is your friend. You may have to say, "Look, I need your help. I feel like I'm doing this whole thing by myself, and it's wearing me down. Please help me out." There are many ways that your friend can help you.

Fewer Demands

Your friend can think twice about asking you for things, especially things he may not need or has no real use for. Discuss requests at first, but then, when you feel his demands are unreasonable, ask, "Are you sure you want me to do this?"

James had to confront this problem with his brother Earl. "When Earl came home from the hospital after he had toxoplasmosis, he was pretty weak. He didn't do much; in fact, he just slept and watched a lot of TV. He wasn't out there like he used to be—making things happen. Then Earl started calling me at work and asking me to bring him sports magazines or food like fried chicken and 'a pound of his favorite potato salad.' After a while, I noticed that the magazines were never moved from where I put them down and all the food was still in the refrigerator. So I said to him: "You know how much money I make. I can't be spending money on magazines you don't read and food you don't eat.' 'I want them,' he said to me, but I think he understood.

"After that, he'd call me, and I'd bargain with him until I got him down to one magazine, and I'd bring him as much food as I was willing to eat the next night. So when he didn't eat the food, I'd eat it the next night as my dinner. He didn't seem to mind, and that worked for both of us."

Less Complaining

Your friend does not have to tell you about every feeling and every pain in his body all the time. You know his condition. He does not have to complain to you about *all* the problems in the hospital, or at home, or with his doctors—especially those problems you can do nothing about. In other words, he can set boundaries that will respect your limits and the amount of time you can devote to his problems. If constant complaining or haranguing becomes a problem, you should discuss the situation frankly with your friend. He may not even be aware of what he's doing. Try to come to a joint resolution; you'll both be much more content.

Jeffrey and Paul went through a very difficult time when Paul seemed to focus entirely on himself and his illness. "For a while after Paul moved in, he was doing well," Jeffrey recalls. "He did telephone work at one of the AIDS agencies in town, and we went out fairly often. Then something happened. Maybe he got really depressed. But he started telling me about every little ache in his body. He would call me at work to tell me that the joint in his knee hurt or that he'd just had a pain flash across his forehead or that his guts were growling. And he almost never stopped. He would even wake me up in the middle of the night to tell me that he couldn't sleep. Finally, we went to his doctors, but no one could find anything, and then we went to a therapist to see what *he* could tell us. He said Paul was depressed, but we already knew that. It was driving me crazy. I said to him, 'Paul, you have to start thinking about something else besides your aches and pains. You have to talk to me about other things.' It took a while, but he became conscious of when he was complaining, and the more conscious of it he became, the less he did it."

Giving You More Free Time

Your friend can demand less of your time. He can be understanding if you need an occasional evening out, or if you can only spend a short time in the hospital now and then. If your whole life is made up of going to your job and taking care of him, you are going to need to make time for yourself.

Hugh and John had a particularly difficult problem because Hugh's work as a contractor made many demands on him, and John was very jealous of Hugh's time. One day, the conflict came to a head. Hugh recalls: "When I got to the hospital, John sent me out for a sandwich. It was the beginning of the old go-out-and-get-it routine. When I got back, the doctor was there interviewing him, so I told John I'd be back in the morning, and I left. When I got there the next morning, John started crying. 'How come you left last night?' he asked. I said, 'You know, the doctor was here.' He said, 'I thought you left because you wanted to go out. You didn't want to stay here.' So I stayed most of that day, mostly out of guilt. But as I sat there, I knew things had to change. I started to be conscious about exactly how much time I would spend at the hospital.

"Every night, I'd go by the hospital at visiting hours and stay an hour or so. John would get mad and ask why I couldn't stay longer, and I'd tell him that I had things to do. I think that after a while he got used to that, because I just couldn't spend all my time there. At least he didn't complain about it as much."

Demanding Less Attention

Sometimes it's not enough for you to be physically present; your friend may want all your attention, too. If you're cleaning his apartment or doing some work, he will interrupt you to tell you about an item in a newspaper or magazine, call you to look at something on television, or otherwise let you know that he wants you to be focused on him. Meanwhile, you're getting frustrated because you're not getting done what you wanted to do.

The two of you can solve this problem in several ways. If you wish, you *can* simply focus on him. Or he can invite a friend over for an evening to keep him company. Sometimes he can participate in whatever it is that you are doing to whatever degree he is able and that you want. Or he can develop some projects of his own, like volunteering, getting involved in politics, taking a class at a local college.

Jack and Bruce had to solve this problem. Bruce didn't know what to do with himself when he was alone, and he wanted all Jack's attention when Jack was around. Bruce was too healthy to have nothing to do but not well enough to hold down a job. "You know," Jack remembers, "we lived in this big old house I had bought for the price of an old car when I first came to Houston, and there were millions of things that needed doing. Finally, I told Bruce, 'Look, I'm going to teach you how to do things around this place, and you're going to make this a decent house to live in.' At first he grumbled a lot, but after a while he got into the swing of it. He could work with wood. He could take off and put on wallpaper. He could paint, scrape, repair windows, fix the porches. I just taught him how to do it as we went along. What a change it made. I'd come home and he'd have been working, and he'd be so proud of what he'd done. I can tell you, during the times he was well, Bruce really made that house a place to be proud of. He also made my life a lot easier. And I found I was able to give him more in other ways, too."

Showing Appreciation

Your friend can let you know that he is aware of what you are doing and that he appreciates you. He can let you know that he loves you, and that he knows you love him. Sometimes, these things are hard for people to express, but in these extraordinary circumstances, they need to be said. You need to hear that he is concerned about you, just as much as he needs to hear that you are concerned about him.

Marilyn tells about her confrontation with Tim when she told him she was prepared to leave him because of the way he had been treating her: "All he was doing was moping around the house, sulking and feeling sorry for himself, and ordering me to get him this and get him that. Meanwhile, who was I? I work all day, I pay the bills, and at night I get to be the maid, without so much as a thank-you once in a while. Finally, one day I said to him, 'Remember me, Tim? I'm Marilyn. I was Marilyn before you got sick, and I'm still Marilyn right now. Around here, you act like I'm the maid.' He gave me a look and said, 'But everything's changed. Don't you realize what's happened? This terrible thing has happened. We're outcasts.' I said to him, 'I realize better than you what's happened, but I'm still Marilyn, and you're still Tim.' I started to get angry. 'I'm still here,

Tim. You want me to leave? I'll run out the door. Start paying attention to me. I need you to pay attention to me.'

"But he just sat there staring at me, so I got dressed and went out for the evening. When I got back, he was waiting up for me, and he snuggled up to me when I got into the bed. 'I've been thinking about what you said. You know, you're pretty special to still be here. When I think of all the shit I've laid on you, and you're still here. You didn't walk out the minute you heard I was sick.' "

Marilyn smiles, saying, "He actually made me feel good that evening for the first time in months. That was the beginning of something. A few things started to get better for us after that."

When You Both Need Help

You and your friend must communicate openly. You must tell each other your needs and feel that the other is listening and is willing to make room for your needs.

If you find that you cannot talk, and it seems that the tension is rising in the relationship, involve a third person—a friend, a therapist, or someone you both trust—to mediate. The purpose of speaking to a third party is to express your true feelings to your friend—and vice versa. Be sure that you can do this. It's easy not to. It's easy to be a martyr.

You may also find at this time that you and your friend need to pursue therapy individually or join a group. Often, attending a group for caring friends, carepartners, or people with AIDS is all the help that a person needs. Sometimes, however, it is not. Groups have limitations. Some people cannot express their intimate feelings in front of other people, or their problem can be so complex that the group cannot deal with it adequately. Support groups are generally best at helping a person deal with immediate problems.

Setting Up Support Systems

Discuss with your friend whether he wants to tell members of his family or any of his other friends about his illness. Help him make this decision. It can be an important step in gathering the help you both need.

When they learn they are sick, some people do not want anyone else to know. They may be denying that they're sick at all; telling others would be admitting their illness to themselves. They may not want to be treated differently because they're sick; they want other people to relate to them as they always have. They may be afraid of being abandoned. Any of these is a valid reason to keep the illness a secret—at least for a time.

For some people with AIDS and their carepartners, whom to tell about the illness is not an issue. If a person was infected for a long time before diagnosis, or has been very open about his health with family and friends, everyone who needs to know may already know.

Eventually, *you both* must agree to tell at least some people that your friend is ill. This is always risky. If you are abandoned by some, so be it; try not to worry about those people anymore. There will be others, people you may never have expected to care, who will be there for you. Only under the most extraordinary circumstances will you have to go through this alone. Help will come from unexpected quarters.

After Mirabel had been hospitalized for nearly two weeks, she came home weak and extremely worried about how she would care for her family. With her husband working every day and some evenings to help pay the medical bills, she recalls, "I thought I would have to do it all myself. But the day I got home, my oldest girl, Eliza, came into my bedroom and explained how she wanted to help. 'I know I used to be lazy around the house, Mom, but I want to be there for you now. When you get tired, I'll take care of the younger kids. I'll do some of the shopping and the laundry.' I could hardly believe my ears. And from that point on, I had a lot of help from Eliza, day after day. You know, I never would have expected it to happen, but it did."

Informing Your Family

As a friend, lover, spouse, carepartner, there may come a time when you must talk to your family. The response from some relatives will be to support you and your friend in this difficult situation. Others will do more than express sympathy—and phone once or twice in six months. (Of course, a few will not do even that much, but they are the exceptions.)

Tom tells about his trip to the Midwest when he told his parents about Mart. "We were gathered around the breakfast table, my mother, my father, and I. My mother started asking me about Mart and the business. They had been very concerned about his health. I told them that he was getting ready to sell the business because he really couldn't face the stress of another tax season. So I finally said, 'Listen, there's something that I really have to tell you.' My mother said, 'I think I know.' I said, 'Mart has AIDS.' And she said, 'I was afraid of that.' I asked my father if he had suspected, but he said he hadn't, although he knew about AIDS.

"They made it easy for me to tell them. We began talking about what his illness meant for us, for Mart and me, and how we were coping. They were wonderfully supportive. They kept saying, 'If there's anything you need from us, just let us know—if there's anything we can do.' I said, 'I can't tell you how much this means, just to know that. I don't know what you can do. But just to know that you're available, that you're thinking about us, is the support we need.' "

Sometimes when you tell members of your family that your friend has AIDS, they may feel at a loss. What should they do? Is there anything they *can* do? In fact, there may be nothing you can ask of them, except to love you and understand what you are going through. If they are nearby, they can provide you with a place to go, a refuge for dinner or a Sunday afternoon. If they know your friend, they can come to visit. If you are fortunate, they will treat him like a member of their own family. On the other hand, many times your family may wonder out loud why you are doing what you are doing.

There may also be times when your family is already overburdened—with a recent death or another serious illness or some other crisis. You may feel that you cannot add to their burdens by telling them about your friend.

Jack felt that he couldn't tell his family about Bruce's illness because his father had died only a year before and his mother and two brothers were still running the family wheat farm. "I never knew what to expect from my family," Jack says. "I never knew if I wanted anything from them. They all live out in east Texas, and they have their own lives to live—you know, families, businesses, all that. Now my brothers know about me, and they know about Bruce and his illness. They always ask, 'Is there anything we can do?' But what can they do? I don't even know what to ask from them."

Informing Your Friend's Family

Your friend should tell his own family about his illness. It is usually best to give people news of this nature in person. If he is well enough to travel, he could visit them so that he can tell them. If for some reason *you* must telephone them, tell them that he is sick, and ask them to come visit. Only if they insist, or if you have known them for a long time, should you tell them that he has AIDS.

Len tells how Molly, Evan's mother, telephoned and kept asking that he tell her what was happening. Len says, "I had never had a conversation with her, but when I told her that I would get Evan, she said, 'No, I want to talk to you. Evan won't tell me what's going on, and I need to know. Why is he sick all the time?' Evan was in the room at the time, and I put my hand over the receiver and said, 'It's your mother. She wants to know what's going on with you.' Evan shrugged his shoulders as if to say, 'Tell her what you want,' and so I did. I told her about his symptoms, what they meant, what the doctor had told us, and what we were doing. 'You let me know if you want me to do anything,' she said. I told her that I would, and then I gave the phone to Evan.

"She came up to stay with us four or five times over the next year and half. During Evan's bad bouts, I don't know what I would have done without her. She even slept in the hospital with him."

The position and obligation of your friend's family should be much clearer than that of your own. You can and should make demands on them. You can ask them to come to visit—even for extended periods. You can ask them to help out with your friend's care in the hospital and at home. You can ask them to share all the financial burdens of his care—emotional as well as physical.

If your friend was a drug user, you may have great difficulty explaining this to his family. In many instances, however, the family has already had to deal with your friend's drug problem long before he got sick. They may have denied that he used drugs, and they may still deny it to you. But no matter what: Don't let them blame you. If it is apparent that your friend became infected by using needles, acknowledge it if they ask you. This is not the time to make up stories. But remember, too, that it does not matter how your friend became infected. What matters is that *he is infected* and needs the love and support of his family and friends.

Marilyn was very angered by Tim's father's reaction. "He just sort of barged into the hospital room like he was the Gestapo or something. To the doctor, he said, 'What's going on here? Are you sure this is AIDS? What are you doing to cure him? Should I call in a doctor who knows what he's doing?' To me, he said, 'How did he get it? Did you give it to him? I hear that soldiers in Germany are getting it from prostitutes.' To Tim, he said, 'Maybe there's a mistake here.'

"I wanted to say, 'Take your choice, Mr. Win-Friends-and-Influence-People. Your son has shot up occasionally. He has had sex with male prostitutes and sometimes with male models. That's one of the charming lessons he learned on Daddy's knee. You tell us how he got it.' But I didn't say anything. He's such a selfish son of a bitch. All he could hear was what he was saying, anyway. Before he left, he had Tim crying."

156

Of course, sometimes disclosure of an AIDS diagnosis can have unintended results. Mirabel remembers telling her mother, only to be told, "Oh, that's nothing. Take care of it, and you'll be all right in a couple of days." Mirabel talks bluntly about her mother's reaction: "We had never had a good relationship, and this certainly didn't help it. I think part of the reason I even wanted to tell her was to hurt her, hurt her for abandoning me all those years ago. But it didn't work. I didn't get anything—no support, no love, no caring. And I guess she really didn't get anything, either. I look back, and I wonder if it wasn't a mistake."

If you and your friend are in a loving gay relationship, that fact will become clear to the family when they are told of the disease (if it wasn't clear already). They may accept this knowledge with little overt fuss, but don't necessarily expect them to want to discuss it with you or their son. It may be better not to try to force members of his family, who are under the stress of coping with his illness, into accepting a gay relationship. Under these circumstances, you have a right to expect them to express their care and concern for their son, but changes in attitude or conviction are much harder, if not impossible, to elicit. Yes, his parents should treat you as the most important person in your friend's life and should consult you as they would any significant other in matters pertaining to your friend, but they may not be ready or able to accept you as they might a son- or daughter-in-law. However, they may recognize what you are doing from the outset, and they may be grateful.

Jack says, "I told Bruce that he had to do something about telling his family. He said, 'I've been on my own since I was sixteen. My family's got a tough enough time scratching a living out of that stingy soil up in the Panhandle without my laying this on them.' But I insisted anyway, because he really couldn't see how sick he was, and finally he did call his mother and brothers. I think their reaction stunned him. His mother flew down to Houston, and she stayed at the house with us for two weeks. She needed to know everything that was going on. I can tell you, too, the house sparkled for those two weeks. When she left, we were both sad. The whole thing, from the phone call till she left, was something really special."

Families may have various reasons for not embracing or even tolerating you and your relationship with their child. For many, the main reason is a so-called moral one. They may believe gay and lesbian relationships are wrong. They may be ashamed and guilty that one of their own is involved in such a relationship. If they say anything to you indicating their disappointment, simply say, "The problem is that your son is sick. The problem is not my relationship with him. I am here because I am helping your son deal with a life-threatening illness. What we have in common is our concern for your son's health.'' Such a response at least sets the ground rules and can be quite effective.

Families may also be frightened of the social stigmas they believe will be attached to them if their neighbors learn that their son not only has AIDS but is also gay or a drug user. This, too, is their problem. Do not try to deal with it, and do not let them shift the problem to you. Given time, they may find the courage or resources to deal with any ostracism they encounter and still care for their own.

Joan and Barry had avoided their greatest fear—that they would become outcasts in their own town because of the stigma of AIDS—when they told their son that he could not come home. But their problem did not go away. ''One day, after he'd been living in San Francisco for about six weeks,'' Joan recalls, ''David called me. He told me that he really couldn't live in his friend's house anymore. He started crying on the phone and yelling at me. 'I've got nowhere to go and nobody to help me.' When he said that, I couldn't stand it, either. I had felt so rotten and so guilty so long, but I felt Barry was right that we couldn't bring David home. So I said to him, 'Just calm down. I'm still your mother. You can count on me. I'll come out there on the very next plane. I'll get everything straightened out for you.'

''Barry and I had a good cry together as I packed to leave. I hadn't seen him cry since his father's funeral, almost ten years before. 'When will you be back?' he asked. 'What am I going to tell everybody?' I told him he knew as much as I did, but if I didn't do this, the rest of our lives wasn't going to be worth anything. I said, 'The reverend can say anything he wants to about God's punishment for their weakness, but when it's my son lying there so frail and weak, then I just know it's not true. God wouldn't do that to David. I read the other day that babies get AIDS. How does the reverend explain that?'

''When I got to San Francisco, I went to the house where David was staying. He was in a room with two other people, and they were all very sick. David was sleeping, so I didn't wake him. But he looked so sick and weak I could hardly believe my eyes. I went out immediately to find an apartment.''

David was fortunate. Others are not. Your friend should be prepared for abandonment and rejection. Some parents reject outright their child with AIDS. If your friend's family says that they will not come to visit and that they do not want to see him at their home, your friend will feel that rejection deeply and painfully.

Marilyn talks about Tim's father's rejection: "After he came to visit that first time, he just didn't come back. You know, he lives right here in New York, and he works about twenty blocks from the hospital and only a little farther from where we live. So Tim would call him, and his father was always in a hurry to get somewhere. Then he started with his secretary, saying he was never in the office. Tim said to me one day, 'I was always his go-getter son. He was always slapping me on the back and parading me up and down in front of all his friends. Now what am I?' I didn't say it, but I thought it—'To him, you're a sick, drug-addicted, faggot-loving jerk married to a whore, and you'll be lucky if you ever see him again at all.' But instead of talking, I sat on the bed and held him and told him I would be there. But he could never get over his father's reaction of him. His father just confirmed to me every rotten thing I had ever thought of him."

If your friend has been rejected by his family—to any degree—you should assure him that you are there. Draw closer to him if you can, and be as strong as you can. Physical intimacy may be very important right now. If you watch TV together, try to sit where you can touch each other. Call friends and invite them over. Realize, though, that some pain will remain in your friend, and there is nothing you can do about it.

Not every member of a family will act the same way, and you and your friend will probably maintain contact with those who did not abandon him. Often, when parents cannot deal with the situation, siblings or other relatives can. Don't be surprised if you feel great anger toward those family members who abandoned your friend. If your friend wants to express anger, he should. So should you, although neither of you needs World War III with your families right now.

What to Expect from Your Families

Once families have been told, experience has shown they will react in any of several ways:

- They may accept you and the situation with love, grace, and warmth.
- One of the parents may move in with their child and care for him. These parents are also carepartners. This usually hap-

pens when the child does not have a significant other or close set of friends, and the parent lives in another city.

- They may ask your friend to live in their home, where they can take care of him.
- One family member may begin to take an active role in your friend's care. He may come to spend long periods of time with you to help, and he may make himself available whenever needed. Do not be afraid to ask for whatever you need.
- They may offer some financial help.
- They may grudgingly visit a few times, staying perhaps a few hours or a day. They may make it clear that this is all that they will do, except to bury your friend in their hometown.
- They may maintain limited telephone contact.
- They may reject you and your friend completely. They will tell you that they do not want to see either of you and will not visit. This is unusual.

Most parents love their children, regardless of their sexual orientation or drug history, and all parents, whatever their religious or moral conviction, will suffer great distress upon learning that their child has a possibly terminal illness. But no matter their distress, many families will be reluctant to deal with AIDS, homosexuality, or drug use.

Reaching Out to Your Friends

Much space in this book has been devoted to helping people like you overcome the fears associated with being the friend of someone with HIV or AIDS. Now we need to look at the situation from another perspective. What reactions can you expect when you are the caring friend of someone with AIDS and you reach out to friends and family for help and support?

Many friends will stick by you, and you should not feel ashamed to ask them for help. Stay close to those people. They are valuable friends indeed. Sometimes, your friend has other friends who are more his than yours. Cultivate these people as well. Ask them to come by on a regular basis, perhaps once or twice a week, and if you want, use that time to do other things—even for yourself! If your friend was independent before he became ill and did things with his friends and without you, he should continue to do this as much as he wishes and can.

Hugh tells about some of John's friends: "John had this friend from work, a straight guy, who came to the hospital every day. He used to sit and talk to John and take care of him. And he'd have these great conversations with John. There was another guy, a religious friend of John's, who used to come by and pray with him. An Episcopal priest came, too, and he did touching. He came and ministered to John."

You may find yourself having the following experience; many friends and carepartners have shared it. You may call a friend, one you may not feel particularly close to but with whom you want to talk about what is happening. Much to your surprise, that person visits you and your friend, calls occasionally, returns to visit again, brings flowers, comes over to give you an evening off, brings dinner. You are surprised, even stunned, and very pleased. Stay in touch with this person. You may not know his full motivation, but unless it seems to be unhealthy in some way (and that ought to become clear very quickly), accept it. People who want to help like this are often big-hearted but shy; their kindness is ordinarily hidden but needs to be expressed.

Sadly, not all your friends will stick by you. People in a crisis situation expect friends to rally. Instead, some may run away; some will strike your name from their address book. Many friends, carepartners, and people with AIDS complain bitterly that they have been abandoned by their friends. The scenario might go like this: Upon learning of your friend's illness, an acquaintance of yours voices great concern. He immediately asks what he can do. You think this person has come through, but the initial burst is the total outpouring. This friend does not want to hear about it anymore. He does not come to the hospital, does not come to the house, does not call or return phone calls. You feel, rightly so, that the friend has cut you out of his life. He thinks his obligation to you was fulfilled by his initial show of concern, and he refuses to deal directly with the prospect of recurring illness.

Stella tells of the isolation she felt after her husband, David, was diagnosed with AIDS. "David was a fine person. He always helped everybody out. He always joked with me. He'd say, 'I haven't seen you in three days.' He'd be going this way, and I'd be going that way, visiting people. It's really ironic for the person who helped so many people out that just when you need a friend, nobody's there. I'm not saying that David didn't have any friends after he got sick, but it's people's nature to be fearful. It's the way we were born, and it's the way we'll die, too. Some of it's just plain stupid, and it hurt David. We were in the family room talking one night, about two o'clock in the morning, and he said, 'You know, I can count on my fingers the

161

number of friends who have come up here to see me since I got sick.' That really hurts, especially when you're someone like David.''

Rose, Gary and Linda's stepmother, explains her disappointment in some of her neighbors: "We had lived in the same house since the children were little—right after I married their father—so all of our neighbors knew all our business, and it wasn't long before everyone knew that Gary had AIDS. I was really surprised at some of them. A few of Gary's friends from high school and college came by, but only two of them came more than one time. And my husband's and my friends always seemed a little embarrassed around us. We used to have a bridge game at the house once a month, but that stopped because, I think, people were afraid. Of course, our very closest friends were there whenever we needed them. I have one friend who came every time I had to leave the house and didn't want to leave Gary alone. She took care of him like he was her own son. She spent almost as much time in the hospital as I did.''

Howard also remembers his hurt: "The support we got from our friends was a disappointment. A lot of our friends have just blotted us out. They don't want to deal with the illness or us. Some people wouldn't even return a phone call. I've called them and practically begged them to help Alex during the day, when I'm working; he needed someone to help him with food and medicines and all. But these people have nothing but excuses. You know, they're just excuses. These are people with plenty of time and money, who could adjust their schedules a little bit, but they won't. I believe they think they're safe from this illness if they just don't pay attention to it and never think about it.''

Organizations You Can Turn To

Even if you are not getting the support you need from family and friends, there are alternatives. You can still get help. In many areas, the AIDS community has organized itself to help those whose lives have been affected by HIV. These organizations, which exist throughout the country, have taken on a large number of functions, from educating people about HIV transmission and providing up-to-date information regarding experimental treatments to acting as a clearinghouse for legal advice and governmental assistance programs. Many groups also provide "buddy" programs for people with AIDS as well as a host of different support groups for carepartners and their friends. Appendix C contains a list of organizations that are active in assisting people with HIV/AIDS and their carepartners.

If you need help, call the number of the organization closest to you. If they can't help you, the people there will know where to refer you. If that fails, call one of the large organizations in New York (Gay Men's Health Crisis), San Francisco (San Francisco AIDS Foundation), Los Angeles (AIDS Project Los Angeles), Houston (Houston AIDS Foundation), Miami (Miami Health Crisis Network), or Washington, D.C. (Whitman-Walker Clinic).

Services Available from AIDS Agencies

Following is a compendium of services available from HIV/AIDS agencies. Not all agencies provide all services; many organizations have carved out a particular niche for themselves, such as legal advice, food delivery programs, or telephone hot lines. If you are not finding what you need, always ask for a referral.

- *Support groups and therapy groups for people with HIV and AIDS.* Anyone is welcome to walk-in groups; in closed groups, only members may attend. Specific groups exist for gay men, women, people of color, drug users, older people, and teenagers.
- *Support and therapy groups for carepartners, lovers, and spouses.* Many organizations also have special groups for friends, parents, and siblings. GMHC in New York, for instance, runs groups for carepartners, parents, and couples, support groups for people with AIDS who are also carepartners, and multi-family groups. GMHC runs bereavement groups, too.
- *Medical referrals* to doctors or hospitals experienced in dealing with HIV.
- *Spiritual counseling* referrals for those in need. The agency will put the person in contact with a religious person, of any denomination or faith, who will try to help.
- *Buddies*—both men and women—volunteers who try to help in any way they can: from visiting and cleaning the apartment of a person with AIDS to shopping, running errands, and providing a shoulder to lean on.
- *Crisis counselors.*
- *Referrals to individual therapy.*
- *Financial help,* on a limited basis, when the need is great.
- *Help with finding housing,* both short-term and longer-term.
- *Lawyers or referrals to legal-rights groups* that will assist in drawing up wills, powers of attorney, and other HIV-related legal matters. These lawyers excel in dealing with employers, in-

163

surance companies, and landlords, as well as federal, state, and local laws.

- *Social workers* who will help process applications for food stamps, Medicaid, Social Security Disability, and other government assistance programs.
- *Recreation committees* that arrange theater parties, museum excursions, movie afternoons, bridge clubs, and the like.
- *Education departments* that collect and disseminate information about the disease. These departments also provide information about treatments and experimental drug programs.
- *Visiting nurses* or referrals to home-care workers. These services are often provided by state agencies or the American Red Cross.
- *Telephone hot lines* for people who need almost any kind of information or referral regarding AIDS, or who may need to talk about their fears and concerns about HIV. Special hot lines exist for people with HIV/AIDS.
- *Other services include:* dental and hospice referrals, nutritional counseling, volunteer opportunities, immigration advice, tax information, pet-care assistance, food provided for the homebound, and suicide intervention.

Services Available from Hospitals and Health-Care Agencies

Some hospitals have hospice or outreach programs that can provide many additional services to you and your friend.

- *Visiting nurses and home-care workers* can be arranged when your friend leaves the hospital but continues to need nursing care.
- *Patient representatives* will arrange for social workers who can help you get assistance from city, state, and federal agencies.
- *Hospital workers* may be assigned to serve in the same capacity as buddies.
- *Living accommodations* can sometimes be provided for the homeless.

Services Available from Religious Organizations

Some religious organizations have programs for people with AIDS and their carepartners. Dignity, an organization of gay and lesbian

Roman Catholics, has chapters in many cities across the country, as does Integrity, the Episcopal lesbian and gay ministry. The Metropolitan Community Church, a Christian church for lesbians and gays, has congregations in many cities. New York's Congregation Beth Simchat Torah and San Francisco's Sha'ar Zahav provide a home for their cities' Jewish communities. Find out if your own denomination has an organization for its members with AIDS.

Taking Action

Know that you cannot make this fight alone, that you are going to need help, and that help will be there when you reach out for it. *But you must reach out.*

If you have been following the path that most caring friends and partners take, then you have been assessing your needs and setting up support systems to help you care for your friend and for yourself. If you haven't, the time to start is right now. For many of us, it can be difficult to admit we may need assistance, and even harder to reach out and ask for it. But for your sake and your friend's, you must.

9

TAKING CARE OF YOURSELF AND THE RELATIONSHIP WHEN YOUR FRIEND IS VERY SICK

The longer you and your friend are together and the longer he is sick, the closer you'll be drawn together. If anything, the friendship and love you feel should deepen and grow more profound. You're likely to find yourself sharing more intimate moments than you ever have before. Despite all the problems, this time can be very important for the both of you.

"Evan's sick now," Len says, "and I've fallen back in love with him. How could it have been otherwise? How can you be this close to someone every day, how can you go through this much with someone, and not love him? No, you either love or you go away. And the more difficult things become, the more you love, because love alone makes it possible to bear. So you hold him. You cuddle him. You tell him of your love. And all the while you fear the loss, the fear of the emptiness you might someday feel."

"The relationship got deeper and closer," Michael says. "I think Joe began to love me for who I really am, and I started to love Joe for Joe, not for what we wanted each other to be. We were vulnerable to each other, and we acknowledged our vulnerability to each other as we never had with anybody else or to each other before."

During the times Michelle was very sick, her mother, Suzanne, remembers feeling a certain warmth—despite the overall sadness

166

she was also feeling. "Taking care of Michelle when she was so sick and weak was the most intimate experience I've ever had in my whole life. One day, I walked over to the hospital. It was the beginning of spring. I felt like I was going to meet a lover. I remember thinking, 'What a strange way to be feeling.' I wanted to be alone with her. I could see the time that we had together, and I knew it might not be that much longer. I wanted the intimacy. I wanted it to be mine. I would go to get the things to clean her. I would close the door. I always tried to bring different powders and nice-smelling soaps."

Jack recalls, "It was hard to watch someone so full of spunk and life, and so strong, getting his ass whipped by this disease. Bruce seemed to shrivel up. First he had pneumonia. Then he had something the doctor thought would make him blind. But they had a new drug for that, so he went only partially blind. Then he got a cancer of the lymph glands. I was there, sitting right next to him, when the doctor explained what was happening. 'Bruce,' Dr. Bill said, 'we've got to take a hard look at this thing. If I send you to a doctor to get drugs for this lymphoma, the drugs are likely to make you really sick and knock out what immune system you've got left. What I'm telling you is that the drugs will probably kill you indirectly.' Bruce paused, and then said: 'And if I don't get them, the cancer will kill me directly.'

" 'That's the picture,' Dr. Bill said. Bruce and I looked at each other. He reached over and put his arm around my shoulder and pulled me against him. 'Some choice we got, lovin' Bubba,' he said to me, using a name he never used in public. 'Maybe we should try the drugs a time or two and see how bad it is. I hate to go out not fighting.'

"He was part of me from that minute on. We had shared something so intimate that for a long time I felt like what was happening to him was happening to me. We just got closer and closer. It got so I took him everywhere, and when I couldn't be there, we had a nurse come to the house every day. At night, he curled up against me when he slept. I could feel the tremors in his body. I used to think the tremors were what I could feel of the war going on inside him. Once or twice, I just had to cry when he was around, and he said, 'Be sad, hon. God knows I got a load of it inside me, too.' "

Taking Care of Your Friend

The growing intimacy you may feel toward your friend may be expressed in many ways, either in the hospital or at home. You may find yourself doing things you never dreamed you would do for any person. You may change your friend's bedclothes and underwear when he is incontinent, and clean him. You may have to teach him how to use a bedpan. You may have to learn how to make a bed with someone in it. You will find yourself doing these things out of love. And in among the many chores and the long hours, you may also find yourself talking about things you never imagined you would talk about with anyone.

One of the most concrete ways of expressing intimacy is by touching. As someone who may have long felt like a pariah, whose body is undoubtedly hurting, your friend will find the simple human touch even more important than before. You may touch him simply to hold him or make him feel better, or you may be touching him in the process of taking care of him, by doing for him what he can no longer do for himself.

Massage

When your friend is confined to a bed for a long time and is very sick, he may begin to feel isolated, ugly, even repulsive. The touch of your hands can bring him reassurance and comfort. It does much good just to sit and hold his hand. You might discover that giving your friend a massage not only lets you touch him but also makes him more comfortable and helps to prevent bedsores. You do not have to know how to give a professional massage. All you have to know is how to knead your friend's muscles and skin lightly—he will tell you the correct pressure—and how to show your love by performing this service. You do not have to massage his whole body, maybe only his neck and back or his hands and feet. In fact, you can do a different part of his body every day.

Michael tells how Joe loved massages and asked him for one when he was in the hospital. Massages had become an expression of love between them. "At one point, he asked me to give him a back rub. He'd always loved to have his back rubbed. And that last summer, when he was bummed out about something or just needed a lift or I wanted to give him a treat, then I'd rub his back. And I would always think, 'If I were Joe, how would I like my back rubbed?' And I would always rub his back that way. It seemed to work."

Elimination

Another way that you may show your closeness with your friend is by caring for his need for cleanliness, especially when he can no longer take care of these needs himself. Most likely, your friend feels helpless, embarrassed, and even ashamed when he can no longer control the elimination of wastes from his body. You can help him by not making a fuss when your friend is incontinent and by simply accepting it as a part of the illness. It takes all your love and compassion to perform these services for someone.

If a person has control of his bodily functions but cannot get out of bed, try a urinal bottle for urine and a bedpan for bowel movements. To use a bedpan, have your friend roll gently onto his side, then put the bedpan under him and roll him back onto it. If he is stronger, you can have him lie on his back and slide the bedpan under him by helping him to raise his hips. *Be sure to use gloves during all these procedures.* Empty the bedpan and the urinal bottle into the toilet. Use wet paper towels or disposable washcloths to clean him up after a bowel movement. After washing him, it's a good idea to use a powder or cream to prevent his skin from becoming irritated.

If your friend has lost control of his bodily functions, buy disposable underpants and have him wear them. Also, place a disposable cotton pad under him in bed. Always try to be prompt and thorough in changing the pads when they are soiled. Of course, if your friend loses control of his bladder, his doctor can arrange to have a catheter inserted, but this is sometimes a painful procedure, and your friend may be even more uncomfortable and embarrassed with it than without it. Discuss this with your friend.

Bathing and Cleanliness

Your friend can become uncomfortable when he is not able to bathe regularly and when his bed does not seem fresh. One of the most sustaining things you can do for someone who is bedridden is to bathe him, brush his teeth, shave his face, dress him in clean clothes, put down fresh sheets, and even give him a manicure or pedicure. If your friend is a woman, you can also apply some makeup and do her hair. By doing these tasks, you can raise your friend's spirits tremendously.

Len describes how he and Evan handled cleanliness when Evan was in the hospital, still very sick and weak from PCP. "Evan didn't want to be bathed in bed, but he couldn't stand up in the shower. So we got a plastic chair and put it in the shower. He'd sit up on the edge of his bed, and I'd help him undress. Then he'd lean on me till he got to the chair in the shower. I always had the water going ahead of time to warm up the shower. I also didn't want to be adjusting the temperature of the water while he was sitting there. First I'd wet him.

169

Then I'd push the nozzle against the wall so he could soap himself. He always wanted to do everything that he could by himself. I certainly wasn't trying to make him more dependent on me. When he wanted to be rinsed, I'd aim the water back on him, and turn it off when he asked. Then he'd dry himself sitting there. Later, when he got stronger, he'd dry himself outside the shower. I can't tell you how proud we both were when two weeks later he took a shower by himself.''

If your friend cannot get out of bed, bathe him in bed. It is best to do this in the morning, and before changing the sheets. Use a cotton washcloth that is damp but not dripping wet; that way, the mattress will not get wet. Make sure that the room temperature is not too cool, and that the water in your bucket or pan is not too hot or cold. Use pure soap without deodorants or perfumes, as these additives are likely to dry the skin. First, have your friend lie on his stomach. Wash an area of his back, then dry it and cover it with a towel. When you are finished with the entire back of his body, rub on some skin cream to prevent drying. Then, help your friend to roll over, and wash the front of his body. Be sure to wash his genital area thoroughly, as this part of the body can become especially uncomfortable very quickly. Use powders here to prevent itching and rashes. When the bath is finished, help dress your friend in fresh garments.

Perhaps surprisingly, it is not difficult to change bed linen while someone is in a bed. If it is a large bed, help your friend roll over to one side. Beginning on the empty side of the bed, roll the used sheets toward the person's back. Replace them with clean sheets, and roll these toward the person's back. Then roll your friend onto the clean sheets, pull the old sheets off, and make the other side of the bed. If your friend's is a small bed, be very careful that he does not fall out. If his is a hospital bed, raise the side rails.

It's also important and helpful to assist your friend with brushing his teeth and cleaning his mouth. You can do this with a toothbrush and paste, but if that becomes too messy, use a cotton swab and a mild solution of hydrogen peroxide. If your friend has thrush, be sure to consult with his doctor about how best to clean his mouth for him.

Sometimes you may need to give your friend an alcohol bath to bring down fevers. To do this, put some alcohol, a little water, and some ice into a bowl. Rub the damp but not wet washcloth gently over his body. You will feel the heat being absorbed by the washcloth. Sometimes you must do this for a long time to reduce the fever. Bringing his fever down this way avoids having to administer drugs and may spare him the discomfort of having night sweats.

Grooming

Sometimes, when a person is sick for a long time, his hair grows long, his mustache or beard becomes unruly, and his fingernails and toenails become long and uncomfortable. You can contact your local AIDS agency to see if they have barbers who will come to cut your friend's hair. Even if you're no Vidal Sassoon, you can certainly trim your friend's toenails and fingernails and, if necessary, his hair. (If your friend is a woman, you can also shave her legs and under-arms—and perhaps keep a supply of her favorite body creams and fragrances nearby.) Remember, your friend may be quietly suffering and embarrassed because he cannot do these things for himself but still wants to look presentable, so be sure you do them as best you can, with compassion and love.

Howard describes how Alex felt when he became too weak to take care of himself: "You know, a lot of things that you and I take for granted, like putting on your socks or signing your name, have become an ordeal for him, and it's totally discouraging sometimes. How do we keep our spirits up? It's very difficult sometimes. He feels terrible, but he doesn't want to tell me. He's become so dependent. When I first knew him, he was the most independent of people, very strong-willed, very headstrong, and now he's become very dependent on me and on his mother. It's been very difficult for him. You really have to be very strong to change your entire life so drastically. One day, he complained that the tuna fish was too hard to mash. Watering the plants, cleaning the apartment—forget about those things. He'd be happy if he could dress himself."

Keeping Company

Intimacy takes myriad forms. You might sit with your friend in silence, or read to him as he listens or dozes, and feel yourself overflowing with different feelings: love, compassion, and pain. You might sit or lie on the bed and let your friend lean against you and hold you—or you might hold him—so that he feels secure and unafraid, or so that you are not so afraid. You might have moments of great closeness with each other. With so many barriers lowered, you can never be sure what will come up.

James and Earl found their relationship vastly changed as Earl became sicker. "You know, he and I sort of got wrapped up in the cocoon together, and everybody else who came into our lives just didn't seem to make a lot of difference. After he had toxoplasmosis, he came home and was such a mess. The nurse would come every day to give him his medicine, and this buddy from the agency would come to get him lunch. I put the phone right next to the bed so that he could get it, and I could call him from work during the day. But sometimes he couldn't pick up the phone, or he'd drop it, and then I'd be going crazy wondering if he was all right—but I couldn't just leave my job. We didn't need me on unemployment. Finally, I talked to a neighbor who was home most of the time, and I'd call her to go over to see him when I couldn't get him on the phone.

"Eventually, he and I pulled our beds together so that we were really sleeping together, and lots of times during the night I'd wake up and he'd be holding on to me. Once I woke up, and he was crying, and I said, 'Hey, what's this all about?' He began to tell me how he felt when we were kids and in high school, how sometimes he loved me so much it scared him, and other times he hated me because I always got everything and he got nothing. 'When you'd get those good grades and everyone would be saying how great you were, I'd just want to choke you right there.' I said to him, 'And when you did your thing playing basketball, and the girls would all be gathering around and everyone would be telling me my brother was so wonderful, I wanted to be somebody else.' Earl said to me, 'And now we got each other, and that's what we got.' He was crying. I just felt that I loved him so much."

"Bob started coming to see Gary not only on weekends but during the week sometimes," Linda explains. "He'd drive out on Wednesday evening, then get up very early on Thursday and drive back. He and Gary would just sit for hours talking and reading, and Bob would take care of him while he was there, giving everyone else, especially my mother, time off. She loved Bob and left them alone as much as they wanted, because you could see how important to them the time was that they had together."

"One weekend," Rose remembers, "Bob was visiting, and he was upstairs with Gary. Usually, I could hear them laughing and talking, but this day they seemed quiet and to be talking in soft tones. After a while, Gary called me to come upstairs. When I went into the room, I saw that both of them had tears in their eyes. 'What's going on here?' I asked. 'I've been trying to get him to talk about what's going to happen after I'm gone,' Gary said, 'and it just makes us both so sad. But we've got to talk about it. I need to talk about it. I need to be sure that he'll be all right when I'm gone.'

"In some ways, I felt like I didn't belong in this discussion," Rose says, "but I knew what Gary needed from me, even if he wasn't sure. I said to Bob, 'You're part of our family now. We love you like our own child. You'll always be welcome in this house, and I hope you'll spend holidays with us and things like that.' "

Religion

Perhaps you will find yourself going back to your church, synagogue, or other house of worship. You may not go for the reasons you remember as a child, but extraordinary times often cause us to look back for sources of comfort.

"We went to church this morning," Howard explains. "Although it's not my religion, we prayed. The first time Alex was in the hospital, I even went into a Roman Catholic church to say a prayer for him. If he could go, that's where he would go, so I was just acting as his messenger."

"I have a lot more faith in God now," Suzanne says. "I was quite angry before. As I became more and more tired, I really had to let go, and I just had to hand myself over. I began to see that it was going to be taken care of. Over and over again, I saw things fall into place, and they were taken care of. I was always afraid that Michelle would die without me there. Then Michelle said, 'It's going to be this week, Mom, and I would like you to be here more, because I know it's going to be this week.' I would have to have faith that God would see to it that I was there."

"Evan often goes with me to the Mass that Dignity holds every Saturday night, even though it's not his religion," Len says. "Dignity is the Roman Catholic organization for gay and lesbian people, and we found a lot of comfort there. People there know him from the hospital, and he always gets a warm and loving welcome. We started going maybe two months after he was diagnosed. I remember we went to the Mass on Christmas Eve, and I got such good feeling from that, seeing all these gay people praying together and being told that God loves them as much as He loves any of His children. I thought, 'Why have we allowed ourselves to be deprived of this experience, when we have such love to share?' "

Intimacy with Other Friends

Sometimes your friend has other friends, or relatives, who have stayed by his side through this long process. The same things will be happening in their relationships with your friend as are happening in yours. He may want to share his feelings and knowledge with them, too. Try to leave them alone as much as you can. Let your friends and family draw close to him if they wish. Often, your friend will find he has much to share and wants to share it with all those who are close to him. Be sure to allow it.

When Illness Grows More Severe

More frequent hospitalizations occur as the disease grows more severe and complex. Your friend may have two or more opportunistic infections at the same time; he may be taking an array of drugs that staggers the imagination, many of them toxic and/or experimental. As AIDS progresses, the medical interventions seem to become more desperate, less under control, as the doctors try everything in their attempts to do something to help.

You may be witnessing, slowly or rapidly, the decline of the person you love. You may see him becoming thinner and thinner. He may lose his hair, have terrible rashes, and be afflicted with chronic herpes sores and thrush. His body, which may once have been beautiful, may become little more than a skeleton with skin stretched over it. You will find that looking at your friend is not repulsive, only enormously sad and painful.

Besides the physical decline of your friend, you may begin to notice a mental deterioration as well. He may seem less alert, less able to find words, less interested in anything. All the physical and mental aspects of HIV disease can have a cumulative effect. Your friend may begin asking, "What's the point of living like this?" You may find yourself asking the same thing. There is no right answer. As always, this question and others like it are best dealt with by talking about them.

"John was just wasting away," Hugh explains, "and he was in terrible pain all the time. It was actually to the point that you could see the outline of his spine by looking at his stomach. For the most part, he was totally out of it. I couldn't even have a rational conversation with him anymore. And nothing that anyone was doing was doing him any good. There wasn't anything anyone could do for him. Frankly, the doctors got together with me and everyone else and in accordance with John's wishes, we just decided not to artificially prolong his life. We were going to stop all the medications."

Stella says, "David was so sick toward the end. He had cytomegalovirus in the lungs. His adrenal glands had shriveled up and stopped working. He also had toxoplasmosis, and that caused all kinds of brain problems. The part of his brain that controlled his temperature had just withered away. He had tuberculosis, and just a lot of lung stuff.

"I had decided I wouldn't let them put David on oxygen, or on a respirator, or on anything that would prolong his life artificially. At that hospital, when someone goes on a respirator, the family can't stay with them or anything. And I wasn't going to let them do that to David to prolong his life for just two days or so. He'd have been alone and frightened. David and I talked about it. We had already made up our minds before he got really, really bad that if it came down to the point where he was going to have to live on a respirator, he didn't want it. The only thing I couldn't do was let him die at home."

Suzanne describes Michelle when she finally agreed to go into the hospital: "She could barely walk at this point. She had kept herself going to work—God knows how she did it. When I look back on this, she must have known it in her heart. She did the things she wanted to do. She loved her job. She kept on going to work; she went to the office Christmas party. God, she was so thin and so frail. She was plagued by these huge herpes sores on her face. She tried to cover them with gauze bandage."

Michael explains how Joe was never really sick after his first bout with PCP. "What happened was that life was going on here much as usual, and we had gotten through the summer, and we were beginning to talk about what we were going to do, now that winter was coming. Because our house is a small place, and we knew we were going to be inside a lot, we wondered what improvements we needed to make to be more comfortable. Then Joe started to get little symptoms that something was wrong, like bleeding around his teeth and little blood specks where his capillaries were bursting. So they put him in the hospital, and we found that his platelets were down. I knew what platelets were. I didn't understand that you couldn't live without them. I don't think Joe did, either. He was scared shitless. When we brought him back to the hospital, he knew something was very wrong. We both thought, 'Okay, this is the first of those hospitalizations that are going to happen.' We talked about it, and we expected it. Now it's happened. They were going to put him in the hospital, torture him a little, then send him home a little weaker. And everything will be okay until it happens again.

"So we went on that assumption. He was only in the hospital seven days. But on the fifth day, things weren't happening the way they were supposed to. The situation wasn't getting any better, any clearer. The doctors didn't know why the platelets were down. They not only didn't know why it was happening but didn't know what to do about it, either.''

When Pain Overtakes Denial and Anger

As a caring friend, you will react at this stage of your friend's illness in very complex ways. On the one hand, you will be drawing closer to your friend. At the same time, being more intimate is causing you increasing pain. Moreover, it's becoming harder for you to deny that you are witnessing your friend's decline. For most, it will no longer be possible to rely on denial as a coping mechanism. Your pain is so great because you are realizing that you may soon lose a very important person in your life. Even though you are hurting, you should try to look inward to understand more precisely what you are feeling—and fearing—so that you can face your emotions directly.

Survivor's Guilt

You may feel guilt now, too. You are beginning to realize that you will survive this relationship. You probably know people, perhaps from a carepartners' group, who have already survived the death of loved ones who had AIDS. Now that you have had to face a serious illness and the prospect of death and dying as realities, you will probably realize—consciously or unconsciously—that nearly every person who dies has someone who loves him intensely, much as you love your friend. You should also try to keep strongly in mind that these other people survived the loss. They suffered, but their lives continued.

You should also know that it is okay to go on with your life. At times, particularly when a friend is extremely ill or has recently died, many people feel that they don't have any right to happiness, or love, or any of the good things in life. Think for a moment. Would your friend want you to suffer in your life on account of his illness? After you have given so much, would your friend expect you to deny yourself some simple pleasures and rewards? We rather doubt it.

Separation

You must look after yourself, even as you see your friend slipping from you. Of course, you are taking the best possible care of your friend. Of course, you are loving him to the best of your ability and will continue to be here, holding him, touching him, telling him you love him, no matter what. But you may begin not just to feel but to fear and dread that you are going to lose this person. You may fear not just the loss but the resulting emptiness in your life. After all, you know that you are—and have been for a long time—spending enormous amounts of time and energy dealing with your friend's illness. What will you do with that time and energy if you do not have your friend to care for? You may have heard from other carepartners and friends about the great void they felt when their friend died.

So you begin now to build bridges across that canyon. These bridges may take a thousand forms: new and old friends, work, places to go to feel and be yourself, volunteer activities, family, whatever you need. You are consciously aware that you are turning outside the relationship to meet your future needs. Your friend is not included in these plans. Remember, you are doing this for your own well-being, although sometimes you may not feel good about it.

Pain and Sadness

However intense your pain and sadness, these feelings are natural. You may have to turn to others to express these feelings: a friend, a family member, or a therapist. You shouldn't be afraid to express your sadness or pain. You need to vent these profound emotions. They are certainly not a sign of weakness. Actually, when you allow yourself to recognize these emotions in whatever way you choose, you will feel stronger afterward.

Anger

You *may* be so filled with emotion for your friend, with gratitude toward those friends and family who have supported you, that you find you have little room for anger toward those who have abandoned you or toward the disease itself. Or you may find that as your friend's illness progresses, so, too, does your anger at the disease, at your friend's imminent departure, at the medical establishment, and at the government. Pay attention to these feelings, expressing them in as constructive a way as possible.

Sharing with Your Friend

If previously you had resentment toward your friend because you were carrying more and more of the relationship, that, too, may be fading into the background. Now you accept him at exactly the point where he is, and you ask him for whatever support you need that he is capable of giving. You may need only for him to touch you, to tell you that he still loves you. When decisions have to be made, consult with him, because at this time he may be feeling—he may well *know*—that he has less and less power over his illness, and consequently less control over his life. Help him to feel that he has as many choices as possible. And when he can make decisions, by all means stay on the sidelines.

"When Bruce went into the hospital that August," Jack says, "he had so many problems that it was hard to believe he was still alive. He had tried chemotherapy for the lymphomas for a while, but everything just came apart. In no time, he could hardly breathe, and they started treating him for the *pneumocystis* again. He'd been in the hospital two days when Dr. Bill came in and asked, 'If it comes down to it, do you want us to use a respirator?' Bruce responded, 'What does that mean?' 'It means,' Dr. Bill said, 'that if you can't breathe on your own, then we'll hook you up to a machine that can breathe for you. Tell me later what you want to do,' Dr. Bill said, and he left the room. 'You take a walk, too,' Bruce said to me. 'I need some time to myself.'

"So I went down the hall to the phone, and I called Bruce's brother, and I told him what was happening and asked him to come down. 'Of course,' he said, 'I'll leave on the first plane I can get.' He hesitated for a moment. 'If something should happen to him before I get there, I wouldn't put him on that machine,' he said. 'It's a terrible thing. They did that to our father when he had cancer. He was conscious, and was hurting real bad, and he couldn't talk, and he kept looking at us, with his eyes begging for something. And his wife—not my mother—and I finally figured out that he wanted off that horrible machine. But Bruce should do what he wants.'

"With his brother on the way, I went back to Bruce's room. He didn't move when I came in, and he was lying there with his eyes closed. I pulled a chair up next to the bed and sat on the arm of it and put my head lightly on his stomach and my arms sort of around him. He didn't say anything to me but began stroking my hair and my neck. I wouldn't let them put him on a respirator."

At this time, your friend's health proxy and living will become paramount. If your friend remains conscious and alert, the two of you should discuss any impending medical decisions. If he can participate in the decisions concerning life-support systems, you will be less likely to have regrets later about the choices you made together.

If your friend is not able to participate in decisions at this time, you should attempt to follow his previously stated directives as closely as possible. Remember: At this juncture, you are his only voice.

"When I went to the hospital the next day," says Michael, "Joe told me that the doctor didn't know what was causing his platelet count to be so low, and there was nothing they could do about it. I burst into tears and hugged Joe, and we cried. That was the only time we cried together. And I told Joe that I didn't want him to die. So we just held each other and cried. Then the doctor came back into the room, and we had a replay of her conversation, only this time she outlined all the procedural alternatives. Joe took her through each situation, coming to the same conclusion for each: None of them would make any difference. So he said, 'I just want to let nature take its course.' Joe was not going to fight the inevitable at that point."

Unresolved Issues

In every relationship, there may be many issues between you that you have not forthrightly discussed, for whatever reason. These could be as important as a problem you may have had with your families, an affair that hurt one or the other of you, or the disposition of a favorite object that you owned together. There may be times when your friend will want to talk about these things. If so, allow him. Let him resolve as many of these issues as he can. Talk about anything and everything your friend wants to, even if it is painful to you, so that both of you feel at ease and at peace with each other. The more of these issues that are resolved, the more accepting each of you will be. Sometimes it is extremely difficult for an ill person to let go, no matter how desperately sick he is, if he feels he is leaving behind a lot of unfinished business. You, too, may feel the need for closure on some long-standing issues. Pursue them, gently and at the appropriate time. Use your best judgment about when to bring up difficult matters.

Considering Suicide

As the illness progresses, some carepartners will be faced with yet another agonizing situation: Their loved one is considering suicide. There are many reasons an individual might contemplate taking his life: He may feel he is too exhausted to continue the fight against the virus; the pain and suffering might simply be too much for him to bear; his quality of life might be so compromised by the effects of the disease on his body that he sees no reason to live. For the carepartner, the idea of exploring the possibility of suicide is frightening. It's one thing to watch a loved one die. It's another thing to know he is going to take his own life, and still another if he asks for your assistance in devising his plan.

If your friend begins to talk about suicide, the best thing to do is to listen and talk with him. Encourage him to put forth all the pros and the cons. Try to get him to see the longer view, if, in fact, there is one. Perhaps, even in spite of his pain, he can still take pleasure from a lot of his life. Bring others into the conversation, if that is possible: family members, medical professionals, a therapist. Talk it through. Make sure he knows what he is contemplating.

If your friend asks you to assist him with his suicide—for instance, by collecting certain medications for him—you must be honest with him about your feelings. This is not a transitory situation, but one that will have ramifications for years on the carepartner. Moreover, assisting in a suicide can be construed as illegal. You must not face this issue alone. We strongly advise that if a carepartner or other friend is asked to participate in a suicide attempt, professional help should be sought.

If You Are HIV-Positive

Issues of loss, separation, and the pain involved in watching someone you care about grow more ill will be exacerbated for you if you, too, are HIV-infected. As you watch your friend become sicker, your own fears may increase as well. You will worry more about your own health, about the prospect of facing your own possible illness without your friend's care. You must remember that his illness is not a blueprint for your own. Your health, your hopes, and your body will all be different. Try not to identify too closely with your friend. Take care of yourself. Listen to your inner voice, which will help you maintain your own balance and perspective. Rely on your friends and family for your support. Above all, don't neglect tending to yourself at this crucial time—your health, your mental well-being, the systems and attitudes that have sustained you.

How to Deal with Your Friend's Feelings

As your friend becomes sicker, he, too, may begin to allow himself to confront the reality of what is happening. His denial may diminish considerably; often, he will face the facts before you do. Sometimes, as people with AIDS begin to face the possibility of their own deaths, they try to prepare and even protect their carepartner or friend. They may make jokes about their death. They may refer to your life and what it will be like after they are gone. In the beginning, you need to respond with great diplomacy when your friend does this, because he may be testing you, wanting you to tell him that he is not going to die. You want to hold out hope, yet you want to help your friend and yourself come to terms with the facts of the situation. But he may move past the point of testing the waters with you; he may want to discuss the possibility of his death with you. You will have to be careful and perceptive in gauging your friend's motivations for talking about dying.

Your friend may also need reassurance that you will be all right should he die. He may be afraid for you after he is gone—and he could easily be as worried about you as you are about him.

"Earl started saying things to me," James says, "and I made like I didn't understand at first. But he wanted me to listen. 'This is getting too hard to do,' he told me once, out of nowhere. And I didn't hear him. 'You got to get yourself ready,' he said to me another time, and I just did what I was doing. But one day we had to talk. When we got down to it, he told me that he had to go, but he was scared for me. 'I don't have any memory that you're not there,' he said. 'I can't put your picture together in my head and I'm not there. But that's got to be.' I couldn't talk to him about that. 'I hear you,' I said. 'I've been hearing you all along.' "

The Emotional Stages of Dying

You may witness your partner going through the emotional stages of a dying person. These stages were originally described by Dr. Elisabeth Kübler-Ross, who has worked with hundreds of dying people. In her book *On Death and Dying,* Kübler-Ross described a process that many people go through as they approach death. Of course, such stages overlap, and people may move from one stage to another and then back again. Not all people will go through all stages. Certainly, no one *has* to. Remember, too, that these stages are very similar to what *you* may be going through as you face the approaching loss of your friend. The stages are denial and isolation, anger, bargaining, depression, and acceptance. What follows is a brief description of each, how you can help your friend through the stage, and how knowledge of the stages can help you.

Denial

When your friend was first given the diagnosis, denial was probably a big part of his reaction, and yours. Denial protected you both from a reality that was too painful to accept. By now, your friend has probably long since accepted the fact that he has AIDS, as have you, but denial of death can still be very powerful. "No, this can't be getting so serious," he'll say. "Let's try another treatment. Let's call in another doctor." As the reality of the illness grows stronger, you may discover that your friend becomes quiet, sullen, and even withdrawn. He doesn't want to talk about anything much. He may just be numb. You, too, may be numb. If so, let it be. This phase may pass for both of you, but it doesn't have to. Many people have died denying that death could happen to them. Denial is some people's way of coping with death.

Just let your friend know that you are there. It will be more painful for you if your friend remains in denial, but do not try to bring him out of it unless he is in great emotional or physical pain or is making decisions that could jeopardize his well-being. If this is the case, get professional help. But stay calm. Go off and cry now and again if you feel the need. Try to have friends and family be there to support both of you at this time.

Anger

Denial is often replaced with anger. Your friend may be asking, "Why is this happening to me?" and, in the process, striking out at whoever is close by. Your friend may accuse you of not caring for him; he may accuse the medical profession of killing him. He may hurt you and everyone who has stood by him.

Allow him this anger. Try not to be hurt or to strike back. Most of all, try not to take it personally. Your friend feels angry because he is afraid of dying, and he focuses his anger on you because you are there. Try to empathize. Say, "You have a right to be angry. Being angry may help you. Go ahead and yell at me." But look out for yourself. If you can't take the anger any longer, then withdraw for a while. Simply say, "Your anger is too much for me right now. I'll come back later when I feel stronger." You, too, may be feeling great anger, wondering why you must lose someone you love so much. But you know there is no answer to this question. If possible, go to a place where you can express your anger and other feelings—to your therapist, carepartner, group, or a good friend.

Bargaining

This is a brief stage during which someone who is very ill seems to take a step in the direction of accepting what is happening but is actually grasping at straws to prevent the change. "If this doesn't happen to me, then I'll spend all my life taking care of other sick people." Or "I just want to live until the end of winter. I want to see one more spring." Your friend might seem peaceful at this point. Enjoy this time together, and let him bring up any issues or problems that he wants resolved.

Depression

When your friend stops bargaining and knows that he is dying, he may become extremely depressed: "So this is going to happen to me after all." He is sad, overcome with a great sense of loss. The depression may arise when your friend looks back at all the things he has left undone and sees empty spots in people's lives that he will not be there to fill. He may be very depressed that he is so thin, that he always feels so tired, that a new symptom appears all too often. Try to help him overcome this depression by assuring him that you're there for him, by complimenting him in any way you can, and providing much-needed perspective when appropriate.

The other part of this depression, according to Kübler-Ross, derives from your friend's acknowledgment that he is about to lose everything he has and knows: life, you, his friends, his family, everything. We can only imagine how great this sense of impending loss must feel to him by comparing our own reaction to the loss of only one person in our lives. His is a preparatory depression, a grief over the loss of life and relationships. You, too, may feel this great depression as you prepare yourself for the loss of your friend.

Allow your partner to be sad. Don't try to cheer him up, but sit with him and allow him to express his sorrow. Hold his hand, and if he wants to be quiet and doesn't want other visitors distracting him, then follow his wishes.

Allow yourself to be sad, too. Sit quietly. Try to be there as much as possible, and if you need company, ask your friend if you can have someone sit with you in the room. Tell him that you love him and you understand how he feels. Touch him a lot. Your friend's death may be weeks or months away, but he knows it is coming. So do you.

Acceptance

Often, when someone accepts his approaching death, it is like a giant sigh of relief. "Okay, so it's going to happen to me." Your friend is no longer depressed or angry, nor is he devoid of feeling. He is more at peace, calmer, quieter, more concerned with what's going on inside himself than what's going on outside. Your response is to be there. Hold his hand. Reassure him that you will be okay and that you're there for him.

When the Crisis Comes

Everything in this section that has been addressed to carepartners and caring friends applies as well to all friends of someone with AIDS. It may become very difficult and painful for you to stay around when you are told that your friend is dying. Your instinct may be to run away, to hide, and to emerge again when it is all over. Try not to. Your friend needs you.

Please be careful as you read the remainder of this chapter. You may find some of the information and personal stories too painful to read right now, and not immediately helpful. Read these sections only when you need to—only when facts and testaments about death can strengthen and sustain you.

If someone with AIDS asks you to sit with him as a life-threatening crisis comes, or if his carepartner asks you to be with him, try to be there. Despite your fear, you know that you have been asked to enter the most intimate chambers of someone's existence, to share a most profound time and experience.

James was terrified as he saw Earl dying in the hospital. "He had been paralyzed almost completely for two weeks, and I couldn't stand what was happening to him. He had stopped eating, and they had a feeding tube down his throat. He had huge bedsores on his butt and on his shoulders and heels and elbows. I spent all my time there when I wasn't working. I even slept there on the floor. Finally, I couldn't do it alone anymore. I told Earl that I needed someone there, and he signaled with his eyes that he was okay. We didn't have many friends, but I called my friend Emma, who used to look in on him during the day for me. She didn't hesitate. 'I'll be right there,' she said. When Emma came, we went to the visitors' lounge awhile, and I cried. You know, Emma never left his room without asking Earl first, and she stayed there all day while I was working. In two weeks, I came to love her as much as I ever loved anyone."

Your friend needs to know that you are there, that you can be counted on. He needs you to touch him, to hold him, to comfort him, to fuss over him.

When Your Friend Approaches Death

At some point, you will know that a crisis has arrived. You will feel it. The doctors will inform you. At that point, tell everyone who should be told. If possible, talk to your friend about what is happening. Tell him that you would like some visitors to be with you. Ask him whom he wants to be there. Most people are aware when they are dying, even if only in the back of their minds, so your friend will know what you are talking about when you ask whom he wants you to call. If he doesn't seem to recognize how much in crisis he is, then, of course, don't alarm him.

If you and your friend have been largely abandoned by family and have few friends you can call upon, then contact your local hospice program or your local AIDS organization for support. Or you may choose to be alone with your friend, sharing one-on-one not just the pain but the intimacy.

Although your friend is very sick and may be suffering greatly, he may cling to life. Sometimes he may repeat over and over that he loves you because he may know he is going to leave you and feels guilty about it. He may need assurance that you will be all right, that you do not want him to stay and suffer on your account. Many times he needs to know that it is okay for him to go.

Deciding Where He Is to Die

Sometimes you must decide where your friend should die—at home or in the hospital. This is an important and sometimes very difficult decision to make, particularly if your friend prefers to die at home. Because caring for a dying person is all-consuming, many carepartners decide that is not possible for them to continue their own lives and at the same time allow for their partner to die at home.

Nowadays, many people are choosing hospice care. Hospices, which exist either on a residential basis or through a home-care program, attempt to make patients comfortable physically, emotionally, and spiritually. According to Gay Men's Health Crisis:

> Hospice philosophy is based on the belief that death is a part of life, and it encourages the individual to focus on those

185

aspects of life which are most meaningful. Hospice care concentrates on relief from pain and support for the individual's emotional and spiritual needs. The individual has the opportunity to reflect on life in a way that creates a sense of peace. And hospice [care] allows a person to meet life's end in a more peaceful manner than might otherwise be possible.

If you want more information about hospice care, contact your local AIDS agency or hospice.

Following are some experiences with death:

Michael: "I'll never forget the end. Our friend Cecile came to visit Joe for a while. He got to say good-bye to Cecile. Some people called. He made some phone calls. He spoke to his sister, who was racked with guilt, and tried to make her feel better. We got through the night. He got progressively weaker and weaker, and it became apparent that the estimate of two weeks was wrong. I didn't know how short a period of time it was going to be, but Joe seemed to know. After the third day he said, 'I can feel the energy leaving my body.' I realized that he was not speaking about something metaphorical, but he was indeed describing an actual physical sensation of energy leaving his body. I felt just the opposite of what Joe was feeling. I felt energy pouring into my body from every available corner of the universe.

"Our communication became very basic. We didn't talk about anything. He'd ask for a drink of water. He said he felt sorry for his sister, and he cried about her. But I just sort of helped him through the night. He began to have physical pain. His stomach was hemorrhaging and that was causing a lot of pressure in his bowels, and it hurt him.

"Then, in the morning, his father called. Joe spoke to him and said good-bye. I was totally exhausted; my eyes were burning. I was drained, and I didn't know what was going on because we had made it through the night and it was day again, even though Joe was as weak as a newborn kitten.

"Then, out of the blue, I started having a lot of anxiety about our friend Mark. He and Joe go back a long, long way. The two of them had had a falling out, but they had been patching it up over the summer. Still, Joe didn't trust Mark to be able to deal with the situation, and had sort of kept him away. I knew Mark was afraid, but that he could deal with it. So finally I said to Joe, 'I'm really uncomfortable about something. I think we need to attend to it now.' And

186

Joe said, 'I'm okay,' in a weak voice. And I said, 'Not you, dummy, it has nothing to do with you. It's Mark. I think we should tell Mark what is going on right now.' 'If you have to,' Joe said. So I called Mark up and he said he was coming right over.

"Once Mark got there, Joe opened his eyes—they were sort of rolling around in his head—then he focused on us, and he saw Mark and asked, 'What are you doing here?' Still, he seemed to understand what was going on. They held hands for a while. Not a word was said. Then he closed his eyes and went back to sleep, and his breathing just got softer and softer. And we were crying and amazed, and Mark informed me later that I kept saying, 'This is so beautiful.' He understood what I meant.

"And then Joe stopped breathing. It was hard to say which was his last breath. It was as peaceful as it could be. And then it was over. He wasn't there anymore. Whatever it means to be dead, it had happened to Joe."

Suzanne: "Michelle died a terrible, terrible death. She began to decay, although she was still living. The night before she died, we had asked the night nurse not to turn her again, because we were so sure she was about to die, and it was so upsetting to watch them do it. It seemed to hurt her so much.

"But the next morning, they had to turn her; she had not died. The nurses who had the day off were calling in to find out how Michelle was, and they were terribly distraught. Even one of the doctors cried. Michelle was such a little girl at this point. She weighed maybe seventy or eighty pounds. But amazingly, she still talked. She kept repeating over and over that she loved us.

"The nurses told me to go. They said, 'You're keeping Michelle here. You're making it harder for her to go.' I said, 'I can't go home. I can't leave now. . . .' But sometimes you have to go away and leave them alone. I thought about Michelle and how she had to go upstairs and listen to music and be alone, and that made sense in the overall picture of her life. So I told my other daughter, Camille, that she had to lie down and I would lie down, too. So we lay down on the cot that was in her room, out of Michelle's sight, and I put my arms around her and we went to sleep.

"The last night that Michelle was alive, before I went to sleep, her fever went up to a hundred and five. The nurse was very busy. She had three people on respirators. She was out of her mind. So she set me up with alcohol and all these things, and I washed Michelle and washed her and washed her, with ice and alcohol. I wanted her to die a peaceful death. None of us could cope with this otherwise. I finally got her fever down. The nurse kept coming in and trying to help me. 'I know what I'm doing,' I said. 'Go take care of those other people.' Finally, I said to Michelle, 'You're too sick now. I don't want you to stay. I want you to go.' I knew she could hear me. Then I just lay down and went to sleep.

"When Bob, my husband, woke me up, Michelle was dying. Her hands just unfolded, and she stopped breathing, very peacefully."

Jack: "Bruce's brother Clive had been with us for a couple of days. He stayed in the hospital during the day while I was at work, then he'd leave when I got there after work with the car, and he'd come back about eleven and send me home. He slept on a cot in Bruce's room. Clive looked just like Bruce—this big man who didn't have a pretension in the world. He was a straight man with a wife and two children, but he didn't seem to have any opinion about the relationship between Bruce and me. About all he said to me was 'My brother tells me you been real fine to him, caring for him and all that, and I want you to know that me and my family are real grateful.'

"But one night, after Clive had come back to the hospital, Bruce asked me not to leave. 'I want you here tonight,' he said. 'Both of you. Something's happening. I'm scared.' I think at that moment both his brother and I knew that he was going to die that night. But I was suddenly terrified. I felt my skin crawl. Was he really telling us that was it? What about finishing the work on the house? What about us? So I went down to the lounge and got a comfortable chair and brought it to his room and put it right next to the bed so I could hold his hand. I took off my shoes and tried to get comfortable. When the nurse came by, she brought me a blanket.

"And that's how the night began. Sometime later, when there was only the light in the hall, and the hospital and the world outside were as quiet as the desert at midnight—I was sort of dozing—I heard Bruce sort of gasp, first softly, then loudly, and then he squeezed my hand. I jumped up and saw that he was wide awake. Clive jumped up, too, and turned on a light. Bruce was trying to get his breath. He whispered in my ear, 'Get someone to help me.' His brother went to the door. 'You stay here,' he said to me. 'I'll get help.' So I heard him go down the hall, and I grabbed Bruce and held him because he had begun to go into convulsions. Then I started to cry and I kept saying over and over again, 'I love you, Bruce. I love you, man.' He went limp in my arms.

"Before I realized what had happened to him, all hell broke loose in the room. It was the respiratory team or some group like that that went into action when someone died; I think they tried to revive him. So they shoved me and Clive out of the room, and we both stood there in the hall while all the noise and activity went on in the room.

"After a few minutes, they came out of the room and told us he was gone. Clive rushed back into the room, but a nurse grabbed my arm and pulled me to one side. 'I just wanted to tell you Bruce was dead when we got in there. I want you to know that he died in your arms. I hope, when my time comes, I have someone like you who loves me like you loved him.' Clive and I sat and talked to him awhile. In a while, Clive said, 'I've got to call my wife.' He got up and left the room."

Stella: "I was probably more prepared for David's death than most people. I was prepared by the nurses for every step of David's dying before it happened. When it got down to the last days, they said, 'Do you want to be with him when he dies?' I said, 'David and I started this together by ourselves, and we'll end it together by ourselves.' It was my request that I be in the room by myself with David when he died. That was my time. It took David eighteen hours to die, and I stood by the bed and held him for eighteen hours. Some of his family was there, and of course they poked their heads in and all that. They let me know they were there. But it was my time with him. I told him how much I loved him. I told him how much I cared. I told him I was going to take care of our kids. 'When these girls grow up, I'm going to tell them what a good daddy they had. And I'm going to tell them how proud you were of your girls. The one thing I'll always teach my kids is never, ever, feel degraded because your dad had AIDS—to hold your head up and be proud of your dad.' I said, 'I'll tell them that. You'll never have to worry about that.' About an hour before David died, they came in and told me I could change my mind and put David on a respirator. I said, 'No way.'

"David was in a coma for most of the eighteen hours it took him to die. It was pretty rough because he started having really, really bad seizures. But he could be having a really bad seizure, and I could still talk to him. Then he'd calm down. I always let David know that I loved him.

"David had a close friend, Les, who was a state trooper. They were raised together, went all through school together; he was just like a brother. . . . For those eighteen hours David was dying, I kept praying, 'Just let him live. Just let him live a little while longer.' We called Les. But right before he got there, I started praying for God just to take David on. He'd suffered enough. And when he heard Les's

189

voice, David died. It was like he was waiting for Les to come to take care of me and the kids before he died.''

Fran: ''On Thanksgiving Day 1992, a day I will always remember, I lost my friend Larry. The day began with those of us who loved him gathering at his home to support him and one another. Throughout the day, Larry remained unconscious. Even though we were all aware of his impending death, we feared the inevitable. There was never a moment when someone was not overwhelmed with emotions.

''As much as we were there for Larry's departure, we offered much support and strength to one another through our caring and how intensely we held each other.

''Letting go of Larry, who was always so full of life, was a very difficult thing to do but the greatest gift we could give him. There would be no more hospitals, toxic medications, I.V.'s, or sickness. He would finally be relieved of pain and at peace with himself, his life, and God.

''It was hard to recognize that we could not save Larry but could only fulfill his wish to allow him to die with dignity. Carrying out Larry's desire to die in the comfort of his own home, in his own bed, were his dear friends and his lover of twelve years. Larry was surrounded by eleven people, three animals, candlelight, and soft music. We all encircled his bed, observing every breath and sigh.

''The vulnerability that we all shared with one another and Larry was incredibly beautiful and serene. In the process of letting Larry go, our fear and anger were replaced with strength and faith. We stroked and kissed Larry, guiding him on his journey.

'' 'We love you, Larry.'

'' 'Follow the light.'

'' 'You are safe.'

'' 'You are on your way home now.'

''Larry's life was about laughter, music, theater, friendship, energy, spirituality, and overall acceptance of others. With Larry's last hour of life, he created a powerful bond that will somehow always connect us all and keep Larry's memory alive forever.

''Bill, one of the authors of this book and a loving carepartner, deserves to be commended for the courage, devotion, and love he shared with Larry, always.''

10

RESOLUTION: CONQUERING YOUR GRIEF AND LOSS

When you suffer the loss of someone very close to you, you will probably go into a state of shock and denial. It may last for several days and to some degree for weeks and months. Your mind rejects reality. You want to believe there's been some mistake, that this whole episode will turn out to be a bad dream. This is how many people cope with the beginning of grief.

Even in shock, however, people's reactions are as different as their personalities. You may burst into tears; you may grab the person closest to you and hug him fiercely; you may need to leave the room because you can't breathe; you may feel faint or dazed. Or you may feel very calm, relieved, peaceful, and even thankful that your friend will suffer no more. There is no way to predict what your reaction will be. But from the time of death through to resolution, your grief is *your* grief.

People have been suffering the loss of loved ones since they first learned to love, but still, after thousands of years, each person's grief is always new. Below, some of our friends share their early grief:

Hugh: "John had been lingering between life and death for almost two weeks. Every day, someone different in the hospital would tell me he was going to die that day. 'It's going to be today,' they would

191

say. But one day I went to the hospital around noon and the nurse, Ellen, was crying. She said, 'You better come quick.' I knew she meant that John was dying. And I knew she was right.

"I called our friend Armando and I said, 'Come to the hospital, because John's going to need some help. He's dying.' Armando came and put candles all around the room and then lit them. He even put a tape of some medieval chants on. It was really beautiful. I was in such turmoil that I had to go out and walk. I got back to the hospital a half hour later, just as John died. His eyes were wide open, looking straight up. I was glad for John. He looked unbelievable, so gorgeous. Edith, the nurse who had disconnected all the tubes from John's neck that night, was sobbing. She wanted to close his eyes, but I wouldn't let her. I just stayed in the room, and it was the time when the hospital shift changed, so everyone was there. In a little while, a lot of John's friends started coming by. The nurses said, 'Hugh, why don't you let us change him?' I told them, 'Go ahead and change him.' They said, 'No, we don't want you here. It's bad enough. Go down the hall, and let us get him cleaned up, and then you can come back and be with him.'

"I went down the hall, and I wasn't crying. I felt this incredible relief. I wanted to let people know John died. I called his mother, but she wasn't home. I called his brother. Then I went back to the room. Soon, everybody left, one by one. Finally, I was able to talk to John. I felt very good, you know. I didn't feel terribly sad. Then I went downstairs to the chaplain's office and talked to the chaplain about having the funeral there."

Jack: "I was never a man with a lot of words, but, you know, a carpenter has a lot of time to think about things while he works. I'd thought a lot about Bruce and what we had together and about his sickness. Right after he died, there were just a lot of things I wanted to tell him, I needed to tell him, because I hurt so much. I was in the room with Bruce alone. I felt as if he were still there in some way, but I could see that his body was dead, because the blood vessels in his arm began to change. 'I'll never forget you,' I said, almost in a whisper in his ear, 'not now, not in ten years. I love you, big Mister. You're the man who taught me how to love a man.' I kept thinking about his swagger, about how big and handsome he was, and how proud he was to be a tough man from the Panhandle. I said to him, 'I keep thinking how proud you were of me. You always made sure that everywhere we went, everybody knew we were a couple. I was proud just to be with you, to know that you were mine and you loved me and didn't want anyone else. We had something special. I want to thank you for that, and to tell you that I forgive you for all the times you were a pain in the ass and a big baby.'

"Then I started to cry a little, and I told him how sorry I was about all the camping trips we wouldn't be taking together, all the little projects we wouldn't finish, all the times we wouldn't spend holding each other in bed, and all the pain he had suffered, and that he had died when he was so young. 'You know what's in my heart for you, Bruce, and that my heart just aches and aches and aches. I love you. I love you with my whole heart.'

"I stayed there, crying a little now and then, until the nurses came to wrap him in gauze. I didn't want to stay for that. I went down the hall and talked to his mother for a while, then we drove to my house. In a little while, a few of my friends arrived, and they sat by the bed that Bruce and I used to sleep in, and I lay there and cried and cried. I needed to do that, and I needed them to be there while I did it. Around noon, the four of us went to get some lunch. We hadn't even had breakfast.''

Dealing with Practical Matters

Immediately after your friend's death, even while you are still in shock, you may have to deal with many practical matters, especially if you have been the primary caregiver. Most of these you will do almost automatically. You should take advantage of those around you—both for emotional support as well as to perform specific tasks. These are some items that will need to be taken care of, either by you or someone designated by you:

Top Priority

- *Make arrangements with a funeral home* or for a memorial service. Make sure you have chosen the clothes in which you want the body seen and buried or cremated.
- *Arrange to get the death certificate,* in multiple copies, if possible. You will need many copies for numerous tasks later on, like collecting insurance and closing bank accounts. They must all be stamped and signed by the coroner's office. This matter is usually handled by the funeral director.
- *Begin to notify people.* Call family, friends, co-workers, anyone who you think should know of the death. Be sure to call people who will help you. You will need people around for yourself. And even if it is painful to discuss the death of your

friend, it will grow easier with repetition; repetition will become part of the grief process and help you accept your friend's death. You'll be grateful for the loving contact of others around you.

- *Contact the executor of the will,* if it is someone other than yourself.
- *Arrange for the burial or cremation,* and for any needed transportation if the body will be buried in another town or state (if this is a task you are called upon to do).
- *Prepare an obituary.*

Over the next few days, there will be other duties to perform. You can do them yourself, or people who are helping you can do them for you.

Other Tasks

- *Order flowers* if you choose.
- *Arrange for donations* to be made to a charity in your friend's name.
- *Prepare the eulogy.*
- *Plan to have food at your home* for those who will be coming by after the service.
- *Arrange accommodations* for people who are coming from out of town.

Later, when there is time, you or the executor will have to:

- *Contact insurance companies.*
- *Contact the utility company.*
- *Contact all people to whom your friend owed debts.*
- *Make appropriate arrangements with your friend's landlord.*

There will, of course, be a thousand other things to do, especially if you lived with your friend or were his primary caregiver. You may have to see to the disposal of his clothing and furniture, his papers, medicines, and other personal belongings. This may be a very difficult and painful task, and you may prefer to put it off, as if disposing of the deceased's belongings is disposing of the person himself. But you can draw strength from all these small duties, and however difficult the ritual may be, sometimes it is an opportunity to remember your friend fondly and to ease yourself through grief. Don't hesitate to have close friends or family members assist you during this painful period.

Grief as a Process

Grief is a process of healing. It is a painful process that you may try to avoid but cannot. The more you try to avoid grief, the longer your mourning can take, and the longer your wounds will take to heal. It's hard to allow yourself to feel pain, because nature tells you that pain means something is wrong, and that you should be doing something immediately to relieve it. But this is a time where you must, for your own benefit, allow yourself the pain. Here's some of what you may experience:

Tears

You may remain in a state of shock through the funeral and during the period immediately after, when there are still many people around. Occasionally, during this time, you may cry and otherwise be able to express your sorrow and pain. Many people, especially men, have been told since childhood that crying is a sign of weakness, but crying is actually a sign of health and grieving. You need to cry because you hurt, and tears are a means of relieving hurt and tension. If you can cry with friends, that is fine. If you cry alone, that also is fine. Do not feel ashamed.

Remember, too, that you can't and shouldn't cry and mourn all the time. Even in the first days, there will be times when you and your friends and family will laugh and have fun remembering the person who is gone—and when, perhaps to your own surprise, your life seems to resume of its own accord. You may think this is strange, but it is entirely natural. If you feel angry with the person who has left you, that is common, too. Most people suffering a loss feel this anger at one time or another. You may even feel that your friend has abandoned you. You might think, "If he truly loved me, he wouldn't have left me like this." Express this anger. Get it out and over with.

Sitting on a sofa, with his elbows on his knees and his head in his hands, James cried, "Damn you, Earl. Damn you for your rotten habits. Damn you for getting this disease. Damn you for putting us through this. Damn your leaving me now. Damn you for making me feel so alone."

195

Emptiness

When a person dies, carepartners, family members, and friends feel an intense void. Until the death, your life had been filled with activity and urgency; you were constantly concerned with caring for your sick friend. Suddenly, that's over. Now vast periods of time in the day are empty. You may feel that you have nothing to do, nowhere to go. This sudden vacuum in your life can create another source of pain and sorrow.

"It got to the point, just a few days after John was buried," Hugh recalls, "that I started having panic attacks, like I was going to die or something. I couldn't even leave the house to walk down the street. I couldn't sleep. I couldn't believe it. I honestly couldn't believe that all that had happened. I would lie in bed, playing it over and over and over and over. The situation had been twenty-four hours a day, and suddenly I had nothing—even though I had a million other things to do. It was my job for eight months, and it was over. I felt totally alone."

Preoccupation

This sense of emptiness can lead to your own preoccupation with the image of the deceased. You might hear his voice, or feel his presence in the room, or see him looking through the curtains as you come up to your house. You might see him sitting in his favorite chair, petting the dog, or catch a glimpse of him in the supermarket. You might smell him in his clothes and be very reluctant to throw away any of his possessions. You might find yourself looking into a room to see if he is there. In your mind, you know that he is gone. But however difficult and painful it seems, these images help you to get accustomed to your loss. You are not crazy. You are not losing your mind. The jolt you get makes your loss real to you, more manageable. If your preoccupation becomes inappropriate, someone will notice and say something to you. Or you may notice yourself.

"There are so many memories here in this house," Stella explains, "that we just can't live here anymore. We see David sitting on the couch. It took me up till two months ago to realize that David wasn't coming back. People might think I'm crazy, but it did. I can pull up in the driveway, and it seems like somebody opens the drapes. And at night, I can hear him walking around the house. But it's getting better than it was."

This is an intensely emotional period for you. You are searching for the absent person. Your feelings can range from relief or terror to profound loneliness over the loss. You may feel that your friend is reaching out to you.

"I must have been in our apartment a week after Earl died," James says, "when I realized I couldn't live there anymore. I could see Earl everywhere. I reached for him in bed. I'd wake up and hear him calling me to help him in the bathroom. I called our number during the day and let it ring. Every little thing was a picture of him. I'd get depressed just walking into the place, but I didn't have any money to move. My parents told me I should move, but I told them I couldn't and why. So without saying anything, they sent me a check with a letter, saying it was a loan that I could pay back when I could. I started looking that day for another apartment. It just needed to be. There was no other way to make a separation."

"I always loved my house," Jack explains. "After Bruce died, it was like a refuge to me. I used to love to go look at and touch the things that he'd worked on while he was sick. It was like he had made the place richer for me. He had put little bits of himself here and there. You know, he did everything his own way. I could say, 'No, Bruce, that's not how to miter a corner. Here's how.' Then I'd come home and see he'd mitered all the corners his own way. I love finding those Bruce things in the house now."

What If . . . ?

You may wonder if you did everything possible to help your friend to live. You may have a million "What if . . . ?" questions. You may also question whether you fulfilled all your friend's needs before his death. This experience of questioning is almost universal among carepartners and caring friends.

"I don't let a lot of things bother me, but there are a lot of issues I still wonder about," Jack says. "What if Bruce had stopped work earlier? What if we had tried one of the experimental drug programs? What if he'd just learned to take it easier, and not tried to do so much all the time? But I know we wouldn't do things different now than we did then."

Suzanne tells about a woman in her support group for mothers whose son had died recently. "We asked her to come back to group; we wanted to talk to her. She finally told us that she didn't want to come back. She had seven other children, and she did a lot of volunteer work, and she was able to move on with her life without questioning a lot of things. She was a very religious woman, and she felt that her son was taken care of and was peaceful. I wish I could do that. I mean, there are a lot of things I feel uncomfrtable about, especially as a parent. How I failed. How I didn't do enough. How I didn't listen well enough. The list is endless."

"That's why I went to a grief group," Hugh notes. "I don't think my friends, my family, and John's friends were able to deal with my grief. I don't think I share a lot with people. One of John's friends, the wife of the very religious guy, wrote me a note with a two-hundred-dollar check in it. In the note she said, 'Surely John is in heaven because of you.' I needed someone to say that. Someone had told me I'd done the right things. That's why I just wanted to be in group. I really didn't want to talk about it. I still get very confused about it. I guess that's natural after people die. What if? What if? What if? You know, that stuff doesn't get you anywhere, anyway. What happened is what happened."

Guilt

Sometimes you will feel guilt. But guilt for what? More than likely, you did everything you could, probably more than most people could have expected. You have nothing to feel guilty about. If this remains a problem, talk to a therapist about it. Discuss it with a friend or in a group. The real basis for your guilt may be that you are still here and your friend is not. Deep inside, you may feel unworthy of living and somehow responsible for your friend's death.

Late one night, James begins talking about his dead brother. "I feel like I'm half of somebody. He was there. He was always there. Everything I ever did wasn't finished until Earl knew about it. Now I'm mad at him. I'm mad at me, too. Why am I here? Why didn't I die, too? You know, he and I, we were brothers. Everything was always James and Earl, never just James, never just Earl." James cries softly. "I shouldn't be alive. There should be no James if there's no Earl. What did I do? What could I have done different? I just know, if I'm here, he should be, too. And I keep thinking it's my fault. It's my doing that he's not."

Hugh talks about how greatly he suffered for a long time after John's death. Was there something he didn't do? Did he let John down in some way? "No, I didn't let him down. It was the intensity of it, you know. I did everything I could. I didn't know my way. I took care of everything pretty much alone. I didn't really take good care of myself, my own needs; but some things, I *couldn't* do. They almost overpowered me. I remember when they were going to put that thing in John's neck, he wanted me to stay. I just said, 'No, I can't.' I don't have any regrets about anything I did. I did the best I could."

Depression

Suddenly, you cannot see any future for yourself. The days ahead seem endlessly dreary. "What's ahead for me?" you ask. "More sadness. More loneliness." You may find it hard to concentrate; you might feel exhaustion and dread when you get out of bed in the morning. You may not feel like doing anything. You may want to sleep eighteen or twenty hours a day.

Depression and the resulting lack of will to act are also part of the grieving process. They will pass with time. But you must be patient with yourself. Try to remember events in the past that you thought you would never get over: the breakup with a person you loved, losing the best job you ever had, the death of one of your parents. You survived these events. You know that your friend wanted you to go on after he died. Take your time. Slowly, you will move again, as you realize that *shedding your grief is not the same as discarding the intense memories of someone you loved.*

You can also work actively against this depression. Let yourself feel it, as you must, and then make yourself do things. Do positive things that give you a feeling of accomplishment. Force yourself to call a friend you may be neglecting, and go out to dinner. Make a visit to a house of worship. Take a walk or a bicycle ride. Get more involved at work.

It's important that you not dwell too long on your depression. Activity will take it away intermittently for a while, and ultimately it should play itself out altogether. If after many months you do not feel a lightening of the load, then you should seek professional help.

More Frequent Illness

As you grieve, you may get more colds, more ill-defined feelings of sickness. This may also be a part of the mourning process, and it happens to many people. You may have stomach problems, back problems, headaches. As your grief lessens, your normal health should return. But while you are mourning, take special care of yourself. Your resistance is low. Of course, if you had a sexual relationship with the person who died, you may fear that you're having active symptoms of HIV disease. So see your doctor if you think that will reassure you.

Panic Attacks

Sometimes, too, you may suffer overwhelming anxiety or terror. Suddenly, for no apparent reason, everything seems out of control. You may even feel that you are going to die at that very minute. You may break down crying in the most inappropriate places. You may be seized with the desire to run away. But from what? You may be talking out loud to yourself as you walk down the street, and never realize that you are doing it. Sometimes you do things that you would never do otherwise. "Why shouldn't I vacuum my apartment at four in the morning if I want to?" you say, defending your behavior.

These attacks will also pass. The pressure and strain of your loneliness and grief produce distortions of your mind and your perceptions. As the strain lessens, you will return to normal.

Anger

You might also be feeling anger about the disease itself, about those people who abandoned you and your friend, and you might feel a need to settle things with those people. Let this be. If the opportunity arises and you still want to, then do it, but don't go out of your way, unless your need is very great. Better to direct your anger to activities that are more positive, like lobbying the government for more money for AIDS care, or, when you are ready, being the kind of friend to others that you wish others had been to you.

Looking Back to Move Forward

You know in your heart that you and your friend were strong and courageous for enduring what you went through. Yet you may have a great need to go over in your mind the whole course of the illness, from the time your friend was diagnosed to the end, reviewing the events as they happened; each hospitalization, each crisis, may seem as if it happened yesterday. Many carepartners and caring friends do this.

This review may be necessary to help you to digest what has happened; you may go over your feelings about the events at each stage of the illness to make peace with them. As you look back, talk to your other friends who were around while your friend was sick. You may need assurance from the people who make up your support system that you did everything you could and that your friend did everything he could. You need to accept some facts: that your emotions were what they were, that you couldn't stop the loss, and that you expressed your love for your friend in the hundreds of ways that you cared for him. You may need to be told that you should be feeling the pain you feel. This pain is not a sign of weakness. It is the flip side of the love that you have lost.

"My eyeballs are still intact," Suzanne says, describing how she feels months after Michelle's death. "It's extremely painful. It's like being stabbed a hundred times. I go over every little thing. Night after night, I wake up back in that hospital again and remember every little detail."

"I've been over it and over it and over it," James says. "And it hurt me as much the tenth time as the first. I kept saying, it wasn't like Earl wasn't there anymore. It was like I wasn't there anymore, either. Everything I did, it was like 'I can't wait to tell Earl about this.'

"Then one day, something started to happen. I was going over things, and it seemed like for the first time those things were things *that had happened.* Those things were back there. But I was here. I hurt, but I was right here on this chair. And who was I? I was somebody. I have arms, and legs, and I can move around. I said out loud, 'Okay, Earl, maybe I'm getting ready to go on with my life.' "

When Healing Begins

Gradually, over a period of months, your pain will grow less intense. You will not think about and feel your loss twenty-four hours of every day. Day by day, your grieving will continue—and you will begin to heal.

Eventually, you will become more active in life again. In the period immediately after your friend's death, you might have spent much time alone or, at least, in mental solitude; now you will begin to seek out new relationships, new people, new points of view, and new activities that give you fulfillment. This is part of growing beyond your loss.

This movement away from death has no set schedule. Exactly how long it takes will vary tremendously. But you will adapt to enjoying life again, and you will begin to feel that you have a right to have survived, and you will go on with your life. You have this right because you know you could not have prevented your friend's death; you were not responsible for the course of the disease; you could not have taken your friend's place, even if you had wanted to. You could not have done more for him or loved him more. In short, you gave all to him; now you must do so for yourself. Your life can no longer rest in the past.

Keeping Your Friend Alive in Your Memory

At times, you may feel uneasy that you do not think about your friend all day, every day. In some way, you may feel that you are betraying him, because your love, which had been so intense, now seems a little distant. If you feel this way, understand that it means that you are growing, that you are no longer totally focused on the loss of your friend. Your friend will always be with you—but in memory, not as an everyday presence. But to go on with your life, you must leave him behind—which is different from forgetting him—even though it hurts you to do so.

"You feel guilty about moving away from the person who's gone," Suzanne explains. "Your whole time thing is all mixed up. Michelle would have been twenty-five in May. I'm going to get older, but Michelle is not going to get older. If I move away from her and try to pick up the pieces of my life, I feel guilty. I feel like I'm leaving her in the past. Somehow you want to carry her with you. It prevents your own healing."

Rose describes a visit she had from Bob, Gary's lover. "One day I was home alone—Gary had been dead about seven months—and the doorbell rang. I wasn't expecting anyone. I opened the door, and it was Bob, looking robust and healthy. I almost burst into tears when I saw him, and I just grabbed him and hugged him. I felt then that I loved him like my own because he brought such happiness to my son when he was sick. 'I need to talk to you, Rose,' he said. 'I'm really confused. I don't think anyone but you can understand what's going on with me.'

"He came in, and I made coffee, and we sat in the kitchen. 'Sometimes during the day,' he said, 'I get completely wrapped up in what I'm doing, and I forget about Gary, and what we had together, and how I loved him. The same thing happens to me in the evening. I go out with some friends, and I don't talk about Gary like I did. I don't think about him as much.' He paused for a while, like he was thinking or finding it hard to admit something. 'I feel like that's wrong. He's not part of my life like he was. I feel guilty, as if I'm killing him in another way now that he's dead. You know I love him, and how I loved him. I got rid of some of his things, and I felt like I was betraying him.'

"While he was talking, I thought about my brother who was killed in World War II, about my parents, and about my little girl from my first marriage, who had died at three. Now Gary. I knew Bob had come to me for strength. He wanted Gary's mother to tell him that what he was feeling was all right. I could feel his need. 'I have the same feelings,' I said. 'My son is gone. I can't send him a birthday card this year. He won't call me on Mother's Day. For a while after he died, I wanted to seal his room so nothing would ever change, and I kept the door shut so I could pretend that he was sleeping in there, and I'd even tiptoe by so I wouldn't wake him. But after a while, I knew I couldn't do that forever. The door is open now. I went in one day and rearranged the furniture and took his things off the walls. And I cried while I did it. I thought of his head on my breast when he was a little boy. I thought of all the time with him that I had been cheated out of, the Thanksgivings, the birthdays, those afternoons he'd drop by when he was on his way somewhere. But I had to tell myself that that was over now. It was going to fade into memory, and I had to let it. My husband needs me. My children and grandchildren need me. You need me and I need you.'

"He just sat awhile with tears streaming down his cheeks, and he thanked me. When he got ready to leave, I held him a long time and we cried together, but I knew he was going to be all right. That was the least I could have done for him."

Letting Go

Letting go is perhaps the hardest thing you will have to do. You have to say in your heart to your deceased friend, "I will always love you. You will always be in my heart and in my mind. But I have to go on now, the way you wanted me to." If you are having trouble with this step, if you feel you cannot let go—if, for example, you cannot dispose of your friend's possessions or you cannot bring his affairs to a close—then ask for help. Go to a bereavement group in your area or to a therapist.

"I had so many good times with John," Hugh says, "times I've never, never had with anyone else. John was really proud of me. I was excited about these contracting jobs, and he'd encourage me. He'd talk to friends about what I was doing. He'd talk about working together on projects, and we'd plan things and talk about ideas a lot. I was excited, and I'd go see his jobs. I guess what I'm afraid of most is that I'll never have that again. I keep thinking that I need to see John again, to talk to him. I told that to my shrink once, and he said, 'What would you say to him?' I said I'd walk up to him and just start talking. That's the problem, you know, letting go. I haven't let go. I still talk to him. I say 'Hi' to him. I miss him."

Many times, letting go means admitting that you are not in control of life. If you were in control, you would not have suffered this loss; you would not have this pain; you would not have to remake your life to fill the void left by a friend who is no longer there. You can resolve to yourself, "Today, I will allow myself to go on. I will experiment to see what my new life could be like."

Now Who Are You?

Over time, you will begin to redefine the person you are. For a very long time, you defined yourself as a carepartner or caring friend to a person with AIDS. That was your primary purpose in life; that was what you did. After a period of time in which you simply take care of yourself and your pain, you will begin to look again at yourself and ask what it is you want from your life. You may find that the values you thought important before this experience are not so important now. You will probably find that you place much greater value on your relationships. You know more about these relationships now; you know how to nurture them; you know how to help other people feel good about themselves. This experience will have made you a much more mature and sensitive individual; it will also have taught you about the importance of giving of yourself.

Hugh: "The shrink in my bereavement group said that this was an opportunity to look into our own lives. Everything certainly changes, and it's an opportunity to change your life. I feel like a totally different person since this happened. I'm a totally different Hugh than I was two years ago or four years ago. I feel much stronger. I feel like I could do anything, or nothing. Things that I used to get upset about are nothing now. I think that I'm kinder and more loving now.

"I never thought a lot about other people before. I never, ever, missed people before in my life. I've said good-bye to people and never gave them another thought, you know. I moved out of my house from my parents when I was seventeen and never gave it a thought. I've broken up with people and never thought of them again. That's a big difference. I think more about people now. I'm a lot less selfish."

Suzanne: "I went to a training session at New York Hospital. I was asked to speak about my daughter's illness and then answer questions from the audience. There was another woman there whose son had AIDS, and she had come all the way from California to live in her son's one-room apartment to take care of him. The other speaker was a young man who had AIDS. I remember we were out in the hall when he arrived, and I thought that he couldn't be the one with AIDS because he looked so well. He was winded when he arrived, and he asked for a glass of water, and that moved something inside me. My heart just opened up. Maybe I can't go back to my old life. A boy asked me for a glass of water, and I was moved.

"I like being with people who understand me better than most of my friends, who believe it's okay to have cancer but it's not okay to have AIDS. The people who've had to deal with AIDS are set apart. My husband keeps saying, 'Why don't you quit your job and just see what happens?' But I'm not ready for that. I can't do that yet. I'm just beginning to move a little bit in that new direction. AIDS takes over your life in such a way that it's hard to shake it off. I've grown intolerant of situations that I feel are shallow. I want to say to people, 'Hey, folks, there's something going on out there.' There's lots of people giving in ways that most people aren't even aware that people can give. I don't know where I'm going, perhaps into something where I can help."

Michael: "I'm not nearly as scared as I used to be about whether or not everybody loves me. I know that people love me. They love me because I love myself in a way that I never did before. I take better care of myself. I pay more attention to myself.

"I'll tell you how I identify the change in me the most. I wake up in the morning now, and I know what I'm feeling and who I am. I used to go for days, for weeks, even for years, walking around not knowing what I was feeling. Now in the morning, I know what I feel. I've become very aware of what's going on inside me all the time.

"While Joe was here, I kept thinking, 'I've got a center. I've got a focus. I feel like I've got a purpose in life.' But then I realized I've got to extend this into the future. Did Joe have to be sick in order for me to be well? That didn't make sense. I developed a kind of self-awareness that I never had before. It feels real solid. It doesn't feel like something that's going to evaporate in the next minute. And my going back to school now—that seems to be the result of all this. Finding something I want to do. Something that will satisfy me, where I can contribute."

Stella: "What I'd really like to do is to go get a RN degree, and maybe take care of terminally ill patients. You know, if David's illness has taught me anything, it's taught me patience. When something hap-

205

pens, I don't panic. I take care of that situation. Then, if another one arises, I take care of that one. And I tell you, since David died, it's been one situation after another, especially with the kids.

"One of the biggest things I'm concerned about is people's fear. I do everything I can on the education of this disease. I speak whenever I can. I'm willing to do anything. And somehow, it has been getting better. It's so important that our young children learn about this disease, and how to be safe."

Rose: "The changes that Gary's illness and death made on all our lives have been amazing. I see my daughter Linda in such a different light. She knew exactly what to do. She did all the right things to make us a family and help get through this. My husband had a whole side I never knew existed. He accepted Gary. He accepted Bob into our home like a son. And me, I found all this strength inside me that had been waiting to be called upon. My relationships with all the people in my life now are much warmer, more open, more loving, and more honest."

Coming Together

Suzanne: "The day of Michelle's memorial service was the day of that huge candlelight memorial vigil that they had on Christopher Street. I really wanted to go. But I was also exhausted from Michelle's service. While friends and family were still at my house, Timothy, a gay priest at my church, asked me if I would come to the vigil. So after our guests had left, I went back to New York and went to the vigil. When I left the house, I told my mother, my father, and my daughter Camille where I was going. And do you know what? They all decided to come with me.

"While I was walking with Timothy, he told me that today was the tenth anniversary of his ordination. I thought that was astonishing. We bought these candles—the money went to GMHC—and strangely enough, when we got down to the river, of the people I was walking with, my candle was the only one that hadn't blown out. Camille said, 'Look, Mom, your candle is the only one that is still burning.' When we got to the river, we held my candle up high, said a prayer for Michelle, and then—saying good-bye—tossed the candle into the river.

"Of our group, only Camille and I had made it down to the river, because of the crowd. My mother and father got too tired, so they said they'd sit on a parked car and wait for us to come back. On the way back, we were looking for them—there were people everywhere milling around, and some of them were crying—and then, off in the distance, I saw my mother and father sitting on the curb with a young blond man. He was crying.

"We talked to him awhile and found out that he was from out of town, and he had come to New York with his lover, but his lover had gotten sick and in about two weeks had died of AIDS. He was about Camille's age, so she talked to him, too. He didn't really know anyone, and he was staying at some friend's house.

"I still have a picture in my mind of that evening—the night we said good-bye to Michelle. You never know who is going to come together around this disease, people who would never meet each other. People who would never have anything to say to each other. This disease brings them together."

APPENDIX A

WHAT IS THE HIV ANTIBODY TEST?*

When HIV enters the body, the body produces antibodies in response to the virus. The test detects the presence of these antibodies in a small sample of blood usually drawn from the arm. The test does not detect whether you have AIDS—it only tells you if your body has produced antibodies in response to HIV.

While there is a test that detects whether the AIDS virus itself is in the body, this test is not routinely administered at HIV antibody testing sites and clinics. It is available only upon special request by a doctor.

What Does It Mean to Test Positive?

If you have developed antibodies to the virus, you are HIV-positive. This means that at some point you were exposed to the virus and have been infected with HIV.

Being HIV-positive *does not* mean that you now have AIDS or that you will definitely develop AIDS in the future. Some people may

*Reprinted from "The Test: Understanding HIV Antibody Testing," copyright © by Gay Men's Health Crisis, Inc.

remain completely healthy for long periods of time, possibly even the rest of their lives. Others may develop a condition with some AIDS symptoms but without any of the major infections usually associated with an AIDS diagnosis. Others may develop full-blown AIDS anywhere from three to ten years after infection.

Being HIV-positive *does not* mean that you are immune to the virus. Antibodies to HIV, unlike most other antibodies, seem to provide no protection from the disease.

Being HIV-positive *does not* mean that you can no longer have sex. Just make sure that you always practice safer sex.

In all cases of a positive test result, a second blood test will be performed to confirm the results of the first test. If the second test result is positive, a test called the Western Blot is performed for absolute certainty.

In a *very small* percentage of cases, people will test HIV-positive even though they have not been infected with the virus. A second test will usually show a negative result.

What Does HIV-Negative Mean?

If you have not developed antibodies to the virus, you are HIV-negative. However, a negative test result does not guarantee that you are virus free. Your body can take anywhere from six weeks to a year after infection with the AIDS virus to produce antibodies. If you take the test after you have been infected with HIV but before your body has had enough time to produce antibodies, you will test negative. A negative test result does not mean that you cannot transmit the virus to someone else. You need to be periodically retested in the following year, and you must continue to practice safer sex. Intravenous drug users should never share needles, even if they are HIV-negative.

What Are the Advantages of Taking the Test?

There are several reasons to consider taking the HIV antibody test.

If you think that you may have been infected with HIV, consider taking the test as a first step toward a healthier life-style and taking control of your health. Several new therapies have shown promise in delaying the onset of AIDS in people infected with HIV. These treatments, which suppress the virus and strengthen the immune system, may be most effective at the early stages of the disease. It is often recommended that you begin these therapies as early as possible after HIV infection.

Knowing that you are HIV-positive will, in most cases, help you to practice safer sex all the time. This is important since repeated exposure to the virus seems to play a large role in the development of AIDS.

If you are thinking about having a child and think that you or your partner may be infected, you and your partner may want to consider getting tested. Confirming that you and your partner are HIV-negative before conceiving a child will reduce the chance of transmitting HIV to the child before or at birth.

What Are the Disadvantages to Taking the Test?

People sometimes feel depressed and anxious when they find out that they are HIV-positive. People who learn that they are HIV-positive may also feel afraid, helpless, and worried about being shunned by their lovers, families, friends, and co-workers.

To help you cope with your reactions to your test results, it is important to set up a support network of people you trust before you take the test.

Discuss your questions and fears about the HIV test and AIDS with a trained counselor both before and after you take the test. The purpose of pre-test counseling is to make sure that you understand what the test will and will not tell you, and whether you should take it. Pre-test counseling will help prepare you in case you test positive. Post-test counseling will help you deal with any negative reactions. Then you can begin to take control of your health and, if needed, begin preventative medicines.

Another possible disadvantage of taking the HIV antibody test is that you may be denied services or suffer discrimination if you are HIV-positive. If insurance companies find out that you are HIV-positive, or even that you took the test, they may attempt to deny or take away your health- or life-insurance coverage. Some doctors, dentists, landlords, employers, and schools have also discriminated against people who are HIV-positive, even though this is illegal in many locales.

If you do not have health insurance, try to get it before being tested. Many group-insurance programs available at the workplace do not require medical screening. Once you have been granted medical coverage, it is very difficult for the insurance company to discontinue it because you test HIV-positive. However, your application for individual medical-insurance coverage will probably be rejected if you have tested HIV-positive before applying.

How Can I Make Sure That My Test Results Are Kept Confidential?

The only way to make sure your test results will be kept confidential is to take the test anonymously. Many cities have set up free testing centers where they do not require you to give your name, address, or any other identifying information. Many private doctors and public and private hospitals also administer the antibody test, but not anonymously. For instance, New York State law requires that you sign a form indicating that you understand the test and agree to be tested. Your test results will probably be permanently recorded in your medical chart. While these test results are supposed to be kept confidential, there have been instances in which a patient's HIV status has been disclosed to insurance companies and others without his or her consent or knowledge. As a general rule, to protect yourself against possible discrimination, you should be cautious about disclosing that you took the test and your test results to anyone other than trusted friends and family, sexual partners, and health-care professionals. . . .

Should I Take the Test So That I Can Stop Practicing Safe Sex?

Some people use the HIV test as a basis for making decisions about their sexual relationships. Some people will not begin a sexual relationship unless their partner has tested HIV-negative. If someone has asked you to take the test, you should do so only after carefully weighing the possible advantages and disadvantages.

Couples who decide to remain monogamous (to have sex only with each other) sometimes want to be tested to know if it is safe for them to have unprotected sex. If you and your partner want to use the test for this purpose, you both must remain absolutely monogamous and continue to practice safer sex for at least a year before taking the test.

If you are both HIV-negative and stop practicing safer sex, you and your partner must continue to be absolutely monogamous. Unprotected sex with even one person may expose you and your partner to HIV infection. It is safest simply to continue practicing safer sex, even if you think that you are in a monogamous relationship.

Under What Circumstances May I Be Required to Take the Test?

Unfortunately, some forms of HIV antibody testing are mandatory. Insurance companies may require applicants for life and health insurance to take the HIV antibody test.

The armed services, Job Corps, foreign service, and Peace Corps routinely subject new recruits to the test, and federal prisons also test all inmates. Persons applying for permanent resident status (green card) will be required to take the test.

In all these cases, persons who are found to be HIV-positive may be excluded from insurance coverage, employment, or permanent residence.

Who Should I Tell If I Am HIV-Positive?

Tell your doctor that you are HIV-positive so that he or she can monitor your health and not prescribe any drugs that will harm your immune system.

Also, tell anyone who may be exposed to your blood, semen, or vaginal fluid, including present and past sexual partners or needle-sharing partners. If you do not inform these partners yourself, New York State law allows a physician or public health worker to inform them that they might be at risk for HIV infection. [This is true in other states as well.] However, it is illegal for you to be identified by name as a possible source of infection.

Many people find that telling one or two trusted friends or relatives about their antibody status helps them build a network of support for themselves. If you do not feel comfortable discussing this with anyone you know, you can discuss it with a counselor. There are also group services for HIV-positives and several organizations have been created to provide this support.

How Can I Make Sure That I Will Not Transmit the Virus to Others?

To prevent transmitting HIV, don't let your blood, semen, or vaginal fluid enter another person's body. This means practicing safer sex every time you have sex. Practicing safer sex is also important for your health. Repeated exposure to HIV may further damage your immune system. Also, using a condom during sex will protect you from other sexually transmitted diseases, such as syphilis and gonorrhea, which suppress the immune system. . . . Don't let anyone use anything that has come in contact with your blood or other bodily fluids, such as a syringe, razor, or toothbrush.

If you use drugs, never share needles, rent works, or use rebagged needles. You can clean needles with bleach and then flush them two or three times with running tap water. Never let the bleach enter your body. Cleaning your works will reduce your risk of getting infected from needle use.

Do not donate blood, semen, organs, or tissue. If you are a woman who is HIV-positive, seek counseling if you're thinking about getting pregnant, because the virus can be passed from a mother to her fetus during pregnancy, birth, or breast-feeding. Always practice safer sex, especially during menstruation.

What Else Can I Do?

If you are HIV-positive, you should exercise, eat a well-balanced, nutritious diet, avoid stress, and get enough sleep. Avoid cigarettes and excessive alcohol and recreational drugs because they reduce the body's ability to fight off infections.

Get regular medical checkups by a doctor who is knowledgeable about AIDS, and talk to him or her about beginning one of the medicines that have shown promise in preventing or delaying the onset of AIDS-related infections in HIV-positive people.

Finally, take charge of yourself. Keep a positive attitude. Educate your friends, lovers, and co-workers about HIV. Enjoy life!

APPENDIX B

SAFE SEX GUIDELINES*

What Is Safe Sex?

The San Francisco AIDS Foundation offers this definition:

> Safe sex means any sexual practice that does not let someone else's semen, blood, or vaginal fluids get into someone else's body. The parts of the body where HIV could enter the bloodstream are the anus and rectum, the vagina, the penis, the mouth, and the eyes. These body parts must be protected from contact with HIV-infected fluids. HIV cannot go through skin unless there are open sores or bleeding gums.

The foundation recommends these safe sex guidelines:

- *Always* use condoms for anal and vaginal sex. Unfortunately, *condom use does not guarantee protection from HIV*, since condoms may break or be used improperly.
- Do *not* get semen, urine, feces, blood, or vaginal secretions in your mouth.
- Do *not* have mouth-to-rectum contact.

---

*Reprinted from *Early Care for HIV Disease* and the *AIDS Hotline Training Manual*, copyright © by the San Francisco AIDS Foundation.

APPENDIX C

DIRECTORY OF AIDS ORGANIZATIONS

National Organizations

AIDS Action Committee
131 Clarendon Street
Boston, MA 02116
(617) 437-6200

AIDS Action Council
2033 M Street, N.W.
Washington, DC 20036
(202) 293-2886

AIDS Legal Referral Panel
114 Sansome Street
Suite 1129
San Francisco, CA 94104
(415) 291-5454

AIDS National Interfaith
 Network
110 Maryland Avenue, N.E.
Suite 504
Washington, DC 20002
(202) 546-0807

AIDS Project Los Angeles
6721 Romaine Street
Los Angeles, CA 90038
(213) 962-1600
(800) 553-2437

American Association
 of Physicians for
 Human Rights
 (AAPHR)
2940 16th Street, Room 309
San Francisco, CA 94103
(415) 558-9353

American Foundation for
 AIDS Research
 (AmFAR)
733 Third Avenue
New York, NY 10017
(212) 682-7440

American Public Health
Association
1015 15th Street, N.W.
Washington, DC 20005
(202) 789-5600

American Red Cross
Office of HIV/AIDS Education
1709 New York Avenue, N.W.
Suite 208
Washington, DC 20006
(202) 434-4074

Federation of Parents and
Friends of Lesbians and Gays
P.O. Box 27605
Washington, DC 20038
(202) 638-4200

Gay Men's Health Crisis
129 West 20th Street
New York, NY 10011
(212) 807-6655

Lambda Legal Defense and
Education Fund
666 Broadway
New York, NY 10012
(212) 995-8585

Minority Task Force on AIDS
505 Eighth Avenue
New York, NY 10018
(212) 563-8340

National AIDS Information
Clearinghouse
Box 6003
Rockville, MD 20850
(800) 458-5231

National Association of People
With AIDS (NAPWA)
1413 K Street, N.W.
Washington, DC 20005
(202) 898-0414
(800) 338-2437

National Gay and Lesbian Task
Force
1734 14th Street, N.W.
Washington, DC 20009
(202) 332-6483

Project Inform
347 Delores Street, Suite 301
San Francisco, CA 94110
(800) 822-7422
(800) 344-7422 (California
only)

The San Francisco AIDS
Foundation
25 Van Ness Avenue
San Francisco, CA 94102
(415) 864-5855

AIDS Hot Line Numbers

National AIDS Hot Line. . . . . (800) 342-AIDS
Alabama . . . . (800) 455-3741
Alaska . . . . (800) 478-2437
Arizona . . . . (800) 334-1540
Arkansas . . . . (800) 445-7720
California
  Northern California . . . . (800) FOR-AIDS
  Southern California. . . . . (800) 922-AIDS

Colorado	(303) 331-8305
Connecticut	(203) 566-1157
Delaware	(302) 995-8422
District of Columbia	(202) 332-AIDS
Florida	(800) FLA-AIDS
Georgia	(800) 551-2728
Hawaii	(808) 922-1313
Idaho	(208) 334-5944
Illinois	(800) AID-AIDS
Indiana	(317) 633-8406
Iowa	(800) 532-3301
Kansas	(800) 232-0040
Kentucky	(800) 654-AIDS
Louisiana	(800) 992-4379
Maine	(800) 851-AIDS
Maryland	(800) 638-6252
Massachusetts	(800) 235-2331
Michigan	(800) 872-AIDS
Minnesota	(800) 248-AIDS
Mississippi	(800) 826-2961
Missouri	(800) 533-AIDS
Montana	(406) 252-1212
Nebraska	(800) 782-2437
Nevada	
Reno	(702) 329-AIDS
Las Vegas	(702) 383-1393
New Hampshire	(800) 752-AIDS
New Jersey	(800) 624-2377
New Mexico	(505) 827-0006
New York	(800) 462-1884
North Carolina	(919) 733-7301
North Dakota	(800) 592-1861
Ohio	(800) 332-AIDS
Oklahoma	(405) 271-6434
Oregon	(503) 229-5792
Pennsylvania	(800) 692-7254
Rhode Island	(402) 227-6502
South Carolina	(800) 332-AIDS
South Dakota	(800) 472-2180
Tennessee	(800) 342-AIDS
Texas	
Dallas	(214) 559-AIDS
Houston	(713) 524-AIDS

Utah. . . . . (800) 843-9388
Vermont . . . . (800) 882-AIDS
Virginia . . . . (800) 533-4148
Washington. . . . . (800) 272-AIDS
West Virginia . . . . (800) 642-8244
Wisconsin . . . . (800) 334-AIDS
Wyoming. . . . . (307) 777-7953

State and Local Organizations

ALABAMA

Birmingham
AIDS Outreach
P.O. Box 550070
Birmingham, AL 35255
(205) 322-4197

AIDS Task Force of
  Alabama
Box 55703
Birmingham, AL 35255
(205) 592-2437

Huntsville
AIDS Coalition of Huntsville
P.O. Box 871
Huntsville, AL 35804
(205) 533-2437

Mobile
Mobile County Health
  Department AIDS Control
  Program
P.O. Box 2867
Mobile, AL 36652
(205) 690-8167

Montgomery
AIDS Outreach
1209 Mulberry Street
Montgomery, AL 36106
(205) 269-1432

Tuscaloosa
West Alabama AIDS Outreach
P.O. Box 031947
Tuscaloosa, AL 35403
(205) 758-2437

ALASKA
Alaska AIDS Project
730 I Street
Suite 100
Anchorage, AK 99501
(907) 276-4880
(800) 478-AIDS

ARIZONA

Phoenix
Arizona AIDS Project
919 North First Street
Phoenix, AZ 85004
(602) 420-9396

Tucson
AIDS Project
151 South Tucson Blvd.
  Suite 252
Tucson, AZ 85716
(602) 322-6226

219

ARKANSAS

AIDS Foundation
5911 H Street
Little Rock, AR 72225
(501) 663-7833

CALIFORNIA

Bakersfield
Kern County AIDS Task Force
P.O. Box 10961
Bakersfield, CA 93389
(805) 861-3631

Fresno
Central Valley AIDS Team
625 North Palm Avenue
Fresno, CA 93701
(209) 264-2436

Garden Grove
AIDS Response Program
128-32 Garden Grove Blvd.
Suite B
Garden Grove, CA 92643
(714) 534-0961

Guerneville
Face to Face
P.O. Box 1599
Guerneville, CA 95446
(707) 887-1581

Los Angeles
AIDS Project Los Angeles
6721 Romaine Street
Los Angeles, CA 90038
(213) 962-1600

Merced
Loving AIDS Management
  Program
711 West Main Street
Merced, CA 95340
(209) 723-0405

San Diego
AIDS Foundation San Diego
4080 Center Street
San Diego, CA 92103
(619) 686-5050

San Francisco/Oakland
AIDS Project of the East Bay
565 16th Street
Oakland, CA 94612
(510) 834-8181

San Francisco AIDS Foundation
Box 6182
San Francisco, CA 94101
(415) 864-4376

Santa Barbara
Santa Barbara Health Care
  Clinics AIDS Services
300 North San Antonio Road
Santa Barbara, CA 93110
(805) 681-5120

COLORADO

Colorado AIDS Project
Box 18529
Denver, CO 80218
(303) 837-0166

CONNECTICUT

Hartford
AIDS Project Hartford
30 Arbor Street
Hartford, CT 06106
(203) 523-7699

New Haven
AIDS Project
254 College Street
New Haven, CT 06510
(203) 624-0947

DELAWARE
Delaware Lesbian and Gay
  Health Advocates
800 West Street
Wilmington, DE 19801
(302) 652-6776

DISTRICT OF COLUMBIA
Whitman-Walker Clinic/AIDS
  Program
1407 S Street, N.W.
4th floor
Washington, DC 20009
(202) 332-5295

FLORIDA

Ft. Lauderdale
Center One/Anyone in Distress
2518 West Oakland Park Blvd.
Ft. Lauderdale, FL 33311
(305) 485-7090
(800) 325-5371

Key West
AIDS Prevention Center
513 Whitehead Street
Key West, FL 33040
(305) 292-6701

Miami
Miami Crisis Network
50-50 Biscayne Blvd.
Miami, FL 33137
(305) 751-7775

Orlando
Central Florida AIDS Unified
  Resources, Inc.
1235 South Orange Avenue
Orlando, FL 32806
(407) 843-3930

Tampa
Tampa AIDS Network
Box 8333
Tampa, FL 33674
(813) 978-8683

GEORGIA

Athens
AIDS Athens
468 Milledge Avenue, So.
Athens, GA 30605
(706) 542-2437

Atlanta
AIDS Atlanta
1438 West Peachtree Street,
  NW
Suite 100
Atlanta, GA 30309
(404) 872-0600
(800) 551-2728

HAWAII
Life Foundation
Box 88980
Honolulu, HI 96830
(808) 971-AIDS

IDAHO
Idaho AIDS Foundation
Box 421
Boise, ID 83701
(208) 345-2277

ILLINOIS
AIDS Foundation of Chicago
1332 North Halsted Street
Suite 303
Chicago, IL 60622
(312) 642-5454

Hispanic Health Alliance
1579 North Milwaukee Street
Suite 230
Chicago, IL 60622
(312) 252-6888

Howard Brown Health Center
945 West George Street
Chicago, IL 60657
(312) 871-5777

INDIANA
AIDS Coalition
1101 West 10th Street
Indianapolis, IN 46202
(317) 634-7221
(317) 257-HOPE

IOWA
Central Iowa AIDS Project
2116 Grand Avenue
Des Moines, IA 50132
(515) 274-6700

KANSAS

Topeka
Topeka AIDS Project
Box 4726
Topeka, KS 66604
(913) 232-3100

Wichita
First Metropolitan Community
   Church of Kansas Care
   Coordination Team
156 South Kansas Avenue
Wichita, KS 67211
(316) 267-1852

KENTUCKY
AIDS Crisis Task Force
Box 11442
Lexington, KY 40575
(606) 254-2865

LOUISIANA

Baton Rouge
Somebody Cares Outreach
6464 Renoir Avenue
Baton Rouge, LA 70874
(504) 924-6025

New Orleans
No/AIDS Task Force
1407 Decatur Street
New Orleans, LA 70116
(504) 945-4000

MAINE
The AIDS Project
22 Monument Square
5th Floor
Portland, ME 04101
(207) 774-6877
(800) 851-AIDS

MARYLAND
Health Education Resource
   Organization (HERO)
101 West Read Street
Suite 825
Baltimore, MD 21201
(410) 685-1180

MASSACHUSETTS

Boston
AIDS Action Committee
131 Clarendon Street
Boston, MA 02116
(617) 437-6200
(800) 235-2331

Cambridge
AIDS Family Support Group
12 Maple Street
Cambridge, MA 02139
(617) 491-0600

Cambridge Cares about AIDS
1493 Cambridge Street
Cambridge, MA 02139
(617) 498-1663

Worcester
AIDS Project Worcester
305 Shrewsbury Street
Worcester, MA 01604
(508) 755-3773

MICHIGAN

Detroit
AIDS Care Connection
4221 Cass Avenue
Detroit, MI 48201
(313) 993-1320

Grand Rapids
Grand Rapids AIDS Resource
   Center
42 South Division
Grand Rapids, MI 49516
(616) 459-9177

MINNESOTA
Minnesota AIDS Project
2025 Nicollet Avenue South
Suite 200
Minneapolis, MN 55404
(612) 870-7773
(800) 248-AIDS

MISSISSIPPI
Mississippi Gay Switchboard of
   Jackson
Box 3842
Jackson, MS 39284
(800) 537-0851

MISSOURI

Columbia
MID Missouri AIDS Project
Box 1371
Columbia, MO 65205
(314) 875-2437

Kansas City
Good Samaritan Project
3030 Walnut, 2nd Floor
Kansas City, MO 64108
(816) 561-8784

St. Louis
St. Louis Effort For AIDS
5622 Delmar Blvd.
Suite 104E
St. Louis, MO 63112
(314) 367-2382

MONTANA
Montana Coalition for Healthy
   Mothers
Box 876
Helena, MT 59624
(406) 449-8611

Out in Montana
Box 951
Helena, MT 59624
(406) 442-1784
(800) 366-GAYS

NEBRASKA

Nebraska AIDS Project
3624 Leavenworth
Omaha, NE 68105
(402) 342-4233

NEVADA

Las Vegas
Aid for AIDS of Nevada
1111 Desert Lane
Las Vegas, NV 89102
(702) 382-2326

Reno
Nevada AIDS Foundation
1225 West Field Avenue
Suite 8
Reno, NV 89504
(702) 329-2437

NEW HAMPSHIRE

New Hampshire AIDS
  Foundation
Box 59
Manchester, NH 03105
(603) 623-0110

NEW JERSEY

New Brunswick
Hyacinth Foundation AIDS
  Project
211 Livingston Avenue
New Brunswick, NJ 08901
(908) 545-4890

Newark
AIDS Interfaith Network of
  New Jersey
505 West Market
Newark, NJ 07107
(201) 481-1412

NEW MEXICO

New Mexico AIDS Services
4200 Silver Street
Suite D
Albuquerque, NM 87108
(505) 266-0911

NEW YORK

Albany
AIDS Council of Northeastern
  New York
750 Broadway
Albany, NY 12207
(518) 434-4686

Buffalo
Western New York AIDS
  Program
121 Tupper Street
Buffalo, NY 14202
(716) 847-2441

Huntington
East End Gay Organization
P.O. Box 2859
Huntington Station, NY 11746
(516) 385-AIDS

New York City
Pediatric AIDS Hotline
1300 Morris Park Avenue
Bronx, NY 10461
(718) 430-3333

Gay Men's Health Crisis
129 West 20th Street
New York, NY 10011
(212) 807-6655

Rochester
AIDS Rochester
1350 University Avenue
Rochester, NY 14607
(716) 442-2220

Syracuse
AIDS Task Force of Central
New York
627 West Genesee Street
Syracuse, NY 13204
(315) 475-2430

NORTH CAROLINA

Charlotte
Metrolina AIDS Project
P.O. Box 32662
Charlotte, NC 28232
(704) 333-2437

Durham
Lesbian and Gay Health Project
Durham, NC
(919) 286-4107

Winston-Salem
AIDS Task Force of
Winston-Salem
Box 20983
Winston-Salem, NC 27120
(919) 723-5031

NORTH DAKOTA

Hot line: (800) 592-1861

OHIO

Akron
Northeast Ohio Task Force on
AIDS
177 South Broadway
Akron, OH 44308
(216) 762-2437

Cincinnati
Ambrose Clement Health
Clinic
3101 Burnet Avenue
Cincinnati, OH 45229
(513) 352-3139

Cleveland
Health Issues Task Force
2250 Euclid Avenue
Cleveland, OH 44115
(216) 621-0766

Columbus
Columbus AIDS Task Force
1500 West Third Avenue
Suite 329
Columbus, OH 43212
(614) 488-2437

OKLAHOMA

Reach Out AIDS Information
Line
1200 NE 13th Street
Oklahoma City, OK 73152
(405) 271-2444

OREGON

Eugene
HIV/AIDS Resources
3477 East Amazon Drive
Eugene, OR 97405
(503) 342-5088

Portland
Cascade AIDS Project
620 SW Fifth Avenue
Suite 300
Portland, OR 97204
(503) 223-5907
(800) 777-AIDS

PENNSYLVANIA

Philadelphia
Action AIDS
1216 Arch Street
4th Floor
Philadelphia, PA 19107
(215) 981-0088

Philadelphia Community
  Health Alternatives
1642 Pine Street
Philadelphia, PA 19103
(215) 732-AIDS

Pittsburgh
Pittsburgh AIDS Task Force
905 West Street
4th Floor
Pittsburgh, PA 15201
(412) 242-2500

RHODE ISLAND

Rhode Island Project AIDS
Roger Williams Building
22 Hayes Street
Providence, RI 02908
(401) 277-6545

SOUTH CAROLINA

South Carolina AIDS Education
  Network
2768 Decker Blvd., Suite 98
Columbia, SC 29206
(803) 736-1171

SOUTH DAKOTA

Sioux Empire Gay and Lesbian
  Coalition
Box 220
Sioux Falls, SD 57101
(605) 333-0603

TENNESSEE

Chattanooga
Chattanooga Care
701 Cherokee Blvd.
Chattanooga, TN 37405
(615) 266-2422

Nashville
Nashville Cares
Box 25107
Nashville, TN 37202
(615)385-1510

TEXAS

Austin
AIDS Services of Austin
Box 4874
Austin, TX 78765
(512) 472-2273

Dallas
AIDS Resource Center
P.O. Box 190712
Dallas, TX 75219
(214) 521-5124
(214) 559-AIDS

El Paso
Southwest AIDS Committee
916 East Yandell
El Paso, TX 79902
(915) 533-5003

Houston
AIDS Foundation Houston
3202 Weslayan
Houston, TX 77027
(713) 623-6796

UTAH
Utah AIDS Foundation
1406 South Street
1100 East
Salt Lake City, UT 84105
(801) 487-2323

VERMONT
Vermont Cares
Box 5248
Burlington, VT 05402
(802) 863-2437

VIRGINIA

Norfolk
Tidewater AIDS Crisis Task
Force
740 Duke Street
Norfolk, VA 23510
(804) 626-0127

Richmond
Richmond AIDS Information
Network
1721 Hanover Avenue
Richmond, VA 23220
(804) 358-6343

WASHINGTON
Northwest AIDS Foundation
127 Broadway East
Suite 200
Seattle, WA 98102
(206) 329-6923

WEST VIRGINIA
Huntington AIDS Task Force
824 Fifth Avenue
Huntington, WV 25701
(304) 525-4357

WISCONSIN

Madison
Madison AIDS Support
Network
Box 731
Madison, WI 53701
(608) 238-6276

Milwaukee
Milwaukee AIDS Project
Box 92505
Milwaukee, WI 53202
(414) 273-2437

WYOMING
Wyoming AIDS Project
Box 9353
Casper, WY 82609
(307) 237-7833

GLOSSARY

Acquired Immunodeficiency Syndrome (AIDS): severe weakening of the immune system caused by the human immunodeficiency virus (HIV). People with AIDS can get many uncommon and life-threatening infections and cancers. (See also *Opportunistic Infection.*)

ACTG (AIDS Clinical Trials Group) trials: ACTG trials are run by the National Institute of Allergy and Infectious Diseases, a government agency. ACTG centers are running clinical trials to study treatments for HIV and related infections.

Acute: rapid and often severe in onset; the opposite of *chronic* or *long-term.*

Acyclovir: an antiviral drug used in the treatment of herpes simplex virus 1 (fever blisters, cold sores), herpes simplex virus 2 (genital herpes), and herpes zoster (shingles).

Administration (or *route of administration*): the way a drug is put into the body (for example, by mouth or injected into a vein).

Aerosolized pentamidine: a drug used as a preventative treatment for *Pneumocystis carinii* pneumonia. It is administered as a fine spray and inhaled.

Amikacin: an approved antibiotic, this drug is being studied in combination with other drugs for the treatment of MAC. (See also *MAC.*)

Amphotericin B: an antifungal drug, used for the treatment of cryptococcal meningitis and other serious fungal diseases.

Amphotericin B lipid complex and amphotericin B colloidal dispersion: two experimental formulations of amphotericin B that are being studied for treatment of cryptococcal meningitis to see whether they are safer and work better than regular amphotericin B.

Amyl, or *butyl, nitrite:* known as "poppers," these nitrites are a fluorocarbon that is inhaled and produces a temporary "rush," or "high," by dilating the blood vessels. Used mainly during sex, poppers, it has been speculated, have an immunosuppressive effect on the body.

Anemia: lower than normal number of red blood cells.

Antibiotic: a natural or synthetic substance that kills or inhibits the growth of bacterial or nonviral organisms and is used to combat disease and infection.

Antibodies: substances produced by the immune system that identify, destroy, or neutralize bacteria, viruses, and other harmful toxins. Antibodies are proteins produced by the B-lymphocytes that combine with foreign substances or microorganisms that invade the body and help destroy them. Once the body has an antibody to a particular substance, the cells remember what happened, and the person is usually immune to that specific substance or microorganism in the future. This is not true, however, in the case of HIV.

Antigen: a substance that stimulates an immune response. The immune system recognizes substances that are antigens as foreign, and produces antibodies to "fight" them.

Antiviral: a drug that kills or suppresses a virus; in terms of AIDS, antivirals such as AZT, ddI, and ddC slow down or stop the production of HIV.

ARC (AIDS-Related Complex): an outdated term once used to describe the condition of people with a variety of symptoms and signs related to all stages of HIV disease. These may include fevers, unexplained weight loss, swollen lymph nodes, and/or fungus infections in the mouth and throat. This condition is now commonly described as "symptomatic HIV infection."

Asymptomatic: without any symptoms.

Azithromycin: an antibiotic approved for the treatment of common bacterial infections. It is being studied to determine its effect against MAC, toxoplasmosis, and cryptosporidiosis.

AZT: azidothymidine; also called zidovudine (trade name is Retrovir). A drug that suppresses replication of all stages of HIV. It is FDA-approved; adverse side effects may include anemia, leukopenia, muscle fatigue, muscle wasting, nausea, and headaches.

AZT-intolerant: a term to describe someone who is unable to take AZT because of its side effects.

Bacteria: microscopic organisms, some of which can cause disease.

Bactrim: one of the brand names for trimethoprim-sulfamethoxazole, a drug used in the treatment and prevention of PCP. Septra is another trade name for this drug.

B-cells (B-lymphocytes): one of the two most important types of lymphocytes. These white blood cells make antibodies specific to fighting an infection.

Beta-2 microglobulin: a protein found in the blood. Higher than normal amounts of this protein in the blood of HIV-positive individuals suggests replication of HIV and progression of HIV disease.

Biopsy: The surgical removal and examination of a small fragment of tissue from a living body for the purpose of diagnosis.

BI-RG-587: an experimental anti-HIV drug that blocks the reverse transcriptase enzyme.

Blood count: an examination of the blood to count the number of white and red blood cells and platelets.

Bone marrow: soft tissue inside bones that is responsible for producing red and white blood cells and platelets.

Brain lesion: any abnormality in the brain tissue.

Brain tumor: a growth in the brain. It is benign if it is self-contained. It is cancerous if it is invading the tissue surrounding it and not just pushing it out of its way.

Bronchoscopy: a procedure for the inspection of the trachea and lungs.

Cancer: the uncontrolled growth of the cells of the tissues of any organ in the body. Cancers can destroy the tissue surrounding them and can spread to different parts of the body.

Candida: a fungus that very commonly infects the mouth, esophagus, or vagina in people with HIV.

Candidiasis: an infection caused by the yeastlike fungus *Candida albicans*. It may be severe and affect the skin, nails, or mucous membranes throughout the body, including those in the throat, vagina, intestines, and lungs. In the mouth it is known as *thrush,* and is often one of the first symptoms of a weakened immune system.

CBC (Complete Blood Count): a screening of important components in the blood, including total white blood cell count, the breakdown and counting of white blood cells, the red blood count hemoglobin levels, and platelets.

Cell: the smallest independent unit of life that is capable of performing all living functions, and the smallest unit making up larger living organisms. Cells are made up of at least a nucleus, surrounded by cytoplasm and enclosed in a semipermeable membrane.

Centers for Disease Control and Prevention (CDC): a federal health agency that monitors trends in the national health and provides safety guidelines as well as statistical information on human diseases, including HIV disease.

Central nervous system: the brain and spinal cord.

Cerebrospinal fluid: a fluid that circulates around the brain and spinal cord.

Cervical dysplasia: abnormal growth of cells in the cervix.

Cervix: the lower part of the uterus that protrudes into the top of the vagina.

Chemotherapy: treatment of cancer with drugs or chemicals, most of them toxic.

Chlamydia: a sexually transmitted bacterial infection.

Chronic: referring to a process—such as a disease process—that progresses slowly and persists over a long period of time; opposite of *acute.*

Ciprofloxacin: an approved antibiotic, currently being used experimentally as a treatment for MAC.

Clarithromycin (Biaxin): an approved antibiotic for common bacterial infections in non-HIV patients. It is being used alone and in combination therapy for MAC, and in combination for toxoplasmosis.

Clindamycin: an approved antibiotic that is being studied experimentally as a treatment for toxoplasmosis and PCP.

Clinical trial: a medical study in people, usually involving experimental drugs.

Clofazimine: an approved drug for the treatment of leprosy, currently being used experimentally as a treatment for MAC.

Clotrimazole: an approved drug for the treatment of fungal infections. It can be used topically as a cream or taken in tablet or lozenge form.

Clotting factors: substances in the blood that cause the blood to change from a liquid to a coagulate, or a solid. This stops bleeding.

CMV retinitis: an opportunistic infection of the eye caused by the virus CMV (cytomegalovirus, a virus related to the herpes family). Untreated, it can lead to blindness. CMV is also found in the colon and to a lesser degree in other organs of the body such as the lungs, esophagus, brain, kidneys, gall bladder, and liver. Symptoms depend on the site of the infection.

Coccidioidomycosis: a fungal infection that usually does not cause disease in healthy individuals. In people with advanced HIV disease, however, the infection can cause a severe, even fatal, disease.

Cofactor: a substance, microorganism, or environmental factor that activates or furthers the action of a disease-causing agent.

Colposcopy: an examination of the vagina.

Combination therapy: the use of two or more therapies administered alternately or simultaneously, in order to achieve maximum results.

Community-Based Clinical Trial (CBCT): a new way of doing clinical trials outside of university hospitals. CBCTs are conducted by personal doctors in close cooperation with their patients and AIDS advocates.

Compassionate use: a Food and Drug Administration classification that allows use of an experimental drug even though there is limited data about its effectiveness. The drug is provided free to people with life-threatening illnesses for which there is no effective therapy; also called *open study protocol.*

Creatinine: a waste product eliminated in urine; creatinine levels are used as a measure of kidney function, particularly during chemotherapy.

Cryptococcal meningitis: a disease caused by a fungus that infects the brain and spinal cord. Symptoms may include headache, confusion, blurred vision, fever, and speech difficulties.

Cryptosporidiosis: an infection of the intestines caused by a protozoan parasite. Usually spread through fecal-oral contact. Symptoms include watery diarrhea, abdominal cramping, weight loss, anorexia, flatulence, and fatigue. Diagnosis is made by either examining feces or a small, surgically removed piece of the intestine.

Culture: the growth of microorganisms of living tissue in the laboratory, in solutions that promote their growth.

Dapsone: an antibiotic used in the treatment and prevention of PCP and other diseases, such as leprosy.

ddC (Hivid): an anti-HIV therapy that belongs to the same family of drugs as AZT and ddI. Adverse side effects may include peripheral neuropathy, ulcers, and, more rarely, pancreatitis.

ddI (Videx): an anti-HIV drug available by prescription. ddI is FDA-approved for the treatment of HIV infection in adults and children over six months of age who are intolerant to AZT or who are experiencing clinical decline despite treatment with AZT. Severe side effects may include a potentially life-threatening pancreatitis and painful peripheral neuropathy.

Dementia: a chronic loss of mental capacity that affects a person's ability to function in a social or occupational setting.

Dental dam, or latex dam: a flat square of latex rubber traditionally used by a dentist, but which can also be used during certain sexual activities to protect against HIV infection. A dental dam can be laid against a woman's vagina or against a woman's or man's anus during mouth-to-vagina or mouth-to-anus sex. The dam acts as a barrier to fluids between sex partners.

d4T: an anti-HIV drug currently in human testing; d4T belongs to the same family of drugs as AZT, ddI, and ddC. Adverse side effects may include peripheral neuropathy, headaches, and nausea.

Diagnosis: the identification of a disease from its signs and symptoms.

Diarrhea: abnormally frequent, loose, or watery stools.

Diclazuril: an antiprotozoal agent available by compassionate use for treatment of patients with proven cryptosporidiosis.

Disseminated: spread throughout the body.

Dose: the measured amount of a drug to be taken at one time.

Dose escalating: a type of clinical trial designed to find the best dose of a drug. The first patients in such a trial will receive a certain dose, and if no serious side effects happen, the next patients will receive a bigger dose. This process continues until the best dose is found.

Double blind: a trial design in which neither the patients nor the doctors know who is getting the experimental drug and who is getting the placebo or other therapy.

Dysplasia: abnormal growth of tissue that sometimes precedes the development of cancer.

Efficacy: how well a drug works.

Encephalitis: inflammation of the brain.

Endemic: continuous presence of a disease in a community or among a group of people.

Epidemic: a disease or condition that affects many persons within a population at the same time when ordinarily they are not subject to this condition.

Epstein-Barr Virus (EBV): a herpes-type virus that causes infectious mononucleosis and possibly hairy leukoplakia. EBV also has been associated with Burkitt's lymphoma, a cancer of the lymph nodes. EBV infection may be a cofactor that accelerates HIV disease progress.

Erythropoietin (Procrit, Epogen): a naturally occurring protein in the body that stimulates the production of red blood cells. This protein has been genetically engineered and is currently being used to treat AZT-associated anemia in some people with AIDS.

Esophageal: relating to the esophagus.

Esophageal candidiasis: infection of the esophagus by the yeastlike fungus *Candida albicans.*

Ethambutol: an approved anti-TB drug being used experimentally against MAC.

Etoposide (VP-16): an approved anticancer drug that is being used experimentally for Kaposi's sarcoma.

Expanded access: ways of giving out experimental drugs to patients who cannot take any other treatment.

Experimental drug: a drug or treatment that has not been proven safe and effective and has not been approved by the Food and Drug Administration for companies to sell.

Extrapulmonary: outside of the lungs.

556: also called 556C80; an experimental drug that shows strong activity against the organisms that cause PCP and toxoplasmosis; currently in phase II testing.

Fluconazole: an approved antifungal drug for the treatment of cryptococcal meningitis and common fungal infections. It is being studied experimentally to see if it can prevent serious fungal infections like cryptococcal meningitis in people with AIDS.

Folliculitis: a bacterial infection of the hair follicles that occurs most commonly in the hairy areas of the groin, armpit, or face.

Food and Drug Administration (FDA): the agency of the federal government responsible for the licensing and regulation of drugs.

Foscarnet: an antiviral drug that is FDA-approved for the treatment of CMV retinitis. It is also under study as a treatment for CMV colitis, HIV infection, and acyclovir-resistant herpes-virus infections. Adverse side effects may include kidney toxicity, seizures, nausea, and genital ulcerations.

Fungus: a class of organisms including yeasts and molds. Fungal infections associated with HIV include thrush (candidiasis), cryptococcal meningitis, histoplasmosis, and coccidioidomycosis.

Ganciclovir (Cytovene/DHPG): an antiviral drug that is FDA-approved to treat CMV. It is being studied experimentally to see if it can prevent CMV retinitis and if it is effective against CMV colitis.

Gastroenteritis: disease of the lining of the stomach or the intestines, usually characterized by inflammation.

Gene: the basic unit in which is encoded the heredity of a cell or an organism. Chains of genes in ordered sequences make up the DNA of a cell.

Giardia: an intestinal parasite once common among homosexual men, which can cause severe diarrhea.

Gland: a group of cells—or an organ—in the body that removes materials from the blood, or alters them to produce a specialized substance, such as a hormone, and then releases it back into the bloodstream to act in the body in some way.

Globulin: proteins found in the blood and cerebrospinal fluid.

Granulocytes: a type of white blood cell that helps kill bacteria and other microorganisms.

Guanfacine: an agent approved for the management of hypertension, currently being studied for use in the treatment of AIDS-dementia complex.

Hairy leukoplakia: a condition that appears to be related to infection with the Epstein-Barr Virus (EBV). Symptoms include white patches in the mouth, often in a striped pattern on the side of the tongue. Hairy leukoplakia has been found primarily in people who are HIV-positive but also in a few HIV-negative organ-transplant patients treated with immunosuppressive drugs.

Hematocrit: the percentage of packed red blood cells in a given volume of blood.

Hemoglobin: the part of red blood cells that carries oxygen to other parts of the body.

Hemophilia: an inherited disease that keeps blood from clotting normally. Many hemophiliacs became infected with HIV during the 1980s because the clotting factor was often HIV-contaminated.

Hepatic: pertaining to the liver.

Hepatitis B: a viral liver disease that can be acute or chronic and even life-threatening, particularly in people with poor immune resistance. Like HIV, the hepatitis B virus can be transmitted by sexual contact, contaminated needles, or contaminated blood or blood products. Hepatitis B is ten to one hundred times more easily transmitted than HIV.

Herpes Simplex Virus I (HSV I): a virus that causes cold sores or fever blisters on the mouth or around the eyes and can be transmitted to the genital area. The latent virus can be reactivated by stress, trauma, other infections, or suppression of the immune system.

Herpes Simplex Virus II (HSV II): a virus causing painful sores of the anus or genitals that lies dormant in nerve tissue and can be reactivated to produce the symptoms. HSV II may be transmitted to a newborn during birth from an infected mother.

Herpes zoster (shingles): a condition characterized by painful blisters that generally dry and scab, leaving minor scarring. Herpes zoster is caused by the reactivation of a previous infection with the varicella-zoster virus that causes chicken pox, usually early in life. Shingles may be a symptom of HIV disease progression in HIV-infected individuals, and the condition may recur in people with poor immunity.

HIV immunogen: an experimental HIV vaccine preparation made from killed HIV. It is being studied to determine whether the vaccine can prevent asymptomatic HIV-positive individuals from developing symptoms.

HTLV-1: human T-cell leukemia virus, a human retrovirus that causes a rare form of leukemia after a long period of asymptomatic infection. The organism spreads through sexual contact or the sharing of unclean needles by injection drug users. HTLV-1 infection may be a cofactor for HIV disease progression.

Human growth hormone: a protein made in the body in the pituitary gland. It is being used experimentally to see whether it can help people with AIDS gain weight and to determine whether it can bolster the immune system.

Human Herpes Virus type 6 (HHV-6): a previously unknown herpes virus discovered in 1990 at the National Cancer Institute. Some researchers believe that HHV-6 is a cofactor that accelerates HIV disease progression. HHV-6 has also been linked to Chronic Fatigue Syndrome.

Human Immunodeficiency Virus (HIV): the virus that causes HIV disease. Infection with HIV is acquired through exposure to genital fluids or blood containing HIV. This infection causes no symptoms of disease for a period of time (called the incubation period) that lasts an average of about ten years. During this period, however, HIV multiplies and spreads throughout the body, destroying important cells of the immune system. Eventually, HIV infection makes people vulnerable to opportunistic diseases, such as other infections and forms of cancer.

Human Immunodeficiency Virus type 1 (HIV-1): the virus that causes AIDS. HIV-1 is known as a retrovirus.

Human Immunodeficiency Virus type 2 (HIV-2): a virus very similar to HIV-1, which has been found to cause immune suppression.

Hypericin: a chemical substance that in laboratory studies inhibits HIV replication and intercellular spread, and that protects mice from the lethal effects of HIV-like mouse viruses; found in low concentration in the Saint-John's-wort plant. Clinical trials of hypericin for treatment of HIV infection are under way with both a synthetic version and with a highly concentrated Saint-John's-wort extract.

Hypersensitivity: when an immune response to certain substances is exaggerated in the body.

Immune system: the complex natural defense system that protects the body from infection by viruses and microorganisms and probably also from the spread and survival of cancerous cells.

Immune Thrombocytopenic Purpura (ITP): decreased levels of blood platelets resulting from an unknown cause.

Immunity: a natural or acquired resistance to a specific disease. Immunity may be partial or complete, long-lasting or temporary.

Immunization: the introduction into the body of a weakened form of a disease that cannot cause sickness, but which induces the body to form antibodies against the disease. This is also called *vaccination.*

Immunoglobulin: any of the structurally related glycoproteins that function as antibodies.

Immunomodulator: a substance capable of modifying one or more functions of the immune system.

Immunosuppressed: a weakened state of the immune system. This can result from diseases (such as HIV infection) or certain drugs (such as certain anticancer drugs).

Incubation time: the time between the introduction of a germ into the body and the first sign of symptoms.

Informed consent: a process that all people entering clinical trials must go through. Before entering the trial, patients must sign a consent form saying that they understand important facts about that trial.

Institutional Review Board (IRB): a group of doctors, experts, and other concerned members of the community (including people with AIDS/HIV) that protects the rights of the people in a clinical trial and makes sure that the trial is ethical and as safe as possible.

Interferons: alpha, beta, and gamma interferons are proteins produced naturally by the body. These substances have antiviral and immunomodulating activity and "interfere" with the infection of cells by viruses. These and other interferons have been synthesized by genetic engineering, and can be produced commercially. Alpha interferon is now available by prescription for KS and other illnesses, and is under study as a treatment for HIV infection. Gamma interferon is being studied experimentally as a treatment for PCP.

International Unit (IU): a standard way of measuring the amount of activity of a biological substance.

Intramuscular: injected into the muscle.

Intranasal: sprayed into the nose.

Intravenous (I.V.): injected into a vein.

In vitro ("in glass"): an artificial environment created outside a living organism (for example, a test tube or culture plate) used in experimental research to study a disease or process.

In vivo ("in life"): studies conducted within a living organism (for example, animal or human studies).

Isoniazid: an approved drug for the treatment and prevention of TB.

Itraconazole: an experimental antifungal drug that is being studied for treatment of histoplasmosis and cryptococcal meningitis.

Kaposi's sarcoma (KS): lesions caused by the massive growth of tissue on the walls of blood vessels. Sometimes found in people with AIDS, KS lesions are usually pink or purple painless spots on the skin, but they may also develop inside the body.

Latency: the period between the introduction of a germ and the first symptoms. (See also *Incubation time.*)

Lesion: any abnormal change in tissue caused by disease or injury.

Letrazuril: an experimental antiprotozoal drug being studied as a possible treatment for cryptosporidiosis.

Leukocytes: white blood cells.

Leukopenia: a lower than normal number of white blood cells in the blood.

Liposyn III-2%: a food supplement made of egg lipids. It is being used experimentally as a treatment for HIV-related weight loss.

Liver enzymes: proteins produced by the liver. Abnormally high levels of liver enzymes in the blood indicate liver damage or inflammation.

Lumbar puncture (spinal tap): a small hole made in the spinal column to take out spinal fluid for study or to inject drugs.

Lymph: a clear fluid containing white blood cells (mostly lymphocytes), antibodies, and nourishing substances. Lymph circulates throughout the body.

Lymph nodes: Glands located in the groin, neck, underarms, and various locations on the body, which fight infections by filtering out microorganisms and by producing hormones, and which contain large numbers of lymphocytes.

Lymphadenopathy: abnormality of the lymph nodes. Lymphadenopathy usually refers to enlargement of the lymph nodes.

Lymphocyte: a type of white blood cell. There are B- and T-lymphocytes. Each type has a specialized and important role in the immune defense system. T-4 lymphocytes (also called T-helper or CD4 cells) are one type of cell that HIV infects and kills.

Lymphoma: a cancer of the lymph nodes. Of the many different kinds, non-Hodgkin's lymphoma is most common in AIDS.

Macrophage: a cell of the immune system that takes in and destroys dead cells and infectious organisms (like bacteria). Macrophages also work with the T-cells to fight infectious organisms.

MAC (Mycobacterium Avium Complex): a disease caused by two bacteria found in water, soil, and food. In people with AIDS, it can spread through the bloodstream to infect lymph nodes, bone marrow, liver, spleen, spinal fluid, lungs, and intestinal tract. Symptoms of MAC include prolonged wasting fever, fatigue, and an enlarged spleen.

Mbacod: a combination of approved anticancer drugs (methotrexate, bleomycin, adriamycin, cyclophosphamide, vincristine, and dexamethasone) being studied as a treatment for lymphoma.

Meningitis: infection and inflammation of the membranes that cover the brain and spinal cord.

Microbes: organisms that can be seen only under a microscope.

Microsporidiosis: an infection of the small intestine by a parasite. The most common symptoms are diarrhea and weight loss. Diagnosis is difficult because the parasite is very small. Special stain and electron microscopes are needed.

Mitoxantrone: an approved anticancer drug being used experimentally for Kaposi's sarcoma.

Monoclonal antibodies: antibodies produced ("cloned") from a single cell that recognize specific antigens as foreign to the body and "fight" them.

Myalgia: pain in one or more muscles.

Mycoplasma: microorganisms that may cause disease. Mycoplasma infection is under study as a cofactor that may accelerate HIV disease progression.

Mycosis: any disease caused by a fungus.

Myelosuppressive: anything (usually a drug) that decreases the bone marrow's usual production of red and white blood cells.

Neoplasm: a new growth or tissue in which the growth is uncontrollable and progressive.

Neurologic or neurological: pertains to the central nervous system (brain and spinal cord) or to the peripheral nervous system (the nerves in tissue and organs) and/or to diseases of the nervous system.

Neuropathy: a disease of the nerves; the symptoms can range from pain and "burning" feelings to paralysis. HIV can cause neuropathy. Some anti-HIV drugs can also cause neuropathy as a side effect. *Peripheral neuropathy* usually means neuropathy in the hands or feet.

Neurosyphilis: syphilis that affects the nervous system.

Neutropenia: a shortage of neutrophils in the blood. Neutrophils, the most common white blood cells, are essential in fighting bacterial infections.

Neutrophil: a white blood cell important in defending the body against infections. Neutrophils take in and kill infectious organisms.

NIAID: The National Institute of Allergy and Infectious Diseases. One of the many institutes of the National Institutes of Health (NIH), which is part of the Public Health Service of the federally funded national AIDS research program.

Nimodipine: an approved calcium channel blocker that is being studied for the treatment of neurological problems caused by HIV.

Non-Hodgkin's lymphoma: a type of cancer of the lymph nodes.

Nucleoside analogue: a man-made compound that is similar to one of the building blocks of DNA or RNA; many antiviral drugs are nucleoside analogues (for example, AZT and ddI).

Nystatin: an antifungal agent approved for the treatment of candidiasis.

Ocular: pertaining to the eye.

Oncology: the study and treatment of cancer or tumors.

Open-label trial: a clinical trial in which both the patient and the doctor know which drug a patient is getting and at what dose.

Opportunistic infection: an infection in a person with a weakened immune system. These infections usually do not cause disease in people with normal immune systems.

Pancreatitis: inflammation of the pancreas that can result from several causes, including infectious diseases and alcohol abuse. Some anti-HIV drugs can also cause pancreatitis as a side effect. Symptoms include severe abdominal pain, nausea, vomiting, constipation, and, possibly, jaundice.

Pandemic: denoting a disease affecting the population of an extensive region, i.e., HIV disease is a pandemic disease, affecting an extensive area of the world.

Papillomavirus (PMV): a virus that may cause oral, skin, anal, and genital warts or nipple-like growths on the skin. There are many kinds of these viruses. One of them is implicated in cancer of the cervix.

Pap smear: a test commonly used to detect abnormalities or cancer of the cervix.

Parasite: an organism that feeds on or lives in a different organism; some parasites cause disease.

Passive immunotherapy: a treatment in which high HIV antibodies from donors are infused into HIV-positive patients.

PCP: see *Pneumocystis carinii pneumonia.*

Pediatric: having to do with children.

Peptide T: an experimental anti-HIV drug under investigation to see whether it can help improve mental functioning among people with HIV.

Periodontal disease: any abnormality of the tissue around teeth.

Peripheral neuropathy: a disorder of the nerves, usually involving the feet or hands, and sometimes the legs and arms. Symptoms include numbness, a tingling or burning sensation, sharp pain, weakness, and abnormal reflexes. In severe cases, paralysis may result.

Pharmaconkinetic: how a drug behaves in the body (for example, how long the drug stays in the body, and where it goes in the body).

Phase I trial: a small clinical trial that mainly studies the safety of a drug and what doses of the drug would most likely work best.

Phase II trial: a clinical trial involving several hundred people that mainly studies how well a drug works and what its most important side effects are.

Phase III trial: a large clinical trial that studies how well a drug works. Phase III trials usually compare the experimental drug to a standard treatment, or to a placebo when there is no standard treatment. (In AIDS research, some trials are called *Phase I/II* or *Phase II/III* trials because they are studying at the same time how safe a drug is and how well it works.)

Placebo: a "sugar pill" that won't have any effect on a disease. Experimental drugs are sometimes compared to a placebo in a given clinical trial. In these trials, neither the patient nor the doctor will know who is getting the experimental drug and who is receiving the placebo.

Platelet: a component of the blood that plays an important part in helping blood to clot. Without platelets, any wound could result in death by bleeding.

Pneumocystis carinii pneumonia (PCP): a life-threatening form of pneumonia that occurs in people with suppressed immune systems. It is the most common opportunistic infection in AIDS.

Prednisone: an approved steroid used to reduce inflammation. It is being used experimentally to see whether it reduces muscle wasting sometimes associated with AZT use.

Preexisting condition: a medical problem that existed before or at the time of a defined date, e.g., the date of an insurance application; individuals with a preexisting condition such as HIV infection may be denied health or life insurance by insurers.

Prophylaxis: a treatment that prevents disease.

Protease inhibitor: a compound that blocks the ability of HIV to produce the enzyme protease. HIV must produce this enzyme in order to replicate.

Protein: a large group of substances that are formed naturally by plants and all living organisms. Proteins provide the structures essential for the growth, function, reproduction, and repair of living tissue.

Protocol: a plan that explains how a clinical trial works. Before the trial begins, many things must be described in the protocol, including the purpose of the study, the drugs that will be given and how they will be given, criteria for participation, and statistical analysis.

Protozoa: a group of one-celled organisms. A few protozoa may cause disease.

Psychosis: usually referring to a disorder in which mental function is greatly impaired.

P24 antigen: a protein component of the core of HIV. The p24 antigen test measures the amount of this protein present in the blood. A positive result for the p24 antigen suggests active HIV replication and increased likelihood of a serious complication of the HIV disease.

Pulmonary: relating to the lungs.

PWA: person or people with AIDS.

Pyrazinamide: a drug approved for the treatment of TB in combination with other drugs.

Pyrimethamine: an approved antiprotozoal drug that is standard treatment, combined with sulfadiazine, for toxoplasmosis. It is also being studied experimentally to see whether it can prevent people with HIV from developing toxoplasmosis.

Radiation therapy: treatment of cancer with intense beams of radiation. The radiation actually kills the cancer cells and any cells it must pass through to get to the cancer cells.

Randomized trial: a kind of clinical trial in which patients are divided into treatment groups by chance (usually by computer). When this process is used, the two groups will be as much alike as possible.

Relapse: recurrence; the return of the manifestations of a disease after an interval of recovery; also used to describe a return to unsafe sex.

Renal: pertaining to the kidney.

Resistance (to a drug): the ability of an organism, a microorganism, or a virus to lose its sensitivity to a drug. For example, after long-term use of AZT, HIV can develop strains of virus in the body that are no longer suppressed by this particular drug, and therefore are said to be resistant to AZT.

Respiratory: relating to the process of breathing.

Retinitis: inflammation of the retina (a part of the eye).

Retrovirus: a type of virus that carries genetic information in RNA instead of DNA (HIV is a retrovirus).

Reverse transcriptase: an enzyme found in retroviruses that copies RNA into DNA. Some anti-HIV drugs, such as AZT and ddI, work against reverse transcriptase.

Rifabutin: an experimental antibiotic being studied to see whether it can treat or prevent MAC.

Rifampin: an approved antibiotic being used experimentally as a treatment for MAC.

Risk factor: some condition in the environment or in a person's behavior or makeup that increases the probability of contracting a particular disease.

Risk group: a group of people at a higher risk of getting some disease than the general population.

RNA: genetic material that is the analogue of DNA.

Salmonella: a bacterium sometimes found in raw meat, poultry, or eggs that can cause severe diarrhea and even, if untreated, death. There are many types of salmonella. People with suppressed immune systems are more susceptible to salmonella poisoning.

Sedimentation rate: the speed at which blood cells settle to the bottom of a long, narrow tube. The lab test that measures it is an indicator of an inflammatory process in the body, e.g., viral activity or bacterial infection.

Septra: one of the brand names for trimethoprim-sulfamethoxazole, a drug used in the prevention and treatment of PCP.

Seropositive: positive on a serological test, i.e., a test done on blood. The term is used for people infected with HIV because their infection was diagnosed by a blood test that detects antibodies to HIV.

Shingles: see *Herpes zoster.*

Side effects: unintended effects of a drug. The term usually refers to undesired or negative effects, such as headaches, rashes, or liver damage.

Somatostatin: a drug being used experimentally to see whether it will stop diarrhea caused by HIV infection.

Sparfloxacin: an experimental antibiotic being used to treat MAC.

Spermicide: a substance that can kill sperm; used as a contraceptive.

Sputum: mucous or other matter ejected from the throat by coughing or spitting up.

STD: sexually transmitted disease.

Steroid: any of numerous natural and synthetic chemical compounds that include steroids, certain hormones, D vitamins, and some carcinogenic substances. Steroids are often used to reduce inflammation in the body.

Subcutaneous: underneath the skin.

Suppressor cell: a type of lymphocyte (white blood cell) that helps regulate the body's immune response to an infection.

Syndrome: a group of symptoms and diseases that together are characteristic of a specific condition.

Synergy: the action of two or more drugs that when taken together have an effect greater than the added effect of the individual drugs.

Syphilis: an infectious, sexually transmitted disease caused by a microorganism called *Treponema pallidum.* If left untreated, syphilis can cause severe nervous-system and cardiac disorders and death.

Systemic: affecting the whole body.

T-helper lymphocytes (T-4 cells): white blood cells in the body that are a key component in the body's defense against invading organisms. They help the B-lymphocytes to produce an antibody that enhances immunity.

T-lymphocyte: a type of lymphocyte that matures in the thymus gland and helps protect the body against a number of microorganisms, such as viruses, fungi, and parasites. T-lymphocytes also release substances that cause B-lymphocytes to proliferate.

T-suppressor lymphocytes (T-8 cells): a group of T-lymphocytes that regulates the antibody production of B-lymphocytes.

Thrombocytopenia: an abnormally low number of the blood platelets that are needed for blood clotting.

Thrush: the oral form of candidiasis, a fungal infection, characterized by white spots or patches in the mouth or back of the throat.

Thymus gland: a gland in the neck that helps in the development of T-lymphocytes and produces hormones that help in maintaining the immune system.

TMP-SMX: trimethoprim-sulfamethoxazole. A drug used for prophylaxis and treatment of PCP; marketed as Bactrim, Septra, and under other names.

Toxic: a substance that is poisonous or harmful.

Toxoplasmosis: an opportunistic infection that is caused by the protozoan organism *Toxoplasma gondii.* It most frequently causes focal encephalitis (inflammation of the brain). The organism is passed by contact with feces of infected cats and ingestion of raw or undercooked meat. The organism can cause severe problems in people with suppressed immune systems. Symptoms include headache, motor changes, seizure, tremors, shakiness, blindness, personality changes, confusion, disorientation, and coma.

Transfusion: the introduction of whole blood or blood products into a person who needs them because of loss of blood or because the blood lacks a particular substance.

Treatment Investigational New Drug (Treatment IND): an FDA classification that allows a still-unapproved but fully tested drug to be obtained from the drug manufacturer by a patient's physician.

Trifluridine: approved for the treatment of a viral eye infection; it is also being studied for the treatment of herpes infections that are resistant to acyclovir.

Trimethoprim: an approved antibiotic that is used in combination with other drugs for the treatment and prevention of PCP.

Trimethoprim-dapsone: a combination oral drug regimen for PCP. It appears to work as effectively as TMP-SMX (Septra, Bactrim) but is much less toxic. It also appears to be more effective than dapsone alone.

Tuberculosis: an infectious disease caused by *Mycobacterium tuberculosis* that may affect any tissue or organ in the body.

Tumor: any abnormal growth, whether it is cancerous or not, whether it is a threat to health or not.

Tumor Necrosis Factor (TNF): a protein made naturally in the body that some researchers think is an important cause of weight loss in people with AIDS. TNF may also help HIV replicate in the body.

Vaccine: a weakened or dead virus or bacteria that is introduced into the body to cause it to make antibodies and increase immunity against a particular disease that a virus or bacteria may cause.

Varicella: Chicken pox.

VDRL: the standard blood test for syphilis. VDRL stands for Venereal Disease Research Laboratories.

Vidaribine: a drug sometimes used to treat acyclovir-resistant herpes infection.

Viremia: the presence of virus in the bloodstream.

Virus: a type of infectious agent that can be reproduced only inside a living cell. Viruses may take over the cell's normal functions, causing the cell to behave in a manner determined by the virus.

Wasting syndrome: a condition characterized by involuntary weight loss of more than 10 percent of baseline body weight, plus either chronic diarrhea or chronic weakness and fever for more than thirty days, when these conditions cannot be explained by any illness other than HIV infection.

White blood cells: blood cells whose primary function is to fight infections.

APPENDIX E

SELECTED BIBLIOGRAPHY

The AIDS/HIV Treatment Directory. AmFAR, 733 Third Avenue, 12th Floor, New York, N.Y. 10017. To subscribe, write or call 212-682-7440; a one-year subscription of four issues is $44.

AIDS Treatment News. ATN, P.O. Box 411256, San Francisco, CA 94141. A semi-monthly newsletter published by John S. James reporting on treatments of HIV disease.

Altman, Dennis. *AIDS in the Mind of America.* New York: Acorn Press, Doubleday, 1986.

Baker, Ron, et al. *Early Care for HIV Disease.* San Francisco: San Francisco AIDS Foundation, 1992.

Becker, E. *The Denial of Death.* New York: Free Press, 1973.

Callen, Michael. *Surviving AIDS.* New York: HarperCollins, 1990.

Coren, Gena. *The Invisible Epidemic: The Story of Women and AIDS.* New York: HarperCollins, 1992.

Cousins, Norman. *Anatomy of an Illness.* New York: Bantam Books, 1979.

Duda, Deborah. *Coming Home: A Guide to Home Care for the Terminally Ill.* Santa Fe, N.M.: John Muir, 1984.

Eidson, Ted, ed. *The AIDS Caregiver's Handbook.* New York: St. Martin's Press, 1988.

Hitchen, Neal. *Voices That Care: Stories and Encouragements for People with AIDS/HIV and Those Who Love Them.* Los Angeles: Lowell/Contemporary, 1992.

Hunter, Nan D., and William Rubenstein, eds. *AIDS Agenda: Emerging Issues in Civil Rights.* New York: New Press, 1992.

Katoff, Lew, ed. *Living with AIDS: A Guide.* New York: Gay Men's Health Crisis, 1989.

Kübler-Ross, Elisabeth. *On Death and Dying.* New York: Macmillan, 1969.

Levine, Stephen. *Meetings at the Edge.* Garden City, N.Y.: Anchor Books, 1984.

————. *Who Dies.* Garden City, N.Y.: Anchor Books, 1982.

McCormack, Thomas P. *The AIDS Benefits Handbook.* New Haven, Ct.: Yale University Press, 1990.

McKusick, Leon, ed. *What to Do About AIDS: Physicians and Mental Health Professionals Discuss the Issues.* Berkeley, Ca.: University of California Press, 1986.

McNeill, William. *Plagues and Peoples.* New York: Anchor Press, 1976.

Moffat, Betty C. *When Someone You Love Has AIDS.* Santa Monica, Ca.: IBS Press, 1986.

Monette, Paul. *Borrowed Time.* New York: Harcourt Brace Jovanovich, 1988.

Nungesser, Lon. *Epidemic of Courage: Facing AIDS in America.* New York: St. Martin's Press, 1985.

————. *Axioms for Survivors: How to Live Until You Say Goodbye.* New York: HarperCollins, 1992.

Petrow, Steven, *Dancing Against the Darkness: A Journey Through America in the Age of AIDS.* Lexington, Mass.: Lexington Books, 1990.

P.I. Perspective. Quarterly newsletter of Project Inform. Donation appreciated. National hot line: 800-822-7422; California hot line: 800-334-7422.

Pohl, Mel, et al. *The Caregivers' Journey.* New York: HarperCollins, 1990.

Sankar, Andrea. *Dying at Home: A Family Guide for Caregiving.* Baltimore: The Johns Hopkins Press, 1991.

Shelby, R. Dennis. *If a Partner Has AIDS.* New York: Haworth Press, 1992.

Shilts, Randy. *And the Band Played On.* New York: St. Martin's Press, 1987.

Simonton, Carl O., et al. *Getting Well Again.* New York: Bantam Books, 1984.

Sontag, Susan. *AIDS and Its Metaphors.* New York: Farrar, Straus and Giroux, 1988.

ACKNOWLEDGMENTS

David Groff, editor at Crown, recognized good intentions and a very imperfect idea and molded that idea into a book that we hope will prove to be greatly useful to those for whom it was written. I thank him for his constant and continued encouragement, his suggestions for improvement, and his hard work and important contributions to the development of the manuscript. This book would not exist without him.

Joyce Wallace, doctor and AIDS specialist in New York City, was more than just a doctor to Evan and me, but a friend when we were in need of all her encouragement, inspiration, and caring. And to Barbara Starrett for being there when Joyce could not be.

My Carepartners' Group—these men and women, and their friends and lovers—has opened my eyes to a depth of human love and dedication I would not have guessed existed before this crisis.

St. Vincent's Supportive Care Program—Sister Patrice, Sister Pat, Joan Blanchfield, Carol, Cathy, and especially Jim Earley and Roger Smith—have watched over Evan and me, cared for us, and loved us.

—L.J.M.

Carol Mann, our literary agent, for her unending support and guidance both professionally and personally.

Alan Dolber, Ph.D., for his review of some of the more emotional aspects of this book.

—W.M. and F.D.P.

Paul DiDonato, legal director at San Francisco's AIDS Legal Referral Panel, for his careful and constructive reading of the manuscript and for his friendship over many years.

Joel Thomas, with Project Inform, who edited this book with all his heart and soul and who provided much valuable information to me.

Carol Taylor, at Crown Publishers, for her dedication to this project and her steadfast good cheer.

Fred Morris and Jodi Redmon for their attentiveness to the details of the making of the book.

Charlotte Sheedy, literary agent extraordinaire, whose wise counsel and deep caring for me are greatly appreciated. (Thanks also to Regula Noetzli and Victoria Sanders.)

And to my friends and family who supported me throughout: Jack Burrus, Nancy Clarke, Maddy Cohen, Charlotte Eyerman, Susan Ostwald-Barnes, Cynthia Perry, Jay Petrow, Julie Petrow, Margot Petrow, Richard Petrow, Michael Seltzer, and Ralph Tachuk.

—S.P.

INDEX

fear of, 38–39, 54–55, 125–26
guilt feelings after, 198–99
healing of carepartner after, 201–7
hospice care, 185–86
joking about, 181
practical matters after, 193–95
regrets after, 197–99
sharing with patient, 177–79
suicide, 179–80
talking about, 180–81
unresolved issues before, 179
where to die, 185–86
delusional behaviors, 76
dementia, 16, 76–77, 105, 126
denial, 30, 33, 57–59
in AIDS patient, 57–59, 182
in carepartners, 57, 136–37
of death, 182
dental care, 11
depression, 183, 199
Destiny of Me, The (Kramer), 60
dextroamphetamine, 77
D4T, 71–72
diagnosis, 1–4
reactions to, 16–18, 40–42, 43
see also tests
diarrhea, 12, 16, 29, 78, 81, 82
DiDonato, Paul, 105
diet, 19, 90, 214
eating habits of patient, changes in,
131–32
disability insurance, 95–96
discrimination, 26–28, 211
AIDS agency and legal clinic assistance regarding, 112
Americans with Disabilities Act
(ADA) protections, 109–10,
111–12
business and service provider discrimination, 112
legal protections against, 109–13
by medical professionals, 34, 47
and privacy rights, 113, 212
tenant's rights, 110–11
in workplace, 111–12
doctors, *see* medical professionals
doxorubicin, 81
drugs, 7
antibiotics, 19
antifungal drugs, 73, 85
antiviral drugs, 68, 70, 71, 73–75

approval process for, 86–88
for bacterial infections, 77, 78
for cancers, 80, 81
for cryptosporidiosis, 82
for diarrhea, 81
experimental drugs, 71–72, 86–90
for fevers, 82
government subsidies for, 108
immune-modulating, 68–69
IV-drug users, *see* IV-drug users
for neurological problems, 75–77
for opportunistic diseases, 72–73
for PCP, 69
for PID, 86
for rashes, 83
recreational drugs, 19, 68, 214
unapproved drugs, use of, 89–90
for yeast infections, 85
see also specific drug names

E

elimination of wastes, 168–69
ELISA test, 11
ethambutol, 78, 79
experimental treatments, 25, 43, 47–
48, 71–72, 86–90
getting into a program, 88–89

F

families, 172–73
of carepartners, 154–55
children, protections for, 101–4
reactions of, 154–60
rejections by, 31, 32–33, 118–19,
120–21, 156–59, 160
telling about illness, 154–59
fatigue, 12
FDA (Food and Drug Administration),
87–88, 89
fears, 35
of abandonment, 140
analyzing of, 51–57
of carepartners, 28–29, 35–39, 50,
51–57, 139–40, 176–77, 180
confronting and overcoming of, 39,
51–57
of death, 38–39, 54–55, 125–26, 180
discussing with patient, 52–53, 54–
56, 57

fears (*cont.*)
of helplessness, 38
of infection, 28–29, 36–37, 53, 140
of past activities, 55
of separation and loss, 176–77
of similar life-styles, 37–38
of unknown, 52, 53–54, 140
see also discrimination
feces, 169, 215
fever blisters, 29
fevers, 12, 72, 76, 78, 79, 82
financial matters, 130
children, protection of, 101–4
government benefits, 104–8
personal planning, 92–101
fluconazole, 73, 85
flucytosine, 75
flu symptoms, 13
food stamps, 107
foscarnet, 74
friends:
other friends, sharing patient with, 173–74, 184
reaching out to, 160–62
see also support systems
funeral arrangements, 101, 193–94

G

gait, changes in, 16
gamma-interferon, 80
ganciclovir, 74
Gay Men's Health Crisis, 9, 43, 60, 163
genital warts, 83, 85–86
glossary of terms, 228–45
gonorrhea, 214
government benefit and entitlement programs, 18, 25, 104–8
grief, 191–93
anger and, 200
crying and, 195
depression and, 199
emptiness, feelings of, 196
guilt feelings and, 198–99
illness and, 199
panic attacks and, 200
preoccupation with deceased, 196–97
questioning yourself, 197–98
grooming, 171

guilt feelings, 55, 140–41, 176, 198–99
grief and, 198–99
survivor's guilt, 55, 176

H

hairy leukoplakia, 15
health-care workers, *see* medical professionals
health insurance, 92–95, 211–12
arguing with insurers, 25
care in submissions to insurer, 17–18
health maintenance regime, 19–20, 68, 214
hearing, changes in, 16
helplessness, 56–57
hemophiliacs, 2, 8, 26–27
hepatitis, 29
herpes simplex, 74, 75, 83
herpes zoster (shingles), 15, 29, 74–75, 83
heterosexuals, AIDS among, 9
HIV (human immunodeficiency virus), 1, 5
antibody test, 11–12, 209–13
children, infection in, 8–9, 26–27, 28
early detection, benefits of, 12
effect of, 6–7
primary HIV infection, 6–7
in saliva, 10
T-4 cells and, 6
testing for, 11–12, 209–13
transmission of, 10–11, 214
treatment of HIV disease, *see* treatments
HIV antibody testing, 11–12, 209–13, *see also* tests
HIV encephalopathy, *see* dementia
holistic therapies, 68
homeopathic treatment, 43, 90
hospice care, 185–86
hospitals, 185
choosing of, 44–45
services provided by, 164
tensions of hospital stays, 132
see also medical professionals
housing, 163, 164
decision to stay at home, 117–22
housekeeping, 121–22